SPORTS
NETWORK

Also available at all good book stores

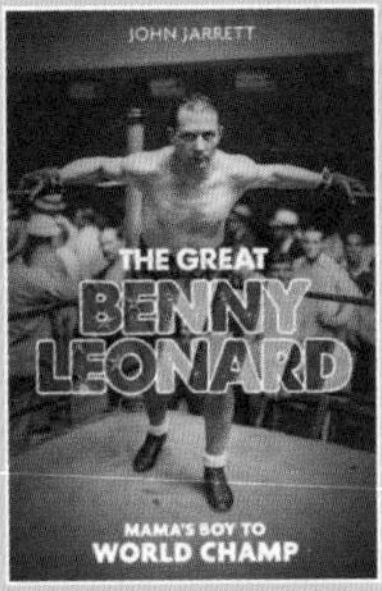

9781785317866

9781785313813

9781785312960

9781785310317

9781785316272

9781785316371

9781785316425

9781785315350

9781785315404

King of the JOURNEYMEN

King of the JOURNEYMEN

The Life of PETER BUCKLEY

with Chris Akers

pitch

First published by Pitch Publishing, 2021

Pitch Publishing
A2 Yeoman Gate
Yeoman Way
Worthing
Sussex
BN13 3QZ
www.pitchpublishing.co.uk
info@pitchpublishing.co.uk

A CIP catalogue record is available for this book from the British Library.

ISBN 978 1 78531 785 9

Typesetting and origination by Pitch Publishing

Printed and bound in India by Replika Press Pvt. Ltd.

Contents

Foreword

I received a message on Facebook that left me at a loss for words. Peter Buckley, aka The Professor, The Legend, the ultimate journeyman, two times Midlands Area champ, asking me to write the foreword for his upcoming autobiography.

Of course, I said yes without even hesitating and then I was told I had a 500-word limit. Is that even possible? This man had 300 professional fights. How do you describe someone like that in 500 words?

People will wonder why I was asked to write Peter's foreword when there are plenty of better-qualified people in boxing and much better people with a keyboard who could do it. As Peter put it, 'Jon, you know my career better than anyone, even me.'

I don't know if that's true but there is a link and a reason why I know so much about the man dubbed in boxing circles as 'The Professor'.

Thirty years ago Peter, along with his trainer Nobby Nobbs and fellow pro boxer Rocky Lawlor, was looking for somewhere to train, as Rocky had a title fight scheduled and Peter was getting ready for his third or fourth bout.

My amateur gym in Birmingham, Irish ABC, was offered but there was no one to open it. So, the keys were handed to me and I was given the job of letting them in. Peter and Rocky allowed me, a young amateur, to train alongside them and chew their ears off talking boxing. A week later, their gym was fixed or reopened and they went back to train there. But the seed had been planted.

Already an avid fan and scrapbook collector, to meet, sit and train with two real pros was a dream come true for me. Peter became one of the fighters I followed and tracked down results for, in the local paper and in *Boxing News*.

Fights were won and lost on the road and I still remember the picture in *Boxing News* when Peter suffered his first stoppage loss to Duke McKenzie, and how gutted I was when it happened. Even though I hadn't seen him since our training week, when Peter won the first of his Midlands titles against Brian Robb, I was buzzing reading the result.

I continued to follow Peter and his second Midlands title win against Matt Harris was also received with jubilation when I picked up the *Birmingham Mail* for the result. (As happens in boxing, I became very good friends with both men years later.)

On the pro scene as a fan, I was sitting in the crowd watching a show at Wolverhampton Civic Hall. I was chatting to a loud bunch next to me who were very excited about their friend having his second bout, having won his first bout by first-round knockout.

The lad I was talking to seemed a bit confused as Rob Hunt's opponent had pulled out that afternoon and they had just found out he had a substitute, who was on his way to the venue but still hadn't arrived at 7pm.

It was then I saw Peter quietly walking along the aisle, bag over his shoulder and saying hello to people in the crowd who recognised him. I told the lad that I thought that's who Rob was boxing instead. His response was, 'Rob will smash him. He's tiny and he's only just turned up.'

I just smiled and said, 'I think you might be surprised.'

Ninety minutes later, Pete was in the ring doing his thing. Making the much bigger Hunt miss. Feinting, slipping and sliding and at the final bell leaving the ring without a mark on his face.

As Pete walked up the same aisle he had arrived down two hours earlier, bag over his shoulder and a smile on his face, the Rob Hunt supporter turned to me and said, 'How did you know?'

I told him there's not much I don't know about that guy.

A few years after, when I had become involved in pro boxing myself, Peter and I struck our friendship back up and liked nothing better than being at shows sitting and talking about old fights and fighters from around that era. It always made me smile that my intimate knowledge of Pete's career seemed to surprise him more than any left hook or right cross from a young contender ever could.

Pete's record of 300 post-war professional fights would never be beat, many said. Indeed, I was there for that final fight, on a TV show at Aston Villa Leisure Centre promoted by Frank Warren, who had graciously put Pete in the home corner for his services to boxing.

I had managed to get the job of house second and was in the home corner, so was looking forward to helping out in his final fight.

As people walked to the ring for the 300th and final time, the older, experienced house second waltzed round the ring and said, 'Swap over. I know Pete well and I want to do the corner.'

Not wanting to argue our Buckley credentials, I walked round to the other side and prepared to put the stool in for the other boxer. It wasn't quite what I wanted, but looking back I am still happy I was involved in Pete's final fight (which he won).

Finishing up, I trained a lad called Kris Laight, who was getting close to the 300 mark and people were speculating would some day beat Pete's record. Pete got asked about it a lot and would merely say, 'If anyone can do it, Kris will. But he didn't box the quality I did.'

Which was totally true but looking back I don't think anybody boxed the quality that Pete did.

Kris made it to his 300th fight and a fuss was being made. I rang Peter and asked if he wanted to come along and do the ring walk with Kris for his fight.

Some fighters would be pissed off at somebody equalling their record, would have blanked the call or been annoyed. But Peter does not carry himself like that. He turned up on the night, had a great chat with Kris, walked him to the ring wearing a Kris Laight T-shirt and even presented him with a bottle afterwards in celebration.

Then, in a twist of fate, a small medical query prompted Kris to retire. So, although the 300 was equalled, it still hasn't (and won't) be beaten. I was proud a lad I worked with equalled that record. But I'm also glad that it wasn't beaten as Pete deserves his place in the record books for everything he has achieved.

There is a thing in boxing that is above wins, titles and everything else, and that is giving and earning respect. In that category, Peter Buckley is the undisputed champ.

This has gone on a little longer than I planned but like his career, where Peter Buckley is involved, things never go the short or easy route.

I hope you enjoy his story as much as I have enjoyed watching it unfold.

Jon Pegg

Prologue
In the changing room

I had mixed feelings during my last fight. I knew it was the end of a career that I had been doing for 19 years. Yet I had been fighting for longer than that and I knew that once the bell rang for the final time that I would not be fighting in any capacity ever again. I didn't really know what I was going to do with myself once this fight was over.

Don't get me wrong, I knew it would stop one day. Yet here I was, sitting on my own thinking, 'What now then, Pete?' Boxing was a way of life for me. It *was* my life. More or less every week or month, I would have a date for a fight. The phone would ring and it would be a promoter or my trainer asking me if I would be willing to fight someone the following week, or if I would be willing to be booked for a fight at the last minute. I knew that was all coming to an end after tonight and I felt a bit empty.

Although I would feel empty after I'd retired, I had seen plenty of bad things happen within the sport. I've seen boxers who have been used as pieces of meat, who were quickly forgotten once their sell-by date was up. I'm lucky that I had a good woman in my life, but not everybody has that. I've known boxers after their fighting career was over. They just go downhill as they feel they have nothing left. You see that a lot. I also saw plenty of lads get ripped off like fuck. It's easy for the managers. They just get new fighters as there will always be lads who want to fight.

I have watched lads being put in well over their heads in fights where they can get hurt. I was a bit different as I knew my way around in boxing terms. But seeing lads well overmatched and their managers not giving a fuck, that's always going to happen in boxing.

There were plenty of good things in boxing that I saw, especially with Nobby, my trainer when I became a pro. I saw the lads that he got off the streets doing something good with their lives. Nobby always had time for people no matter what their background, colour or religion. That's the great thing about the sport in my eyes. At our gym, we were like a family. We didn't always get on great, but we all had respect for each other and looked out for each other. In my opinion, those involved with boxing are a different breed of people. You get to know boxers and trainers at shows and they become friends for life. It really does change you as a person.

With myself, I'm a different person and a better one for boxing. It saved my life. That's a fact. It taught me to respect people when I was growing up; I didn't really respect anything. I was a bit of a horrible lad when I look back on my life. Boxing made me a better human being.

I always had respect from people within the sport. From fighters at the very top of the sport to the lad having his first fight and asking me for advice, everybody knew me. Sitting there in the changing room the night of my last fight, people were coming in and wishing me well, saying, 'Good luck tonight, Pete. Get the win,' and so on. Yet I felt a bit lost knowing it would be the last time I would be doing what had basically been my life.

CHAPTER 1

Charlie Magri's jab

'Oh, that was a nice jab from Charlie Magri.'

Me and my brother David would always do commentary when we were boxing, trying out different moves on each other. This was a daily thing me and him used to do in the house in those days. The minute our mom left the house, I'd say, 'You wanna spar?' At that point, we would push the settee out, put the gloves on and start sparring in our living room.

Our mom used to go mad when she came home as both our noses would be bleeding. 'I told you no fighting when I'm out,' she would shout. But it always happened.

The fights between us would start off nice and easy. But they would always escalate. They would turn vicious. I'd hit him hard, then he'd hit me hard and I'd be like, 'What the fuck?' Gloves would be torn off and before you knew it, we would be on the floor fighting. That happened with most of our fights. My mates would tell you that growing up, when I was 13 and 14, me and my brother used to spar. Even though I was a better boxer than him, he was bigger and stronger than me and could punch a bit. If I caught him with a few good shots, I'd say, 'You prick!' I would get a broom handle and smack him and chase him with it. Now we get on really well but when we were younger, we used to really fight each other a lot. I've chased him with knives, cut his hand, and chased him with milk bottles. Just some mad things like that. We never used to really get on until we were older.

David wasn't a bad fighter. He would win two and lose one, but he was always in a good fight. Like me, he liked to have a fight. He would tell you himself that I was a better boxer than him. Even when we sparred I would jab his head off, though he was stronger than me.

Another thing we used to do, as loads of us in the area used to box, is go over the park during the summer and get the gloves on and spar each other. About 20 of us. Fucking loved it, I did.

My dad's attitude to all this was, 'Ah, they're just lads.' But when it got out of hand, he'd say, 'You've got to fucking stop now,' only because our mom would be doing his head in telling him that he had to do something about it. But my dad wasn't too bothered about us fighting. He had a big family, so he must have been fighting all the time!

* * *

Me and David sparring in the house and a big group of us sparring in the park when I was younger was not unusual for me. For as long as I can remember, I have always been a fighter. Whether in the playground, the ring, fighting with friends or with my siblings, I have always fancied a good scrap. Having the urge to fight has always been in me. I learned to fight within a boxing ring and made it my living for many years. I also fought on the streets during this time and moved to a 6ft by 8ft prison cell in my mid-teens.

I remember having fights with other kids in infants and in secondary school. I had fights in our house. My sisters used to pin me down and suffocate me. But I was always aggressive, even as a young kid. Even when I was excluded from school, I had fights with anyone. Even when I was in my twenties, I would never back down from a fight in my life.

How I ended up being in a lot of fights started when I was very young. I grew up in a family of 11 with my mom Elsie and my dad John. My mother was originally from Ladywood, an area next to the centre of Birmingham. She had a few main jobs during her life. She first worked at a factory and then she moved to Hall Green Dog Track, working there for more than 20 years. She served behind the counter in the canteen and as kids we used to hang around the dog track, eating burgers and chips while my mom worked. My mom always worked hard. After she left the dog track, she worked at my brother's father-in-law's catering shop for several years. They would cater for functions such as wedding parties, as well as sell food like bacon and eggs and ready-made meals, which my mom would make. At Christmas time, the shop would have orders for turkeys and my mom would cook about 20 of them during the holidays. My mom was a great cook and it was a great shop she worked at. It was a place that was always busy and everyone in Acocks Green knew who my mom was. My dad John came from Dublin and had a lot of siblings in his family. Fourteen sisters and six brothers to be precise. He and his family came over to the UK to settle and though some of them moved to Liverpool, most of them settled in London.

My dad lived in London for a while but ended up making his roots in Birmingham. How he ended up in my hometown, I don't know. He may have been doing some jobs up here or had mates that lived here.

My dad was a plumber and gas engineer. My relationship with him was solid. I got on with him really well and he was a hard-working bloke. He never talked about politics or religion, but when the pub bombings happened in Birmingham in the early 1970s, he was a target because he was Irish. He couldn't get on the bus for work when we were kids and I think that's why he went to London later on to earn money for us, as his family from Ireland were all there. He was a good man who worked hard for his family and I always got on with him.

My dad used to take me down to London in the six weeks of summer holiday. When I would go and visit family there, they all knew that I was boxing as my dad used to take clippings from the local newspapers with him and show the family. He was very happy about what I achieved in boxing. I was a good amateur, so any time he came to watch me I didn't really lose, I mostly won. He was very proud of how I had performed in championships and he was always telling his mates what I had done. Some of his mates would sometimes come to the house after work or after leaving the pub and he would show them all my trophies and certificates. My dad used to mainly work in London, Monday to Friday. His family had their own jobs down there. He had nine kids to pay for, so he had to go where the money was.

How he met my mom I don't know, but when they became a couple, they both moved to Ireland. While there, my dad became severely ill with tuberculosis and ended up in hospital for 22 months. During his recovery, he lost his lung and had to have surgery to remove two of his ribs, ending up with a big scar on his back. While he was in recovery, my mom would stay with my dad's aunt in Ireland for a few weeks at a time, visiting him in the hospital before returning to England. She did this for a couple of years. Once my dad recovered he moved to Birmingham. Initially, they lived in Ladywood, which is near the centre of the city, before moving and settling in Acocks Green, where I was born.

* * *

As I mentioned earlier, there are nine of us – five sisters (Ann, Pat, Phyllis, Tina and Jean) and three brothers (Noel, John and David). Me and John in particular were really close and he was always a scally, always up to mischief, though he died of a heart attack a week after his 40th birthday. David has his own business as a builder and Noel, who is the eldest, works as a roofer.

Noel was 15 or 16 when I was born, so I don't remember him much. He got married young and is still married to the same woman.

Our family was large, though we lived in a house comprising three bedrooms, meaning the rooms were shared between the 11 of us. My sisters shared the largest room, my parents had the smallest room and me and my brothers slept in the backroom. The kitchen was small but we had a big garden, which led out on to a park. We have always been a tight-knit family and even though my parents have since died, we still help each other out and all live close by.

Christmas day in particular was a great day in our house. Eleven of us would be sat round the table and it was crazy! *Top of the Pops* and the Queen's speech would be on the TV, but the only thing we liked was *Top of the Pops*. My mom always tried to get us to be quiet when the Queen's speech was on. She loved the royal family and always had Union Jacks out when the England football team played and also during the jubilee. We used to slag the royal family off but she would cut us down straight away.

I get on with my sisters really well. When I was younger, they used to beat me up. They used to suffocate me by putting a pillow over my face. Don't forget, I was the youngest out of nine, so my sisters were older than me. We all had nicknames for each other and my nickname when I was a kid was Jealous. Jealous balls, to be precise! That's what my brothers and sisters used to call me because I was the baby of the household and my mom used to dote on me. Even now, me and my sisters get on really well and they phone me all the time.

I always wanted my own way and most of the time I got it. I was the apple of my mom's eye. She'd be like, 'Give the baby this and give the baby that.' But when my mom used to go out, it was payback from my sisters. If I was cheeky to them, they would pin me down. In a funny way, there was nothing malicious in it! Tina had a dart board in the house. One day, I was cheeky to her and she threw a dart and it pierced my back.

'Wait 'til mom comes home. I'm fucking telling her what happened,' I screamed.

'Oh, you little bastard,' she replied.

When my mom came home, I told her what happened and Tina got a bit of a hiding from her. My mom used to dish out the punishments in our house, not my dad. If my dad had had a drink after work, he would come in and go upstairs to have a lie down. Within ten minutes of him lying down, because he was drunk, he would come back down the stairs.

'What's going on here?' he would say.

'Oh shut up! There's nothing going on,' my mom would reply.

He used to imagine we were fighting downstairs, just because of how he was feeling. But if our mom told our dad to sort us out, he would go upstairs for a belt, but would tell us to pull the quilt over us.

'You bastards!' he would say as he hit the quilt, not very hard. 'You better not be playing your mom up again!'

My mom had big, long fingernails. When she grabbed you, she would dig them into you. Every now and then, when we were really playing up, she would say, 'Right. I'm fucking off out of here.' When she did this, we used to shit ourselves as she would do it at nine o'clock at night and we'd be wondering where she'd gone. But she would be back in 15 minutes. All she had done is just walk around the block to cool off.

* * *

Both my grandmothers were very different people. My nan, my mom's mom, didn't have the time of day for me growing up. When we used to go to her house, me and my brother would go straight into the back garden. She wouldn't even give us a cup of tea. But my mom used to say she had a hard life. With my dad, I never really knew my nan on that side. When his mom moved over from Ireland, she moved to London like most of their family. When I visited her in London, she was very kind to me.

When I was in prison as a teenager, my mother's mom had Alzheimer's. My mom used to catch the bus every day to her house to look after her. She would do her washing, her ironing and other chores. My mom was an angel. My nan used to call my mom Rosie as she used to think she was her other daughter.

'Our Elsie never comes to see me,' my nan used to say to my mom.

'Oh, don't she?' my mom would say. She never got upset over it.

I was in prison when my nan died. I never knew my grandad as he died before I was born. Even though my nan and grandad on my dad's side lived in London, I had more to do with them than I did my mom's mom, who lived in Birmingham, as bad as that sounds.

Growing up, I always had fond memories of my mom. She used to be a smoker but stopped when she was 50, due to having a slight heart attack. She was our life and we all looked after her. My mom always put us first. No one came before her kids. After my dad died, my mom never had a relationship or married again. It sounds really selfish of me to say it now but I don't think we would have allowed it. Our dad was our life and we couldn't have had another man come into our house and tell us what to do. He would have had his head taken off and I think our mom knew that. She was all about her kids and her grandkids and where she lived was an open house for them. She was a diamond.

I went to her house every single day unless I was working away from Birmingham. Every morning I went there, I would bring bread and milk. My mom only wanted a certain small loaf. She would never want a full loaf. I'd have to go to three or four shops before I would find the exact small loaf that she wanted. Then I would go into her house and she would say, 'I'm a fucking nuisance.'

'No you ain't,' I would say. 'You're never a nuisance to me.'

The day I found out my mom died, it was the week before Christmas. I had been to work the night before at the NEC. I was with my wife Tania and my twin grandkids, who were one year old at the time. When we walked in and found her dead, we were devastated.

Tania and my mom got on really well and my mom thought the world of her. If me and Tania ever had a row, my mom always took Tania's side. She had also worked at the same catering shop as my mom for about ten years, and it was my mom who taught her how to cook, which is why they got on so well. It broke her heart when my mom died as Tania loved my mom to bits.

* * *

I was also close with my brothers. I don't really remember my older brother Noel because I didn't grow up with him, though he always used to call me Rocky from when I was 15 years old. His son is only six years younger than me, so I knew him more than I knew Noel. Regardless, I phone my brother all the time as we both bet on the horses and he's always sending me tips. I pop down to his house now and again.

My other brother David works as a builder. I used to work with him a few years ago and every now and then, if he had a bit of work on the side, he'd call and ask if I wanted to help out and I would go down and help. We get on now but when we were younger, we never got on. We used to fight all the time. It was only when we grew up and I had my daughter and he had kids that we became closer. Even then, at times, we would fall out.

One day about 15 years ago, when I was still boxing, I was at a job doing a load of digging for him. It then started to rain, followed by thunder and lightning.

'Let's call it a day now,' I said.

'No, no, we won't,' he said.

'Look. I've been here since seven o'clock and it's nearly four now. I'm fucking off,' I replied. He then started moaning, so I told him to stop being a fucking prick.

We started arguing and I told him, 'Stick your job up your arse.'

I walked off, heading back home. I had no car as David had picked me up. It was still pissing down with rain and I became soaked. My brother phoned me as I was walking. I answered the phone, told him to fuck off and hung up on him.

It was quicker to go to my mom's house than my own. So, I arrived at my mom's and knocked on the door. She opened it and saw how wet I was.

'What the fuck's up with you?' she said.

'I had an argument with that prick,' I replied.

'Why?' she asked.

'I was working with him and he was doing my fucking head in.' My mom always took my side in situations involving my brothers.

'That fucking bastard,' she said. 'You know what he's like. Don't work for him.'

'I won't. I won't,' I said.

From then on, whenever my brother called to say he had a bit of work for me, I'd say, 'I've told you. I'm not working for you again.'

'Come on now. Fucking grow up,' he would say.

'I'm not working for you.'

It was only after about five years that I started doing a little bit with him now and again. If I had no graft, he would phone me up. He always looked out from me. I ended up doing some work with him in Leamington. I was there for about three months. While I was there David had a slight heart attack, so he stopped doing that job but the gaffer still wanted me to carry on working there. I was getting the train as that was quicker than driving there.

My parents always made sure that we were fed, that our clothes were clean, that we never went to school scruffy and that our house was always clean and spotless. We never wanted nothing but we never asked for nothing. We just got what we could. We always got presents for Christmas and always had birthday parties. My dad used to come back from London with a big bag of sweets, throw them on the floor and say 'scrambles!' and we'd all be like animals, trying to grab the sweets. He used to bring his mates back and put on the Irish LPs. It was a happy time in my house, never sad times.

* * *

Back then, Acocks Green was a bit of a rough area. There were a couple of Irish families who my dad knew, so we used to say hello to them. There were also a few black families and we all used to hang out with each other. There were a lot of Irish kids and black kids, that's what our street was like. Colour wasn't a thing in our street. I always hung out with black kids and it wasn't a big deal. On the road I lived on, we all used to get on. We would all meet on the street and hang around with who was out and about really. We would all be over the park most nights, playing football and the old games like tracking and British Bulldog. Even while playing football, I always wanted to do a dirty tackle. We were just rough and ready, always getting up to no good.

David had mates who were a couple of years older than him. He started boxing with a few of them. The Shippereys, who were the same age as my two brothers, they were mad boxers. Desi Lane, a guy on our road, was a really good boxer. George Richards, who turned professional and fought future world champion Harry Simon on the undercard of a Prince Naseem [Hamed] world title defence at Wembley Arena. We all boxed and mingled together. We would play football and I'd probably end up having a fight with one of my brother's mates, and then we'd forget about it after five minutes. We all had fights. I had fights with the brothers of my brother's mates, who were my age. My brother would come in and give me an ear slap and say I was causing trouble. It was just how we were. Fighting every day, just mischief. Minor fights really.

* * *

It would be fair to say that I used to be in quite a bit of trouble when I was a kid, especially at school. From infants through to juniors and senior school, I was always cheeky, always in fights and always playing up. Not the class clown, but I would backchat teachers all the time. I generally didn't give a shit at school and always rebelled. Teachers even banned me from school trips as I was always in trouble.

An example of this took place when I was at junior school. There was a teacher who wouldn't let me and another kid go on a school trip as we had a fight in the classroom. The school had a garden at the back of this wooden hut where they used to grow strawberries, and it was this teacher's pride and joy. One morning as revenge, on the day the kids were going on the school trip, me and my mate woke up at about half-seven in the morning and we totally vandalised the garden. Just wrecked it to bits. We dug up all the plants and just smashed everything. The teachers knew it was us, but they couldn't prove it.

In assembly, the teachers were talking about the damage to the garden and we were just laughing. They asked me if I did it, but I said that it wasn't me. I lied to my mom and also told her that it wasn't me. I bare-faced lied to her as I knew that if I told her the truth, I'd have got a hiding, not off my dad but my mom. My dad would shout at us but he never hit us. Although my mom was the one who dished out the punishment, her bark was worse than her bite.

It wasn't the first time I had been mischievous as far as gardens were concerned. As kids, we used to go scrumping, where we would go into people's gardens and rob apples from their tree. The irony is that I would chase away anyone who would try to rob apples from the trees in my own garden!

* * *

Fighting other juniors was a regular thing for me. When I first went to junior school, there was another school that was over the park from where I lived. Kids from both schools used to share the park. During my time in juniors, I used to have fights with the kids from the other school all the time and would beat them up.

I remember once there was a kid who had just started at our school. He was a traveller and was very small. I remember me and him having a fight in the classroom and the teacher broke it up. He was like, 'Ah fucking hell. I'll get you after school.'

We later went over the park after school and me and this kid started having a fight. While we were fighting, these older lads came across to watch. They were probably about 16 or 17 years old, while me and this kid were 10. The fight with this kid went on for ages. The older lads ended up breaking it up, but I did manage to beat the kid up. We had a good fight. After that, we became not friends as such but we had a mutual respect. We didn't have any more fights between us. He thought he was a bit hard, probably because he was a traveller and he had fought a number of times, but I didn't give a fuck. It didn't bother me that he was a traveller. It was just a good fight for me. I had plenty of fights when I was a kid.

* * *

The mischief and backchat wasn't just aimed at the other kids. It was also aimed at the staff at the school. I remember one day in junior school telling a teacher to fuck off. In those days, they used to give you a slap across the palm of your hand. Well, I refused it.

'You're not giving me it,' I said and ran home.

I came home and my mom asked me what was the matter.

'The teacher wanted to give me the pump,' I said.

My mom always said that if they tried to give me a slap across the hand or any other corporal punishment, that I was not to have it.

'What did she want to give you a slap for?' she said. I said that I didn't do anything.

My mom always stuck up for her kids. She marched up to the school and went to see the teacher in the classroom. She started going mad at this teacher.

'You want to slap my son? No one gives my kid the cane. I don't give him the cane so you're not going to do it. He hasn't even done anything,' she shouted.

'Oh, I think he has Mrs Buckley,' said the teacher.

'Well, what's he done?' she said.

'He told me to fuck off.'

Our mom's face just dropped and she looked at me, as she always taught us to respect others. She asked me for my side of the story. I said some bullshit, but she knew that I was lying.

'I'll deal with him,' she said as she grabbed me out of the classroom. As soon as we got home, I can't remember if I got a slap from her. But just my mom going mad at me was enough to do my head in.

CHAPTER 2

Move to the big school

After years of giving both the kids and the teachers grief at primary school, it was time to move to a secondary school. The move to big school was not difficult as I already knew some of the pupils. They were mates of mine who were a couple of years older than me. The kids from the two local junior schools ended up at the same senior school, which at the time was called Heartfield.

When I first attended Heartfield, I was fighting these kids from the other junior school (which was called Oaklands) straight away as a way of establishing myself. Even though I was small, everyone knew that I did boxing as I'd been doing it since I was ten at Talbot ABC. I used to bring my trophies into school just to show them to the kids and the staff.

'Ah look, I won this,' I would say as I showed off my awards.

Yet the fights and mischief that happened at junior school followed me when I went to senior school and started from the first day I arrived. And for once, I was minding my own business.

My first day at seniors, I was waiting by the classroom and some ginger kid from the third year started coming up to us new kids trying to show off. He saw me and walked towards me.

'What you looking at?' he asked.

I looked at him. 'You. Why? What you going to do?'

Break time arrived and he came over to me, still trying to give it the big 'un. Little did he know my older brother David was in the same school, as well as plenty of lads from round by my road. He was standing in front of me, being loud and acting like he was a big man.

I just started punching him.

He was shocked, maybe because I was a new lad and he didn't think I would do that. I kept hitting him and my brother and his mates were like, 'Go Pete, fuck him up!' I found out the kid was just all mouth and he didn't come near me again.

I got on with most lads at school but would not take any shit from any of them and they knew it. However, there were times when some kids would try their luck.

One day, a lad knocked into me outside of class. This kid was in the year below me but was big for his age and a lot of the kids were scared of him. But I didn't care. When he knocked into me, I told him to fucking watch it. He got mouthy at me, so I banged him in the mouth. We started fighting but our fight got broken up. He kept shouting to me as we were getting separated.

'You're dead after school,' he said.

'Fucking sound, you prick. See you over the park after school,' I replied.

For the rest of the day, all people were saying to me was, 'You fighting that big lad? He's hard you know.'

'Fuck him,' I replied.

After school, everyone headed over to the local park to see who would win this fight. As soon as he came towards me, he started getting mouthy again. I just cracked him straight on the jaw and dropped him. Everyone was cheering and shouting as he fell to the ground. As he was getting up, I booted him in his chest and he went down again. He got back up and I was standing in my boxing stance. He took a few swings at me, but I ducked them.

Left. Right. Left hook. Bang!

I put him down on his arse again, then he put his hands up.

'Leave it out!' he shouted.

But I gave him one more dig and dropped him again. That was the end of that.

* * *

When I went to senior school, quite a few people were scared of me. My missus is two years younger than me and went to the same school I did. When I was in school in the third year, she said that when she saw me she would do a U-turn as I was quite aggressive and loud.

Everyone knew who I was at school, and also at the other senior schools. A few of us from the school would go to another school and have a fight with the hardest kids from that school. Or a few of us would be on a bus and lads from another school would get on and it would just kick off. If someone had a beef with a lad from another school, we would arrange a fight between them at the local park to sort it out. Even when I wasn't at school and fights were going to happen, I would still turn up as in a silly way I classed it as my school and I wanted to back my mates up.

My name was quite well known around Acocks Green as I used to have quite a lot of fights. People used to arrange fights for me to have with other people, so I would be fighting all the time.

Once, there were these kids from Shaftmoor Lane and there was one lad in particular in the group who was about a year older than me. He used to hang around with all these older kids and I would hang around with older kids also. We got along with them but I remember one of my older mates saying about this kid, 'Ah yeah, this Timmy's hard.'

Someone else said, 'Ah, Peter would batter him.' So they arranged a fight between me and this kid.

We went to Fox Hollies Park and basically had a fight. It was a good fight and I beat him up while the rest of our group watched. I wasn't in a gang as such but a lot of us used to hang about with each other. There were about 11 of us in the group, which today would be classed as a gang. But we didn't class it as a gang. We were just mates who all hung about with each other.

I used to hang about with people who were in trouble as they grew up around me. If one of my mates had a fight in a pub, a load of us would go down and I'd be there with them. And they would vice versa to me. They are still my mates now.

These moments of fighting and just being up to no good, though happening during school hours, weren't just limited to inside the school. When I was about 12 or 13 I went on a school trip to the Severn Valley railway, which is a train line that stops off at various towns. Not long after we arrived there, I was caught robbing out of their shop. I was taken back to the school and the headmaster phoned my mom. She came to the school and gave me a right telling off in front of the headmaster. She was going mad. As we were walking home from the school, my mom was still angry.

'You're showing us up and making us look like lowlifes,' she said. 'What were you robbing anyway?'

'Some fridge magnets for you.'

She looked at me and said, 'Fucking fridge magnets?' as she slapped me up the head and called me a 'dopey little prat'.

About a week or so later at school, there were letters going out about a trip for a week in Germany. Me being me, I put my hand up. The teacher laughed.

'What you laughing at?' I said.

She replied, 'You're barred from every school trip from now on.'

'Why? Cos I got caught robbing?'

'Yes,' she said.

When I got home, I told my mom about the trip and what the teacher said. She laughed.

'Why you laughing, mom?'

'Hold on,' she said. 'Your dad works down in London, Monday to Friday every week, and you think you're going abroad for a week?' She was still laughing as she said it.

'You can't even go to Severn Valley railway without getting into trouble, so you won't be going overseas,' she said, still laughing her head off. She kept breaking into little fits of laughter.

'You going abroad? Where did I get you from?'

* * *

When I was about 12 or 13, I joined the army cadets. I did it for about eight months. I was given a uniform and used to go once a week. I joined because a few lads from school were going and it sounded good. I liked that I would end up shooting a rifle and camping and all of that, plus I was fit and had good endurance for the activities. It also helped a bit with my discipline as I did love going every week.

I would go twice a week sometimes and would even miss boxing training to attend if I wasn't in the championships, as it was getting quite hard to match me on some club shows. We would go on trips to places like to the Brecon Beacons, as well as learn how to strip and put back together a Lee Enfield rifle 303. I couldn't wait to shoot it. I can remember the first time I was at a rifle range. I got two bullseyes out of five shots and was buzzing.

I used to go camping for the weekend doing drills and stuff like that. One time, there was a lad there who me and the cadets decided, while he was asleep, to put Imac remover all over his eyebrows.

The next morning when we were having a cold shower, he was going mad as he realised that he had none of his eyebrows left! The sergeant in charge gave us all a bollocking. Yet afterwards he admitted to us that the lad needed to man up and that he found it funny himself. After some time at cadets, I got bored. It was too much shouting for me and I couldn't be arsed. I was always thinking of joining the army but after I had spent time in a detention centre, I was told that as I had been in trouble I wasn't allowed to join. I would have loved the army.

* * *

My life outside of school was just as eventful, especially when I would hang out with my mates. Two mates of mine are Ada and Morris.

Me and Ada have known each other since we were kids, since we were ten years old to be precise. Our first encounter was at the local youth disco, where the two of us were both break dancing, doing our moves on the dance floor. We parted ways and it wasn't until a couple of years later that we met back up, this time in school. The rest is history. Well, we skipped history to get up to no good!

Ada and I speak every day on the phone more or less. We were in the nick together, though we knew each other before that. He was never really in trouble. I got him in trouble actually, as he was robbing with me. We got caught robbing a shop. We went into custody. I got 12 months and he got six months as he had never been in trouble. Me and him got into trouble after that, such as going robbing or jumping on the bus. He is a real good mate of mine. As is Morris. Me and him have been mates since we were 12 years old. Later on, we were in prison a few times together. I don't see him as much as I used to but speak to him on the phone. A hard geezer. Not many people messed around with him. He was a person you didn't fuck around with. But me and him were tight. We had loads of fights on people together. He was a geezer who was right by your side if you were having a fight with someone. Me and him have been in clubs and had fights in which we were well outnumbered. But he'd have my back. He wouldn't leave me. Same with Ada as well.

Once, me and Morris were at a club in Knowle, near Solihull. It was me, Morris and another geezer called Robbie, and there were a load of geezers out that night from a part of Solihull called Damson Wood, as the club was near their manor. I came out the club and a geezer tried to get in my taxi. Seeing this, I dragged him out and banged him. The group from Damsel Wood ran out of the club and were firmed up. There were a few of them. We were just beating them up as they ran out of the club to fight us. We left them all on the street. They all shit themselves.

On another day, we were in Solihull the one night, having a drink there. A few of them came in the pub, saw us and just done one.

Me and Ada, when we were about 15 or 16, walked past a club in Acocks Green. We noticed that there was a bouncer on the door on his own as his mate didn't turn up. He was throwing a couple of pissed-up blokes out of the pub and they in turn were giving him shit. As me and Ada were walking past, we saw what was happening. We both came over and chinned these two blokes, who looked in their thirties. I bumped into the bouncer recently and he said that at the time though he wasn't scared, he was a bit worried as he was on his own that night. We done him a favour, so he used to let us in the club after that.

With Ada, a geezer tried to rob his flat one day. They caught the guy who done it, but he managed to run off. So, I went into a pub one night in Solihull. It was just me and a couple of lads I don't really drink with and I noticed the guy there, playing pool. There was a few of them. I went over to him.

'You fucking tried to rob my mate's flat?' I said.

'Nah nah,' he answered.

I just whacked him and knocked him out in the pub. His mates just froze as they didn't expect it. They didn't say fuck all.

We used to go up Solihull quite a bit. On one occasion, we were up there and Ada asked a geezer for a light.

'Fuck off, you black c***,' the geezer said back to him.

As this guy stood up, I slipped in between them and just hit him with an uppercut, which left him sparked out. But another mate of mine, who was a taxi driver, saw what happened, pulled up and said, 'Quick, jump in.' We jumped in the taxi and he dropped us off.

We were about 25 when this happened. We're still good mates now. I don't even have to see them all the time. We keep in good contact. Ada don't live far from me, so I do pop down to see him quite a bit. Morris lives further, so I don't see him as much. He always works. Morris is a painter and decorator. He used to sort me out and he used to decorate my flat for next to nothing.

CHAPTER 3

Fighting in and out of the ring

The fighting continued outside of school, although this time it was in a more disciplined setting. The boxing gym.

I first went to a boxing gym when I was ten years old. My dad used to put boxing on the TV when I was a kid. I used to love watching the likes of Barry McGuigan, Tony Sibson and John Conteh, though my favourite fighter was Charlie Magri.

As much as I was a fan of the sport, David was really the reason why I went into boxing. He joined a boxing club with his mates before I did. Eventually, most of the kids on our road started to go to this boxing club and I started following them. As all the kids on my road done boxing, I also wanted to go.

'You're not fucking coming up,' David groaned. The big brother didn't want the little brother following him around everywhere.

'You're taking him,' said my mom, and she would give both me and my brother the 50p it cost to get the train.

My brother was the inspiration to start boxing. He had about 25 amateur fights and won about 20. He was quite a good boxer, though he would tell you himself that he wasn't as good as me. He'd win two and lose one, but he was always in a good fight.

There used to be about ten to 15 of us who would walk into the gym every Monday, Wednesday, Friday. We would all play football together, all hang about with each other and all go boxing together. Quite a few of them boxed in the end.

* * *

The amateur club we all went to was called Talbot ABC, which was a fairly new club at the time. It used to be a car centre and the kids would train in the canteen upstairs.

It was a decent gym. Les Barnet was the trainer and he done a lot for us there. He's dead now, though in his time he did a lot of good for the sport. He was from the Black Country and he used to help train Pat Cowdell when Pat was going to the Olympics. He was a very good trainer, a pure boxing man through and through. He would teach the kids who attended how to actually box and not just fight, as well as work on our technique. He wanted us to hit and not be hit, and didn't like us engaging in a brawl. Whenever I went to Talbot, I would go into the canteen, put the tables out of the way and get the bags out of the cupboard. On the ground, we had a canvas floor.

My first time at Talbot, I was really looking forward to it. I thought I would go there and just fight but it wasn't like that. First, they had you skipping and doing drills such as shadow boxing and going on the pads. Although I was good at skipping, I found it boring and didn't really see what good it was doing me. I knew that it was supposed to help get your feet and balance right, but I didn't really like it, though I had to do it as it was part of the training. I never really liked the speed ball either, so I rarely used it. But the rest of training I loved, especially the sparring and the pad work. I used to go three times a week.

After six months we got a canvas, a ring, no underlay, but three ropes were put up. I was buzzing, ready to spar in what was to me at the time a proper ring.

The first time I went there and sparred, I was up against an older kid who was around David's age. During our spar, I got caught with punches a lot. He jabbed me silly and was really taking the piss a bit. I got hot-headed but the lad I was in with had had a few fights. My brother saw this and got the hump. He jumped into the ring and ended up giving this kid a bit of a battering. My brother had also had a few fights by then.

After a few weeks, I picked up on all the skills you needed to learn to become good at the sport and started to become good at sparring. I got better and better at sparring and started to love it. I would spar anyone I could. I would spar older and heavier lads. Even when I was a pro, I would spar heavyweights, even though I weighed around the nine-stone mark during my pro career. I didn't give a fuck. I used to like testing myself and I liked fighting bigger geezers. Even if I was just having a move around with a new kid, I loved sparring as it was more physical than skipping or hitting a punchbag. It was my favourite bit of training.

Later on, when I bumped into people I knew at boxing shows, they would say, 'I bet you never have to spar because you are fighting all the time.' I would tell them that I didn't spar much, though that wasn't the case. Sparring was the main part of training I used to do, though I would stop sparring about a week before an area title fight as I couldn't risk getting a cut.

* * *

While I was enjoying boxing, there was still tension between me and a lot of people at school, especially the teachers. I didn't really like a lot of them. There were only a few of them that I got on with. I got on with the PE teacher and the art teacher was alright. Certain subjects like maths and history I enjoyed and was good at. I was also good at geography and RE but English I found hard. My reading was sound but my writing was terrible. I couldn't put pen to paper. The teachers never picked up on my dyslexia. I could read but couldn't spell, yet the teachers just classed me as a bit dopey. I guess that is why I was rebellious at school as no one taught me in a way that took that into account.

There was an English teacher called Mrs Brown, who was on a placement at the school. She took the piss out of me because of my struggles with spelling. This teacher embarrassed me in front of the class and made me feel really small.

She used to have a spelling test to assess your spelling age. I could read all day long and words were not a problem. But when it came to spelling, I could not put the letters together. I just couldn't do it. In the second year, I did the spelling test and from that she worked out my spelling age. When I was 12, my spelling age was something like nine. Like I say, I was dyslexic but at this time it wasn't picked up on.

'What's your spelling age?' Mrs Brown said. I just ignored her. She came over to my desk, turned my test paper and saw my spelling age.

'Nine!' she said as she belittled me in front of everyone.

Because I was fiery anyway when I was young, I just told her to fuck off. I then picked up a chair and threw it across the room. As it smashed into the blackboard behind her, I told her to fuck off again as I walked out the classroom. Everyone used to like her but I never got on with her. After I did it, I just fucked off out the school. I went home and my mom was going mad at me.

'Look mom. She embarrassed me in front of everyone. Made me look like an idiot.'

Yet Mrs Powell was different. She was my English teacher in the third year and I got on with her well. She was a real nice lady and easy to talk to.

She went to the headmaster and explained that I had a spelling disorder [as dyslexia wasn't diagnosed then]. She was the one who worked out that I was dyslexic, which was great.

One day Mrs Powell said to me, 'I'm hearing all these things in the staff room about you, Peter, and that is not the same Peter Buckley I deal with.'

'Yeah, 'cos you don't treat me like an idiot,' I said.

'You're not an idiot, are you?' she asked.

'Well, I don't think I am,' I replied.

She was persistent. 'Well, you need to show them that you're not, then.'

'Yeah, but they haven't got the time of day for me.'

'Well, make them have the time of day for you,' she said.

'Certain teachers just piss me off. It's too far gone now. They don't like me,' I replied.

Some teachers, I would go into their lessons and straight away they'd be like, 'Out!' They just didn't want me in their class.

Because I was dyslexic, they never had time for me. So I compensated by playing up.

She asked me why and I said that I was frustrated and told her about the teacher that embarrassed me.

'What's the problem?' she asked.

'I can't spell,' I replied.

'You can,' she said.

She was the only teacher there who figured out what was wrong with my writing and she used to teach me how to spell. She would sit me down and give me one-to-one sessions to help me improve my spelling. She knew I could read, it was just putting the spelling together. I can read well but spelling-wise I really have to take my time. Over the years, I have taught myself how to spell. Texting on my phone I'm OK. But when it comes to putting pen to paper, I struggle.

* * *

I was still enjoying going to Talbot at this stage. Working on the pads, sparring in the ring, hitting the heavy bag. I just loved it. Soon, I was ready to have my first fight.

I was 11 years old when I fought for the first time. I always remember the name of my first amateur opponent, Ray Petite from Castle Vale. I boxed him on Castle Vale's own show. I won not only my first fight but the best fighter of the night award.

For my second fight, I was supposed to box on our home show at Talbot ABC but my opponent didn't turn up. Yet there was a kid from Nechells called Lee Williams who was there and needed an opponent. He'd had six fights and won them all. A big lad, he was between half a stone and three quarters of a stone heavier than me, which is a lot at that age. My trainer said I could fight him but told me straight about his record, how good of a boxer he was and that I would be giving away weight.

'I'll fight him,' I said. He beat me but I thought I beat him. Again, a fight I was in won best fight of the night.

I won my next 19 fights on the bounce, which included a run in the schoolboy championships when I was 13. I reached the semi-finals of the tournament and was scheduled to meet Nigel Wenton. Nigel went on to become a good pro who signed with Don King, I believe. People rated him and were saying to me, 'You're boxing Nigel Wenton?' But I didn't give a fuck who Nigel Wenton was.

When he got into the ring, he had England badges on his shorts as he had won two schoolboy titles. His dad was a boxer and he came from a big boxing family in Liverpool. When I turned pro, I boxed his brother Richie.

During our fight, I ended up with a standing count. I'd never had a standing count before. I was thinking, 'Fucking hell.' He beat me by unanimous decision and went on to win the schoolboy title that year. He won three or four schoolboy titles and became a decorated amateur, which included boxing for England. I wasn't disheartened by the loss as I knew Nigel was a good boxer.

I then entered the junior ABAs. Like at the schoolboys, I got to the semi-finals but I lost the fight before getting into the ring. At the weigh-in, I was about half a pound overweight. I was told I had an hour to make the weight. So I put a black bag on, did some skipping and some running. I worked my backside off to lose that half pound. But I couldn't do it. I was a kid and had nothing on me. You couldn't even pinch the weight off me.

As a result, I was out of the championships.

I had a few more club fights, winning most of them. One of these was against a kid from Kings Norton Boxing Club called Dean Beech. Everyone was rating this kid. He was knocking his opponents out. For his age, he could really punch. The Kings Norton Boxing Club was quite a new club when I was about. It didn't really gain the respect other clubs had at that time. But Dean Beech was a real tough kid. I boxed him at the Irish Centre on a Sunday morning show. I was about 14 at the time. The night before, I'd been at a house party. Despite this, I still beat him on a majority decision. He was screaming that he got robbed. I just told him to fuck off.

I got further in the championships than anyone else in the club. I started being a bit cocky as I was winning all my fights and I thought I was the bee's knees. I would be a bit hard on some of the lads in sparring and getting into fights at school. I loved fighting older, bigger lads and beating them up, and I got a bit of a rep for it. My trainer Les told me off at the club about fighting out of the ring. The cheeky little fucker that I was, I told him to fuck off and ended up leaving the club. Now that I'm older, I know how disrespectful that was. But at the time, I couldn't give a fuck.

I was the best boxer at Talbot ABC and I knew it. There were some good lads but I was the best boxer there. Soon afterwards, my mate Joey, who I knew well as my dad knew his dad as they were both Irish, told me to come to Ladywood Boxing Club.

'Why are you at Talbot?' he said. 'Come to our club, an Irish club.' That's how I started going to Ladywood.

I would get the number one bus from Acocks Green to the city centre and walk up to the community centre. I used to do this a couple of times a week. And I'd have fights on the buses all the time when going to training. Nothing major would need to happen for fights to start. It could just be, 'What you looking at, mate?' and I'd be fighting. Sometimes when I arrived at the club with bruises from the fights, some of the other boxers would ask, 'What you been up to?' I'd just say I had a fight on the bus. They'd normally ask then if I won!

The head coach of the club was Dave Tully. He happened to know my dad as he came from Ireland. Sean Keely was one of the coaches. He was very good at getting people fit for a bout. He would go on five-mile runs with the boxers and it was hard to keep up with him as he was very fit. He was 40 when I started going to Ladywood, which to me at the time was old! Not too long ago, I bumped into Sean in the bookies. He is 80 years old now but he doesn't look it. He was always a fitness fanatic. He also knew my dad and I had a lot of respect for him and a lot of time for him too.

The sparring at Ladywood was different to how it was done at Talbot. With Talbot, I developed my skills and technique as well as learning how to hit and not get hit. At Ladywood, Dave was more about having a tear-up, a dog fight with everyone. He was a blood, sweat and tears type of man. Sparring was harder and the fighters went full on each other. Although I left Talbot, after about 20 fights I still knew how to hit and avoid the punches coming back. Yet Dave, the trainer at Ladywood, liked his fighters to have a war at every spar. Now that I'm older and wiser, I think that was wrong. Frank O'Sullivan, who ran Birmingham City ABC, is all about learning to box.

He said to me that when I boxed for Talbot I was a very good boxer, but when I went to Ladywood my style changed as I became a slugger, and that should never have become my style because I was a pure boxer.

The way I see it now, Talbot was a boxing club and Ladywood was a fighting club. With my boxing skills and the Ladywood way of fighting, it made me a good kid in the amateurs.

* * *

As well as boxing for Ladywood I also played other team sports, both at school and regional level. I took part in the pole vault and represented the school in cross-country. I also took part in long-distance events for Sparkhill Harriers, a regional athletics team. I was always playing football and ended up playing for the school football team. I was an aggressive tackler on the field, not that great ability-wise, but I still made the team. Yet I loved rugby also. The only thing I hated was cricket and especially the coach who ran it. He was also a librarian and I always used to get boxing books out the library whenever I went there.

On one occasion, me and him were arguing and I said, 'Cricket is crap anyway.'

'You couldn't bat anyway,' he replied.

'Go on then. I'll play cricket for the team next time.'

I played in the school team in one of their fixtures. I was in to bat but got out for a duck. When in the field, I just used to slide off and the coach would give me loads of stick as I was walking off. I just told him to fuck off and said to him that cricket is a wanker's sport. I got thrown out for about a week then for swearing at him.

* * *

Although I was participating in all of these sports, both inside and outside of school, my main sport at the time was rugby. I started playing the sport when I was 12 or 13. I was a real good full-back for the school team and I loved it as it is a physical sport. Even though I wasn't big, I was good at tackling and kicking as well as taking penalties. Not many players were able to go past me as I didn't give a fuck and would dive straight at them. I was so good that I got picked to play for the year above me and would sometimes play for the year above that. Eventually, I ended up playing for the fifth year.

One of the PE teachers asked me if I wanted to play rugby out of school as he played for this team outside of school hours. He managed to get me into the team for Kings Norton Boys as he used to play for the adult version of it. The teacher would pick me up and take me to the games.

I would play for the school on the Saturday and for Kings Norton on the Sunday. Though I was training at Talbot, boxing wasn't really on my mind at the time; it was rugby. Yet the fighting that I did at school also happened on the pitch.

I was playing a rugby match once and I gave a lad a high tackle round the neck. He started ranting and raving, 'You nearly broke my fucking neck.' He then squared up to me. He was a lot bigger than me and probably thought I was going to shit myself. I just called him a prick and told him to fuck off. As I turned away, he punched me in my back quite hard. I turned round and punched him in his mouth. Before you know it, we were fighting on the ground. The fight was broken up and we both got sent off.

My rugby teacher went mad at me, telling me that I wouldn't be playing again if I didn't know how to control myself. 'But he punched me in the back,' I said. But he wasn't having any of it.

About a week later, I was on the bus going to Ladywood and I was with my mate Joey. The bus stopped and some people got on, one of whom was the lad that I had fought during the game. He got on with two of his mates and looked up at me straight away. I told Joey about the shit that happened with him the week before at the rugby game. I went up to him on the bus and said, 'You remember me?' We soon started fighting on the bus. His mates jumped up to help but Joey jumped up himself and backed me up. Now we were all fighting on the bus. At the next stop, the bus driver came upstairs and threw us all off at Fiveways, which is in the city centre. This lad was still game for a fight and said, 'Come on then. One on one.' There was an underpass nearby, so we went there and had a bit of a fight. He was quite strong but couldn't really fight.

He tried to grab me but I gave him a few shots. His nose was busted up and was pissing out blood.

'OK, OK. Just leave it out. You won, OK,' he said as he eventually gave up and put his hands up. His mates were telling me the same thing. I think I shocked him as I wasn't as big as he was.

During one game, I hurt my shoulder tackling someone and had to pull out of a fight at a club show as a result. My boxing trainer said that I had to choose one or the other as I would be unable to do both. Though I still loved rugby, I picked boxing and that became my main sport.

* * *

The gym at Ladywood was a community centre. We would go in and there would be four cupboards. In each cupboard would be punchbags, which we would get out and hang on to the makeshift chains. There was the usual equipment in storage, such as skipping ropes and pads. Our ring had four posts with three ropes on and we would put the ropes up ourselves. But it didn't have a canvas, so the more we fought the more the surface would get wet. It didn't really matter. We didn't have much in the way of facilities. It was a real basic gym. A big group of us used to do a lot of running round the block before we would spar.

At the time we had a real good club, with schoolboy and ABA contenders and champions. We had Steve Malone, who won everything as an amateur at schoolboys, junior and senior level. But when he became a senior, he didn't do as well as he was fighting men then. He already had man strength when he was 14 but that advantage was lost when he became an adult. We had Melvin Byrne, who boxed for England. Timmy Manning and Lynton Shaw were good amateurs. As was Bobby Mack, who fought Montell Griffin as a pro. Bobby could have been a real good pro but he was into fashion design. Small Heath and Birmingham City were good gyms that were in the city but I'd say Ladywood was possibly the best gym in the Midlands at the time.

Another boxer who was part of the club was Kid Milo. His real name was Winston and he had a good pro career, winning the Commonwealth super middleweight title. I used to spar with him when I was a kid. He was right tough. He would be in the ring and would be sparring three people at the same time. That is one way sparring was done at the gym.

You would be sparring, the coaches would say 'switch' and in would come another fighter. My own sparring sessions were hard. One day, I sparred three lads. Mates really, I'd say, who were older than me, Desmond Dewyer and Lynton Shaw. One of them, I broke his nose, and the other one, I split his eye. Both were sent to A&E. Plus, I fucked up another kid with a rib shot. It was no holds barred. As I said, sparring was hard.

When I was about 15, I was in town to meet Winston on my way to sparring and a guy comes up to me, a big fucker, and tries to rob me, as I used to wear a bit of gold.

'Yo,' he said. 'Take your gold off.'

'Nah man,' I said.

'Yo, I want — .'

'Nah man.'

I thought this geezer was going to batter me. He would have had to kill me to take my gold off me. But then, I spotted Winston.

'Winst,' I called.

This geezer turned around.

'You know him?' he asked.

'Yeah,' I said. 'Winst, this mug is trying to do me here.'

Winston looked straight at the geezer and said, 'Just fuck off. This is me bredrin', you know what I mean.'

'Oh, sorry Winst. Sorry,' the guy said and left.

I said to Winston, 'Fuck me, I'm glad you came as he was a hard geezer.'

Winston was a townie and everyone knew him. They still do now. I knew him because when I moved from Talbot to Ladywood, our club had black kids and Irish kids. It was a rough club.

* * *

Back at school, trouble remained. When I was in senior school, the cane was still in. I remember once I had a fight in school and I was sent to the headmaster's office. He was going to give me five strips of the cane.

'You're not,' I said to the headmaster. 'My own mom and dad don't hit me, so I'm not letting you do it.'

'Well, if you don't you will be suspended.'

'I don't care,' I said. 'You're not caning me.' I was suspended and went home.

The school phoned my mom to tell her I'd been suspended. I told her that they wanted to cane me but I refused to let them do it.

'That's right, but you're in trouble for having a fight at school,' she said.

Because of this, my mom grounded me. I say grounded but we really didn't get kept in in those days as there were too many of us in the house. As I said earlier, our house was at the back of a park. We always used to call it ball park. At the bottom of our garden, there was a fence. You would just jump over the fence to get to the park. So when my mom said that I was staying in, after half an hour I would be getting itchy feet.

I'd be like, 'Mom, can I go out?'

'No you can't.'

'Mom, can I go out?'

'No.'

'Mom, can I go out?'

'No.'

'Alright, I'll just go into the garden.'

Before long, I'd just climb over the fence and go to the park.

I was only a kid. All my brothers, my mates and the kids on my street, they all played football over the park as well as other games. Say I got disciplined. When my mom went off on one I'd shit myself but we never got beatings. We probably got a slap. With some of my mates, their mom used to get the broom and get the belt. Our mom only used to have to raise her voice. Sometimes she grabbed you by the face with her hands, though that was extreme. You would have to really push her over the edge. Her shouting at us was enough as we had respect for her.

CHAPTER 4

Robbing while an amateur

Outside of school and the gym, I had started to go robbing. I started doing it when I was 13. Just little bits like breaking into schools was how it started.

I was robbing a lot of social clubs, emptying the fruit machines and burgling shops. What we used to do was smash the alarms off with a sledgehammer and then go in through the back, knocking the bricks out the walls. Once we were in, we would rob all the cigarettes. We used to do that all the time. Rob social clubs, pubs and anything like that, but never houses. I used to hang around with a lot of older kids who had been in trouble. I just went with them really. I had my own mind but because my dad was working away a lot, I never used to ask my mom for money. She would give me what she could but I never asked her for money. I'd just go out robbing.

Sometimes I was just lucky when it came to robbing. When I was about 13, I found the keys left in an old phone box that were used to unlock the phones in there, so that the change inside them could be released in the change slot to be collected. The same key could be used for every phone in every phone box. For about a week, I would get the bus out of my area and go around different phone boxes and open them to get the change inside. Then one day, the key snapped and that was the end of that.

I used to go to Birmingham City's football ground as well when I was a kid, not to watch the football game but to just have the crack. I was down there when I was a kid when they played Leeds and all the fans ran on the pitch fighting with the police and other fans. But I had a scarf over my face so the police couldn't pick me out as a few people I knew back then got locked up for what happened that day. Though I got away with this, the trouble I was getting myself into was escalating.

* * *

The boxers at Ladywood didn't just have bouts in our home city. We would go to other places and have bouts with fighters that were local to that place. One of the more memorable times this happened was when we went to a place called Speke in Liverpool when I was 13. I boxed a local kid in my fight and beat him, and it felt really hostile in the venue after my fight. After we got on the coach some of the supporters, who were kids, threw bottles at it. Five of us from Ladywood were fighting on the bill, four of us won our fights, and I think they didn't like it. Before the fight, I remember going into an off-licence down there and thinking how rough it was. There was Perspex on the front of the building and literally a slot which was the door and part of it was caged off. That was one of the most hostile places I boxed as an amateur.

I went to box in Ireland as an amateur and I stayed with a guy called Phil Sutcliffe, who later went on to represent Ireland in the Los Angeles Olympic Games in 1984. Soon after our fight, he sent me a postcard signed by himself, Ray Close, Steve Collins and Dave McAuley. All these top boxers had signed it. I had this postcard for years and years. Then when I lived in my flat, I had a fireplace which had a gap away from the wall. The postcard somehow managed to drop down there and I could never get it back. I was 15 years old when they sent it over.

* * *

As I say, the sparring at Ladywood was tough. But while at Ladywood, I also sparred with other boxers from other gyms. One such time occurred when I was 15. I was in the NABC Championships and decided to visit Birmingham City ABC to get some extra sparring. They were based in town and used to have their gym above a bank. One of the first people I sparred at the club went on to have a good pro career, followed by a good career as a trainer. His name was Rob McCracken. I sparred him when he hadn't even had an amateur fight. Me and him are more or less the same age. But I was little, he was really tall and skinny and had a wicked jab. When he was jabbing at me I would think, 'Bleeding hell, he's good for a kid that hasn't boxed.' I also sparred a lad called John Morgan, who was another good lad. After that, I used to see Rob in the championships or I would hear that he was doing well, as although I packed in my amateur career after my NABC final, he was becoming a big name around boxing in Birmingham. He always got far in the tournament. His brothers Max and Spencer also boxed and I still see them about now and again.

I always got on with them but Rob was always the best boxer of them all.

* * *

Between robbing and my amateur career, I hadn't been in school. Me refusing to be caned by the headmaster after I had a fight with another kid meant that I was suspended for about 18 months. That was when the robbing started and I was getting into trouble. My mom said I had to get back to school. That was in the third year. I missed the whole of the fourth year and didn't go back until the fifth year. My mom kept getting in touch with the education department but heard nothing off them. Not even a letter. Yet I would still go up to the school at dinnertime during the break. Teachers used to tell me to get off the grounds and I would tell them to fuck off.

While I was away in the third year, our school merged with another senior school called Heartfield. Later on, that new school would be merged with a school called Pitmaston and become Ninestiles. I remember going up there on the first day of the merger and ended up having a fight with some kid. Everyone said he was a hard kid but I beat him up. I used to just keep getting thrown off the grounds. In the fifth year, I had to go up to town with my mom to an education meeting. The school accepted me back but I had to sign a contract saying that I would behave and that I would attend lessons and all that bollocks. But on coming back, I would still take the piss out of the teachers.

One day, I was in class with a good mate of mine. There was a teacher who used to stink and she was sitting on the table with her legs open.

'You stink!' As soon as I said it, she threw me out the classroom.

So, I'm walking round the school and the headmaster caught me.

'What you doing out of school?'

I told him that I'd been thrown out of a lesson. He then phoned my mom and she had to come down to the school.

He said to me, 'Look, we're not having you in the school no more. You're a nuisance basically.' I'd only been back at school two weeks and I was expelled again!

* * *

When I got thrown out of Ninestiles, I ended up in a school in Newtown called Burlington, which was on the other side of Birmingham from where I lived. I had to catch two buses to get there. On my first day there I was late and the teacher had a bit of a go at me for not coming in on time and tried to show me up while doing so. I told him to fuck off and that I didn't want to even be there. The next thing, I was in the headmaster's room. Now this school was for kids who had been in trouble. The headmaster gave me a speech that this school was more relaxed than the typical mainstream school but that I couldn't speak to the teachers like that. After returning to class, I soon realised that all the kids in the school had been expelled from other schools, so in that sense they were just like me. Breaktime came and I was walking around when some lad comes over and tries to take the piss out of me. He asked me where I was from.

'Acocks Green,' I said.

'Acocks Green is full of pricks,' he replied.

I banged him in the mouth and we started fighting on the floor. He tried to poke my eye out, so I bit his finger until he started screaming. The teachers came in and tried to break us up. Once they did so, we were sent to the headmaster's office.

'We won't stand for this,' said the headmaster.

He also mentioned that they were quite used to fighting on school grounds, so we just got a telling off. I didn't get in any trouble there and even made a few mates. When I was later locked up in Brockhill, a few lads from Burlington were in there. That was just the type of school it was.

* * *

When I attended Burlington, I was training for the NABCs. I used to go to a gym in Hockley now and then on a Friday and do some sparring. There were probably about 60 kids in the school. They knew I was boxing and that I was in the championships. I went into school with a note supposedly signed by my mom, saying that I had to be out of school on certain days as I was training. But the note had been forged by me.

Then one day I forgot I had an appointment with the dentist and my mom actually phoned the school as I had to go. The school said that I didn't have to come in on this particular day as 'she' had sent in a note saying that I had training.

'I don't know what you're on about,' my mom said.

They started telling my mom that I'd been bringing all these letters for training and that they'd been letting me not attend school as I needed the day to do training.

Soon after this I was in a classroom, which was two storeys up, and very bored.

'I'm fucking off out of here,' I said to the teacher.

'No you're not,' he said and locked the door on me.

'I'm going,' I said.

I climbed out the window, went down the drainpipe and walked home. I was expelled from Burlington at 15 years old, so I was out of school then. I wasn't really in education for the last two years of my school life.

* * *

On the positive side, I entered the junior NABCs when I was 15. To win in Birmingham, you had to have two fights on the same day just to get to the final as there were so many entries.

I boxed Ray Petite again and someone else and beat them both on points. My opponent in the Birmingham final was a familiar face, Dean Beech. This fight had higher stakes than when we last fought as it was in the Birmingham final at Nechells.

Dean had stopped all his three opponents and I had beat my three opponents on points to get this far. Leading up to the final, he kept saying, 'I'm gonna stop Buckley.' I'm hearing him say this and thinking, 'No you fucking ain't!'

His trainer then pitched in. 'Dean's gonna do you!'

'When we boxed before, I was out the night before, mate. I'm a different geezer here today,' I said. I was up for it this time and knocked him spark out in the first round with one of the first punches I threw. Knocked him clean out. You don't see that in amateur boxing. I think he was concussed as when he got up, he didn't know where he was.

The next year he moved up in weight, so he wasn't in my division. He was the only one in the Midlands who could really give me a fight.

Funny enough, about 15 years ago I was in Wales boxing on a show against Barrie Jones. Not the Barry Jones who was a super featherweight world champion, but another Barrie Jones. I was just sitting down watching the boxing with my track suit and boots on ready to box and this kid's come over to me.

'Alright Pete,' he said.

'Alright mate,' I replied.

'You don't remember me, do ya?'

'Nah mate,' I said.

'It's Dean Beech. I come to all the boxing matches, Pete.'

'Fucking hell,' I thought.

It had been a while since I'd seen him. I had a good chat with him. Years later when I went on Facebook, he added me on there and I speak to him now and then. Nice lad.

After winning the Birmingham finals, I went on to the West Midlands finals. I remember boxing a kid called Cliff Richards. I stopped him and then I beat another kid on points. His name was Steve McQueen! I always remember these names. I beat both of them on the same day, two or three hours apart.

In the Midlands finals, I also had to box twice in the same day. I stopped one opponent before boxing another kid in the final called Colin Kerr from Northampton. He was a good, tough kid, though I'd beat him before. He boxed for Northampton Boys. Like myself, he had to box twice in the same day to contest the final. He gave me a good fight but I beat him.

When you used to win regional finals, you got badges on your shorts. You got a vest when you won the Midlands title. I wore both of these when I went down to Wales and boxed a kid called Michael Flowers, who was the Welsh champion.

After stopping him in the first round, I then got to the semi-finals and beat a kid from Liverpool.

From there I got to the NABC finals, which were in Newcastle. One thing I used to do when I boxed as an amateur was switch hit. I would box southpaw and orthodox and the referees didn't like it. A kid I boxed in the semi-finals of the NABC was called Tony Mock. I actually boxed on a bill with him when I was pro, though I didn't realise it until recently. But I remember boxing him in the semi-finals and I was switching stances during the fight. I didn't always do it, but I felt comfortable boxing either way. I boxed brilliantly against him. I boxed his head off, out of sight.

My opponent in the final was Mark Tibbs from Repton Boys, a top club in London, whose dad is Jimmy Tibbs, one of the top trainers. Mark beat me on points. He was a good boxer who won a few national finals as an amateur. Nowadays, you could win the Midlands amateur title by skipping the Birmingham final if no one is in your weight. 1985 it happened.

I read an article recently which had the junior ABA rankings from 1986. Number one was Mark Tibbs and number two was Colin Kerr from Northampton. I fought Colin Kerr three times when he was second in the country and I beat him each time. I packed in boxing in '85 because I was in trouble with the police. That could have been me if I was fighting the year after as I had the measure of the kid.

The final against Mark Tibbs turned out to be the last amateur fight I would ever have. I wouldn't box again for five and a half years.

CHAPTER 5

Locked up

After I left Burlington, and after my last amateur fight, all I was doing was just getting into trouble as I was fed up a lot of the time. I just went wild. I was getting arrested for some things I did but also for things I never did. But whenever I would arrive at the police station, I wouldn't say anything other than, 'no comment'.

Most of the time, the police would have to release me with no charges.

This eventually led to me being arrested when I was 15. I was in court for having a fight with a lad from school who lived on my road. I never liked him and I never got on with him. One day as he walked past me, he was staring at me.

'What you looking at?' I said.

He became loud, so we had a fight. He gave as good as he got but I broke his nose. I thought that would be the end of it, but either him or his mom or dad called the police and I got done for assault. I went to court and was told that I had to go to the attendance centre in Boardsley Green. I had to go there every Saturday morning for a few hours. Well, I only went once so got breached for it. After I got thrown out of Burlington, I never heard off them again.

Soon after this incident, I was involved in burglarising a shop as well as car theft. Later on, things would get even worse, this time closer to home.

* * *

While out on bail for the burglary and the car theft, I was caught in a stolen car my mate was driving. We had the car for a few hours, just joyriding. We got chased by the police from Coventry and jumped out the car when we arrived in Solihull. We jumped over gardens and I was caught hiding in a big bin. The cops used sniffer dogs and that's how I was caught. My mate was hiding in a garden. I got remanded to Brockhill.

It was on a Thursday I got remanded in custody. That was on 16 May 1985. The remand was only due to be a week. On 17 May, my first day in prison, my dad died of a heart attack. He was working in London at the time with his brother, coming home every couple of weekends as there was no work in Birmingham. I didn't get a visit from anyone on the Friday and didn't get a visit on the Saturday, which I thought was a bit strange. No one came to see me until the following Monday, when I was visited by my sister and her husband, during which they told me the news.

As I was only on remand, I got out on the Friday on bail and went to my dad's funeral a week later. Two weeks later, I was in court and was sentenced to four months in a detention centre called Eastwood Park in Gloucester. I thought the four months was harsh in a way as people were in the detention centre for six weeks and they had done more things than I had.

* * *

Doing a week in Brockhill on remand was easy. You were just locked up 23 hours a day and could smoke in there, even though I didn't really smoke. But there were four of you in a cell, which had a piss bucket for a toilet. When I was sentenced and sent to Eastwood, they asked me where I'd come from.

'Brockhill,' I said.

'Brockhill isn't here, son,' they replied. 'This is a detention centre. Brockhill is a walk in the park.'

They were right. It was a walk in the park.

When others in Eastwood asked me how long I was doing and I said four months, they called me a lifer. They said that I would lose days there. To 'lose days' means that as a punishment your release date would be extended. For example, if a prisoner was due out on 1 March and lost seven days, they would not be released until 8 March.

'Nah,' I said. 'I'll keep my head down.'

One of the inmates said to me not to ever go to the doctor sick if I could help it. I soon found out why.

A kid went to the doctor one morning with a headache to get out of doing a fitness circuit as people hated doing them. They were brutal. The doctor asked the kid what was wrong with him. The kid said that he had a headache. The doctor put a headache tablet on his head and sellotaped it to stop it falling off. This kid had to keep it on his head all day. It was fucking degrading. It was just done to break you down.

Eastwood Park was the worst place you could be. I saw them beat down on kids, 15-year-old kids, beating them up. When I was there, I never tried to get too friendly with the screws. Some lads thought that because they had a little laugh with them, they would be alright. But the screws could switch like that and fucking slap you up. Because of that, I never got that friendly with them. I just kept my head down and did my time.

I was in the institution for three months and three weeks but just lost days all the time. You couldn't help but lose days. Anyone who's been in a detention centre and says they haven't lost days is talking shit because they mentally made you lose days. They didn't give a fuck. The screws could do what they liked. You couldn't complain about a screw like you can now. It was unheard of. You couldn't go to the government and say, 'That screw's hit me.' They would be like, 'Fuck off and get out.' If you made complaints, you made a rod for your own back.

When I was locked up, my mom got a letter from the England squad. I was picked to go training down at Crystal Palace. My mom sent me the letter in the detention centre for me to read. Obviously, the screws read it and as soon as the gym screw found out that I was a boxer, I got the gym orderly job in Eastwood. The screws were not friendly with me after that, just OK towards me.

All my sisters have said that when I was younger, all they ever heard was about me getting into fights or doing something wrong, but my mom wouldn't really believe it most of the time. They say that I used to get away with murder when I was a kid. I don't remember it like that but I suppose there are always two sides to everything. They also say that I could do anything and my mom wouldn't have a bad word said against me. I do remember one time when I was in jail and she won £1,500 at the bingo. She came to see me and as it was Christmas, she brought me a present, which was a gold kurgan ring. I was chuffed to bits with it. She always cried at the end of every visit and I always went back to my cell feeling bad that I had upset her. She always came in feeling good, telling me what was happening, but always got a bit upset when it was time to go.

Though I would feel bad after she left, after a day I was back to my normal self. I couldn't walk round jail feeling sorry for myself as it would get noticed and taken for weakness. So, I went back to my cell and got on with it. The next day, I would just forget it or it would drive me crazy. I saw the way lads were affected after they had seen members of their family or their missus.

* * *

In those days when you were in the nick, it wasn't like it is now with PlayStations and all that. It was like boot camp in America, but more rigid. You couldn't smoke and you couldn't drink. We had to get up at five o'clock in the morning. You had a towel around your waist and you would go and have a shower. After your shower, you would march back and make your bed. Military style. Toothpaste there, your bed kit here and letters there. You had to clean your cell. Then you would go and have your breakfast, get dressed, come back, then it would be something else. You weren't allowed to lie on your back. If you got caught doing that, you lost days. If your boots weren't cleaned, you'd lose two days. If you were lying on your bed, you'd lose seven days.

If you made a sandwich, you lost seven days. The first time I was in the kitchen, I made myself a sandwich. A screw saw me.

'What are you doing?' he asked.

'Making a sandwich,' I said. He put me on report. I thought he was joking.

When he told the governor what I had done, I lost seven days. I got four months. I done three months, three weeks and two days. Only had five days left in there. If your toothbrush was to the left and not the right, they'd put you on report and you would lose seven more days. If they found dust in your cell, you lost three days. My cell was fucking spotless. They would do a search in the morning and a search in the afternoon.

We also had to do circuits seven days a week that would involve exercises such as sit-ups and star jumps. It didn't matter who you were, if one of the prisoners couldn't keep up with you, then everyone had to do 20 press-ups. If you got caught cheating (which I never did), they'd mentally try and break you down. This would really piss me off if I had nearly finished my circuit and had to start again because another prisoner had been caught cheating.

'Stop. Cheater. He done 14 instead of 15,' the guards would say.

They would then get the kid to write a big C on their chest for cheater and say, 'Everyone start again.' Everyone would have to do 15 press-ups again.

That kid who had that C written on his chest, when he was in the showers next, he got his head punched in. That's how it went. The screws in there were all ex-army or ex-navy and they would not take one bit of shit.

You wouldn't even dare say something bad as they would bang you straight in the mouth. They didn't give a fuck. You didn't have televisions or radios or anything like that. You got association once a week, which meant that the prisoners could mix with each other. We would all be in a big hall watching the telly. They would put programmes like *Songs of Praise* on.

There was never anything good on. It just got you out of your cell. You had a parade every day where you had to march. On the weekend, you would have two inspections. If you failed your inspection, you would be in your cell all weekend. The only time you would get out would be to have your dinner and then you would have to go back in. It was harsh as fuck and I said that I would never do prison again when I came out of there. But when I done youth custody, that was a piece of piss. If they gave you 12 months of what they did in Eastwood, you would never go back to jail again. It was fucking hard.

I saw a kid from my area in there. I learned quickly that you never have a joke with the screws and never have banter with them. Anyway, I never really liked this kid. He came downstairs one morning and tried to have a joke with a screw. The geezer slapped him silly. He had hand marks on his face, his back and chest. It was brutal in there. My nephew Danny (two years younger than me) ended up going in there two years after me and the screws still remembered me. I had told him how harsh it was in there. When I knew he was being locked up, I said to him, 'When you go in there, don't have a joke with them, shut your fucking mouth, keep your head down.' A few years later, one of the screws fractured a kid's skull. That's how brutal it was. It's not like these days where you worked in Tesco's and now you're a prison officer. These people were hard. When I went to Brockhill after that, it was a walk in the park. My experience in there was just madness. But when I came out, I was really fit.

* * *

I was in Brockhill about four or five times during my time in and out of prison as it was a remand jail. Sometimes I would be in there for a few weeks, then get bail, and sometimes my stay would be a few months. The screws in there knew me by my name as I was in and out of there quite a bit.

Jail wasn't a deterrent. When I went to jail at Brockhill, I was in and out of there for a few weeks because of bail and a lot of my mates were in there. When I went in there, I was able to get on the wing I wanted to be on. They would put me on a wing and I would get a little cleaning job or a job in the kitchen. When I went to jail, I'd always try and get either one of those two jobs as you could move around the wings then. You could do deals and move little things for people.

Once, there was a kid in there who was from the same area as me. He said that a lad he was in court with had grassed him up over some incident. I was working in the kitchen when in Brockhill and the kid he was talking about worked there also. On the night before I was back in my cell for lock-up, I had a last cup of tea from a flask that was still very hot. I was in the kitchen dormitory. The kitchen dormitory was a big dorm where the kitchen lads stayed. The cells there were bigger, with a toilet and sink. This grass was in the kitchen dormitory with me on this night.

'You're a grass mate,' I said to the kid.

'That's bullshit,' he replied.

'You're a fucking grass,' I said as I threw the hot tea on his face, which scalded him.

He was shouting and screaming but still tried to run for the buzzer. I managed to grab him round the neck and pull him down. I wouldn't let him get to it. Then I got a wet towel and threw it on his face.

'Shut the fuck up now, yeah,' I said.

Next morning, one of the screws unlocked his door and saw all his face was peeled.

'Who's done this?' the screw said to the kid.

'I ain't saying,' he replied.

Later, I said to him, 'I thought you were going to grass me up then.'

'I said nothing to them,' was his reply.

The screws took me down the block anyway as they had an idea it was me. They interviewed me and I said that it wasn't me.

When this kid came out of the hospital and was back in the kitchen, he said to me, 'Listen, I ain't no fucking grass.'

'Alright,' I replied.

'Wait 'til I get my depositions and statements right, and I'll show ya that I ain't no grass.'

Two weeks went by. Another week went by. Nothing.

He eventually came to me one day and said, 'Here you are, Buckley. Read that.'

Reading through it, the kid wasn't a grass. The kid who told me he was a grass was a grass himself. So, when I next saw that bloke, I chinned him.

Me and the lad who I threw tea over were cool after that and I said sorry to him. That guy wasn't scarred permanently, his skin did grow back. Though we never became mates, we were alright with each other.

That's how it went in prison. Someone you know tells you something about someone else and you acted on it, especially as no one likes a grass.

* * *

One of the times I was in Brockhill, there was a guy called Gerry Murray who was in there at the same time as me. I boxed Gerry as an amateur when I used to box for Talbot and he was at Ladywood. I beat him but he was a real tough kid. He was a small geezer but stocky and he could fight. There was about ten of us in the kitchen dorm. Some of them thought they could box when they couldn't. Some of the guys used to say, 'Go on then, get the towels on.' So, we used to put towels on our hands as makeshift gloves and have boxing fights in the dorm. Me and him used to have some good spars and used to batter everyone in the dorm. We used to knock the bollocks out of them, me and Gerry.

Me and Gerry didn't really spar that much. When I went to Ladywood, he was in my weight class. We were both boxing for Ladywood in the championships and I happened to box him, even though we were in the same club. I beat him then as well.

That happens sometimes. You can box someone from your own club if you're in the championships and in the same weight class. He was also a good street fighter. I saw him in a few fights in jail, although I haven't seen him in years.

When we were in Brockhill together, there was a man in there who was in for battering his baby. Me and Gerry were on the youngest wing as we were only 16 then. This kid thought he was a bully in there. They should not have let him be on our wing as he was 19, nearly 20 at the time. He never said nothing to me. But then one day, he was cheeky towards Gerry and Gerry knocked the bollocks out of him. Really punched his head off. Me and Gerry became real good mates as he was Irish and we had boxed each other.

* * *

I also had a few fights when in Brockhill. During my time there, I was in prison at the same time as my wife Tania's brother Sid. We got on OK outside of prison but never hung about together as he was from Small Heath. But we spoke when we saw each other. Then one day, we were both going to court. They used to take you to court in a coach and you were all handcuffed to another inmate. Then they would take you to Steelhouse Lane police station, which had a prison kind of set-up under the courts.

After the court proceedings were over for the day, we were taken back to Brockhill. As I knew a few of the screws, I said to one of them, 'Any chance you can cell me and my cousin up together?' I didn't call him my brother-in-law at that point as Tania was my girlfriend, not my wife. Plus, saying that a prisoner was a blood relative was a way of getting a mate to share your cell.

'Yeah OK,' he said. I was only blagging him! But then we were put on B wing together.

Neither of us were back in court for a month, so we were put up together. We weren't on the same charges, we just happened to go to court on the same day. We would smoke cannabis every day in there as we both used to get it in during visits.

One day, I had a bit of beef with a lad from Coventry. A big bloke. A lot bigger than me. Now in Brockhill, you would get a lot of banter, slagging this and slagging that off. But as I'm trying to talk to another kid, this Coventry bloke kept on interrupting me.

'Shut the fuck up,' I said. Yet he was giving it the big 'un behind his door all night.

Sid was winding me up all night.

'You gonna let him speak to you like that?' asked Sid. He also said that this guy thinks I'm a dick.

First thing the next morning, as my door opened, I rushed straight out of my cell and into this lad's cell while he was still in bed, and just started smashing him in the head. I dragged his body out of his bed and kept booting him. The next thing someone said, 'Quick! Screws!'

I quickly went back to my cell, shut the door and made out that I was just waking up. The screws never knew it was me. As for the guy I had beef with, he never said nothing to me again. He didn't grass me up neither, though the lad got himself moved off the wing after breakfast. You couldn't let people take the piss out of you when inside.

* * *

When I was released from Eastwood Park, my mom and family, in fact everyone, was saying I should return to boxing and try and win a national title. They were more or less begging me to go back to it as they all knew that's what I was good at and thought that it would help me stay out of trouble. But I liked being in trouble. I wasn't fussed. If I wanted to do something, I just did it. I was in a 'don't give a fuck' mood back then as a kid and always thought I was right, but I wasn't.

I did go back to Ladywood ABC a little after that but I didn't really get into it again. Plus, I was still getting into trouble.

* * *

I was about 16 when I started going to the pub. One night, I'm in this pub with all my mates and a lad comes in and tells me about this bloke I know, who's about 30 years old, that he was slagging off my sister in the Gospel Oak pub. I was a bit wary as he drank with these blokes and I knew they were a bit gangster. But I knew them as they knew my family. So, me and Ada jumped in a taxi but before I left the pub, I grabbed two pool balls off the table, took my sock off and put the balls in the sock. The taxi arrived at the other pub and I jumped out. Me and Ada went into the pub, went straight over to this bloke called Jimmy and just started battering him with the balls in a sock. His head was bleeding.

'What you doing?' he said in shock.

'Don't you slag my sister off, you prick,' I said.

One of these old blokes grabbed me and said, 'Pete, what the fuck you doing?'

'He's not going to slag my sister off!' I shouted back.

As Jimmy got up, this bloke who was also called Jimmy grabbed him and fucked him down in his chair. He went mad at him, saying, 'You ever slag her off again and you're dead.' This Jimmy was really good friends with my sister and family.

* * *

Not long after, I got a 14-day sentence for refusing to pay a fine for common assault. I had a fight with some lad on my road, which he started, though I beat him up in a fair fight. Well, that's what I thought, but he phoned the police. Soon after that I got the fine but wouldn't pay it. I had the money to pay it but on principle I didn't want to pay it. I had been in Winston Green prison for six days before my mom came to visit me. After the visit, she went and paid the remaining money that was owed and I was released. I don't think she liked the thought of me being around some real dangerous criminals.

I was a bit glad in a way as it was my first time in a proper prison. It was different to being in Eastwood Park. There were proper men in there who were doing life, and even though we were younger prisoners that were on a different wing, we still had to go to the main wing to get our breakfast and dinner. It was a bit intimidating.

* * *

Winston Green was unlike Eastwood in many ways. It was in the Green where I saw two lads having a fight in the shower area. Suddenly, one lad pulled out a toothbrush that had a razor blade moulded on it and he just slashed the other lad up. The lad who did the attack was doing life for murder, so he didn't give a fuck. He was letting people know that if you fucked with him, then that's what you would get. There were a lot of young lads doing a long time in there just waiting to get moved to a long-term youth jail, so you stayed away from them a bit as they felt they had fuck all to lose.

In jails such as Winston, you would see fights every day. But if they were nothing to do with you, then you would just carry on with your own shit. You would have to just blank it. Fights would start over anything, what they ate over breakfast, turning the TV over when someone else was watching it, looking at someone funny or someone having a bad visit. It didn't matter. Fights would just start. That's how it was.

* * *

Not long after I left the Green, I would go out with friends and still end up in trouble.

Me and a few of my mates used to go to a blues music night every Friday and Saturday when we were about 16 years old. We would smoke weed and drink while in the club, and I used to love the buzz of the place. One night, me and Ada were at a blues party in Sparkhill when this bloke, who was a big fucker, came into the party and was looking for some draw. I had some cannabis which was squidgy, black and so soft you could roll it out to make it look longer. I just showed him a quick glance of it as it was dark. He gave me a tenner and then fucked off. A few minutes later he came up the stairs shouting, and I knew why – I had just ripped him off! As he was running up the stairs, I booted him straight in the chest and he fell backwards. Me and Ada ran straight over him and out the door. It was a while before we went back to that blues night.

Another time the two of us were out, we had earned a few pounds during the day up town by going into offices and stealing handbags and jackets, most of which had their wallets in the pocket. After that, we were out on the drink, smoking weed and sniffing coke for the rest of the day. We ended up at a place called Mitchell's. It was a club that had quite a few Irish people in there as well as some black lads also.

Once we had left Mitchell's, we flagged down a taxi that was on the street. We always did runners on taxis no matter how much money we had on us. The taxi was driving near to a park.

'Just here, mate,' I said.

Once the taxi stopped, we were out of the door and running through the park, which was about five minutes from my mom's house. Even though it was one in the morning at this point, we still saw a few lads in the park. I was pissed and one of them said something to me. I went straight towards him with Ada and I ended up fighting this lad, who I won't name. I was getting the better of him in the fight and we carried on fighting each other when I started to feel a sharp pain. Looking down, I saw that a screwdriver was hanging out of my side. I pulled it out and straight away I collapsed and struggled to breathe. The group of lads by this point had run off. Ada pulled me through the garden of one of the houses nearby and banged on a door, shouting that I had been stabbed. A woman answered and by a stroke of luck, it turned out that she was a nurse. She put pressure on the wound until the ambulance came. When I arrived at the hospital, the doctors said that I had a punctured lung. I ended up in hospital for about four weeks until I just got up and signed myself out.

For a while, I couldn't run anywhere as I was out of breath all the time. After that, I carried a knife for protection. Soon after, I was involved in a fight and was sentenced to two and a half years in prison. I was in Winston Green for the first six weeks of my sentence before been transferred to Onley in Rugby.

When I first went to Winston Green, I was on a wing called B1A for young prisoners. I was on there for about four to six weeks. When I was in the Green, my mate came in there. At last slop-out, that was when you emptied your piss pot for the night. I had a lad in my cell stay in my mate's cell for the night and my mate came in mine. He had some smokes on him so we had a session in my cell. In the morning, the screws just unlocked the cell and didn't really check them. I did that a few times in there with lads I knew from Brockhill as well.

* * *

My older brother John, who's dead now, was in Winston Green in '86 or '87 and he got a cell visit with me. At the time, I was sharing a cell with some lad I didn't know who seemed a bit of a div.

Anyway, my cellmate was taken out the cell and my brother came in. The screw said that me and John had an hour before he had to go back to his cell. My brother pulled out a joint and we start having a smoke, then started going through my cellmate's stuff like his toothpaste, his shampoo and tobacco. John turned to me and asked if I could handle him.

'Yeah, why?' I asked.

'I'm having his stuff.'

'John, nah man. Don't do that. I've got to share with this prick,' I said. John took his stuff anyway.

The lad came back after John had left the cell and noticed his stuff was missing. 'Where's my shit?'

I told him, 'Listen, you've been taxed mate. So shut the fuck up.'

Next day, the lad got a cell change.

* * *

Arriving at Onley, I was the youngest prisoner there and was initially on E wing. When they told me I was going on D wing, I refused to go there at first as there were hardly any Brummies on there.

'I ain't going on D wing,' I said.

'Why?' the screws said. 'You got enemies on there?'

'Nah,' I replied. 'I'm just not going on there.'

'You can go on H wing then.'

No one wanted to go on H wing. The only people on that wing were paedophile cases of kids who were getting bullied as well as grasses.

'Alright then,' I said. 'I'll go on D wing.'

So, I went on D wing and it wasn't too bad. But a lot of the people on D wing were in for violence and robberies. While on the wing, it was the first time I'd ever heard about heroin. I met some Scouse geezers in there who would talk about 'chasing the dragon'.

'What the fuck's that?' I said.

'Burning the brown,' they replied.

'What's a brown?' I asked. They said it was heroin.

'Nah,' I said. A few of the mates that I made in there were on the gear. I was offered it in there and I was like, 'nah'. I used to have draw all the time but I never would have touched heroin.

Like I said, it was a very violent wing. It was kicking off all the time. In the end, it was alright and I got a red band while I was in there. A red band denotes a trusted person. It allowed me to go on to other wings in the prison without a screw having to be with you. I did a course while in there, City and Guilds Industrial Cleaning. It lasted about 12 weeks and you learned how to clean floors, use the buffing machine, how to strip wooden floors back to the basics and all that bollocks.

From there, I got a job as a wing orderly where I used to go to other wings. But all the cells would be open and what me and this other kid would do is we would be robbing out the cells. Just robbing people's stuff. They never knew it was us as we weren't on that wing. But if you got caught, you got battered as pad thieves weren't allowed. Once, me and this other kid went to the prison church to clean the floor as part of our job, found the wine and started drinking it. After we had drunk about half a bottle, one of the screws came in and caught us. We were sacked from the job and we both had seven days added to our sentence. We were also put on basic, which meant that we weren't allowed to leave our cell, to play pool, darts, watch TV nor mingle with the other lads. All we were able to do is gardening, which was a shit job. Out in the cold and rain, just moving stuff around. I hated it.

* * *

Onley was an OK jail. It wasn't too bad. I was in a single cell. You had slop-out buckets. You never had a toilet in your cell. The only cells that had toilets were on G and H wing. G wing was for the kitchen lads and H wing was for the nonces and grasses. They were the only two wings that had toilets back in the 80s. Everywhere else had slop buckets. Proper old school. You used to have a radio in there, maybe a Walkman, but it was pretty basic.

Some of the screws were bastards who didn't give a fuck. My mate was in there at the time and he was basically walking around smoking spliffs. If you were stoned and kept to yourself, then you were not causing trouble. Just like in Eastwood, when I was in Onley the screws were all ex-army. Now, there are prison guards who used to be security guards at Sainsbury's. It's not the same mentality where back in the day if you got cheeky with a screw, they'd fucking slap you up.

Like with Brockhill and Eastwood, there was a lot that happened to me while I was inside Onley.

* * *

On my 18th birthday, my brother John and Tania came to visit me. John had brought me two £20 wraps of cannabis. He had done a lot of time in Borstal prison from a young age. I put the one wrap in between my bum cheeks and swallowed the other one, hoping to sick it up. John then poured whisky into his coke. I drank it and was half pissed. I came out of the visiting room and there were two screws standing there. One of them was alright and the other was a prick.

'He's having a strip search,' said the one screw.

'Nah, he's alright. Buckley's OK. Let him through. It's his birthday today,' replied the other.

When I went back to my cell that night, I started feeling a bit stoned and I couldn't sick up the wrap of cannabis that I had swallowed. I made a spliff with the wrap I had in my bum cheeks but my arse was red raw. After an hour or so, I was fucking stoned off my head. The solid that I had swallowed had come open inside me. By eight o'clock that evening, I was looking in the mirror in my pad and I just kept laughing and laughing. One screw opened my door and looked at me.

'Fucking hell,' he said. 'You're red-eyed, son.'

'What, what, what?' I said, still high.

'Get out of your fucking bunk,' he replied.

He took a look at me and maybe realised that I was high. He could have grassed me up but didn't. The next day I tried to shit the draw out, but there was none to shit out. Just the clingfilm was hanging out my arse.

* * *

When it came to drugs in prison, I never saw the screws smuggle any drugs or phones. Mobile phones weren't around when I was in jail. But I would sort the odd person out with a little draw.

Even though I smoked some draw in jail, I used to mostly smoke solids. If the screws could smell it, they didn't really bother you as for them it was a quiet life.

If you were stoned, there was no trouble really. In D wing, there was a lot of smoking going on. What you would do is sort out a couple of lads in there with some draw and when it was their visit, they'd sort you back out.

Once there was a guy from Handsworth, who was a nasty bastard.

'You get us a draw?' he said to me one day.

'Yeah, yeah,' I said. 'You look after me, I'll look after you.' I gave him some draw one day.

When he got a visit, he sorted me out. If he were a knob, I couldn't have really done much as he was a big bloke. I was young and he was a geezer on the wing, but he kept to his word and he did sort me out with some draw.

A few years later when I was out of prison, I was at the Hummingbird, which was a music venue and club. While my mate was selling acid in there, a load of boys surrounded him. This same man who I helped out with some draw in Onley was part of the group surrounding my mate and looking to rob him. I saw this and went over to him and said, 'Yo B. He's my boy, man.'

'Oh, he's with you?' replied B.

'Yeah, he's alright.' They backed off.

'You were getting rolled there, man,' I said to my mate.

'Yeah, I know,' he replied.

It's not what you know, it's who you know.

* * *

I remember once the Old Bill were coming to see me about some crimes that had happened. They would always try and write crimes off, so that their crime rate went higher. Now, there was this lad who was on my wing called Tony, who was mad as fuck. I had been with him in Eastwood as well. Before we went out to the visiting room, he said to me, 'Watch what I do on this visit today.'

'What you on about?' I replied.

'Just watch what I do, Buck,' as that's what they called me when I was inside – Buck.

So, I'm sitting down in the visiting area and the Old Bill are talking to me. They tried giving me a couple of fags but I wouldn't take them. As we were talking, I looked over to where Tony was and he just jumped up, whacked the copper straight on the jaw – he actually broke his jaw – and as a result he got another two years on top of his sentence. When I came out and then got another prison sentence and was taken to Glen Parva about a year later, he was still in there. He ended up doing four years in the end.

* * *

I had an argument with this kid from Manchester. Went downstairs to recess, where the toilets were. He had a battery in a sock. As soon as I went in there, he whacked me with this battery and split my eye open. We ended up fighting. There was a bloke from a rough part of Birmingham called

Balsall Heath, who we used to call Yellow Man. He broke it up between us.

'Fucking hell, your eye's gone Buckley,' he said before fucking off.

I heard a screw walking down the corridor, so I threw loads of water on the floor. As I heard him coming, I slipped on purpose and made out that I banged my head on the floor. This screw didn't believe me at first.

I had staged it to look real, though the screw seemed unconvinced. But I went to the hospital and they stitched my eye up and I came back to the wing.

The CO of the wing had me in his office and he knew my older brother John as John had been in there.

'What's going on?' he said to me.

'Nothing. I fell over,' I replied.

'Listen, if you're getting bullied...'

I stopped him before he could finish.

'I ain't getting bullied by no one, mate.'

'Well, I've put you on to H wing,' he said.

H wing. The nonce and rats wing.

'I haven't done fuck all. I slipped,' I pleaded.

'Oh, alright then,' he said and he dropped that plan.

Soon after this, I was paroled and instead of doing two and a half years, I ended up doing 14 and a half months.

CHAPTER 6

How I met my wife

I met my wife Tania was through my brother John. John used to be in a relationship with Tania's sister and had two kids with her, a boy and a girl, though they split up a few years later.

Tania used to go to my school but I didn't really know her too well at that time as I was two years above her. She was really quiet. But I did know her from my brother and her sister and I used to go around her mom and dad's house because of my brother.

There was a pub I used to go to in Acocks Green called Beagles. I used to see her down there and started chatting to her, and walked with her a few times. Nothing happened. Didn't get a kiss off her or nothing. Started seeing her a little bit more but was then locked up when I was 17. By the time she started to visit me in prison, she was my girlfriend. I got out of the nick, then got locked up again and she would still keep coming to see me. The last time I was locked up was for about 12 months at Glen Parva. My brother was always in and out of jail and it didn't bother me, yet she said that she wouldn't visit me in jail all her life and if I carried on being in the nick, that we were done. She was working and doing well. I didn't just knock it on the head like that as even though I was boxing, I was still getting into bits of trouble. I was always having a fight whenever I went out. Bit sad really. I was like testing myself against people. I'd deliberately try and pick a fight with someone. I didn't give a fuck.

* * *

I still didn't learn. I was still getting into trouble. Despite seeing what I'd seen in prison, it was the same old from me since I was first imprisoned at 15.

I was coming back from a pub one night and there was a shop I was walking past. I noticed that its shutter wasn't down, so I booted the door clean off. Me and my mate went in and we took all the fags, but I had no gloves on as I was pissed. The police found fingerprints a few months later and I was caught for it and got 12 months. My mate never got caught.

* * *

When I was in Brockhill on remand for the burglary, Ada was in there with me. We were both remanded to Brockhill on the same day and on the same charge. We shared a cell for one night, then were moved to another wing the next day, but our cells were next door to each other. It was his first time in jail so he didn't know what to expect but was still OK as he wasn't a div and knew a good few lads in there.

The week after we both went to court, we tried to get bail but got fucked off by the magistrates' court. We went back to Brockhill and were placed on the same wing again. There is a process a prisoner can go through when on remand and that is to apply for bail from a judge. Me and Ada asked our solicitors to apply for us. One dinner time, a screw came and opened Ada's door and told him that he got bail.

'Yo boss, my name on there?' I shouted at the screw through my cell.

'You didn't get it,' he said.

I was pissed off but glad that my mate had got out.

He came to visit me on the Saturday half pissed and stoned.

'You got a smoke for me?' I asked.

He pulled out some solids, broke them in half and gave it to me under the table.

'Come on, man, give us the rest,' I said.

'Pete, I need a spliff on the way home.'

'You're a joker man,' I laughed.

When I got my 12 months, he got six months. We were also in Winston Green together, before he went to an open youth centre in Redditch next door to Brockhill called Hewell Grange. Once I was sentenced, I went straight to Winston Green.

* * *

I mentioned Steelhouse Lane earlier when discussing where me and Tania's brother stayed the one night. It was an extension of the police station, a large holding place until you went to court the next day. It was the only place I knew that was like a mini-prison but on a very small scale. It had about two or three levels, was shit in there and smelled of piss. If you got nicked on a Thursday and it was a bank holiday weekend, you were in there until Tuesday as that's when the courts opened. I had done that a couple of times. Other than on a bank holiday, they only kept you in on a weekend if you got nicked, say, on a Saturday until you were going to court on the Monday. It wasn't like this if you got nicked in the borough of Solihull. You would just be kept in a police station until court time.

The food they would give you was really shit. Anyone back in the day who has been in there would tell you. They used to give you a big blue plastic cup of tea. It was like mud and you would get a sandwich with jam or some other shit on it. The spread was thick but tasted like shit. The only good thing about the place was that you could smoke in there. If you were kept in there all throughout the weekend, then someone could leave fags and food at the front of the police station. If the copper on duty was OK, he would allow it. But the funny thing is that there was always someone in there who you would know. Inmates would shout across the landings all the time. But overall, it was a shithole. It wasn't too bad for the night but if you had to stay there all weekend, it would do your head in. You wished you were in jail instead. It was that bad.

* * *

I was soon moved to Glen Parva to finish the rest of my sentence. At the time, it had 14 or 15 wings. It was a clean jail and the prisoners had their own toilet but there weren't that many in there from Birmingham. I had a bit of trouble in there once with some lads who worked in the kitchens. I had sold one of them some drugs for a smoke. Come pay day, he made out that he wasn't going to pay me and he had a few of the prisoners with him.

I asked for some back-up from a lad from another cell, who came from an area by me. But he was a prick and said he wanted no trouble as he was getting out soon. He wasn't a mate of mine but was from my way, so he should have backed me up. A lad from Leicester who was next door to me said that he would back me up instead. Walking down the shower block, I see this lad there. He became really mouthy, so I banged him out. The mad part is that he had half a leg from the kneecap down, which I hadn't noticed before as he looked OK. I didn't really clock it until he fell on the floor.

About a month after I got out, I got nicked for street robbery and was on remand for a month but got it dropped. I didn't do it anyway. The Old Bill were trying to set me up for something I didn't do. After that, I never went to jail again.

* * *

Not long after I was released from Glen Parva, I was at Tania's house. The phone was ringing. It was my mom.

'The police have raided the house. Very heavy police.'

'What?' I said in shock. She said something about a robbery in Leicester.

'There were loads of police just searching the whole house,' she said.

I hadn't been to Leicester. The last time I was there was when I was in Glen Parva, when I was 19. I phoned up my solicitor and told him that the police had raided the house. He later phoned me back and said that I had to go to Bromford police station.

'Alright,' I said.

I went to Bromford, handed myself in and they said that they were arresting me on suspicion of armed robbery of a video shop. They said that the owner had been tied up and robbed, and that someone had been nicked for it and said to the police that I had done it with them.

'I ain't done no armed robbery,' I said.

They cautioned me and put me in the cell while I waited for my solicitor. When he arrived, I told him that I hadn't done any robbery in Leicester and that they were full of shit. I knew it wasn't me as I was in Winston Green at the time the robbery had been committed, so I wasn't overly worried.

Ironically, the name of the shop that got robbed was Buckley's. I'll never forget it.

I was adamant it wasn't me. Normally, I would do a no-comment interview but because I knew it wasn't me, I told the police that I knew where I was at this time. As such, the claims made were full of shit. The police from Leicester came down to interview me. They said that I was in Brockhill that day.

'Yeah,' I said. 'But when I was sentenced on the 17th, I didn't go back there. I went to Winston Green.'

It was impossible for me to be in Leicester at that time.

'Who was it? Who was the kid?' I asked.

They said they couldn't tell me who he was but that he was in Brockhill with me on 17 December.

'He wasn't,' I said. 'Go check it out.'

In the end, they came back and they had to let me go. I again asked them at the end of the interview who it was who'd told them this story. They still wouldn't tell me.

'He's a fucking liar,' I said. I never did find out who it was.

What I think myself is that the kid got nicked for the robbery and they've asked him who he was with. Straight away, he told them my name. Everyone knew me in Brockhill as I'd been going in and out of there for a while. I reckon that was the first name that came into his head. But what he did could have got me a long time in jail.

When I used to finish a sentence, I would go back to the gym. But I never fought as an amateur again. Those five years in prison were just a blur. I didn't really bother learning any new skill. I really had no direction. Boxing was at the back of my mind.

Truth be told, when I went into prison, it didn't deter me. It didn't bother me. A lot of my mates who I hung around with were in prison. Prison didn't stop me because it was hard. When I was in prison, the only thing I really missed was my family but I got used to it. It was just one of those things that I dealt with as I am thick-skinned. It was only getting back into boxing that saved me.

CHAPTER 7

Rocky, Nobby and my start as a pro

Not long after I got out of Glen Parva, I was in my local pub when I was approached by a boxer named Rocky Lawler. He was the Midlands bantamweight champion and a real tough geezer.

'Come to the gym tomorrow,' he said.

'Yeah yeah,' I replied, basically brushing him off.

'Don't talk shit to me, man. Come to the gym tomorrow. I'll knock round for you.'

About half four, five o'clock the next day, he knocked on my door.

'You got your stuff ready?'

'What do you mean?' I said, surprised.

'You coming to the gym with me.'

He was not a person you would argue with. He was small in stature but big in personality. I got some tracksuit bottoms, found some trainers and he threw me a bag.

I always say Rocky got me started. If he didn't give me a dream, I would never have returned to boxing. I'd probably still be in the nick now. I was just in and out of trouble all the time. I have him to thank for putting me on the straight and narrow that way.

* * *

Nobby at the time had a gym over in Kingstanding, which was in a pub called The Charlie. The pub was derelict and was being condemned, but he still had a boxing ring in there and a few bags.

'Fucking hell! What kind of pro trainer hasn't got a gym?' I thought as I looked around.

In later years, before I could drive, I had to get two buses to Kingstanding and The Charlie. But on this occasion, Rocky drove me there.

I didn't know that Nobby was gay, though he was a big doorman for a number of years. Rocky introduced me to him.

'Oh, he's nice,' said Nobby and I shit myself a bit. I was only a young kid and I was paranoid. But he was only having a crack. That was Nobby's sense of humour.

'Come on. Let's stick you on the pads.' Nobby said.

As I'm working on the pads, Nobby turned to Rocky and said that I wasn't bad.

'Well, he was an NABC finalist. He's got pedigree,' said Rocky.

I went to the gym a few times yet soon after it was completely closed down. It was being demolished. I'd been there six weeks. Nobby then took me around little gyms for little bits of sparring. He later got a space in Erdington, which was over a pub called the Red Lion. He had that space for about five years and it was a good gym. Then he had another gym at the back of the Old Central Library in the city centre.

Then there was the gym in Aston on Thomas Street, which was really good. It was a really big space.

* * *

One day Rocky took me over to a gym in Dudley, which was run by Ronnie Brown. There was a stocky guy there, a super featherweight called Lester James. He'd had a few pro fights and was well rated.

'Get in and do a few rounds with him,' Nobby said to me.

'Fucking hell, he's gonna kill me here,' I thought.

He couldn't lay a glove on me. I was jabbing the head off him, and he couldn't get near me.

'Right,' said Nobby. 'I'm gonna get you carded up.'

I thought that this was a bit quick. I thought I would train for about a year before anything happened. I was naive.

I didn't have any trouble getting my licence as Nobby knew all the people on the Midlands boxing board. Two of their officials came to a gym in Dudley to watch me spar, to see if I was able to box. I sparred OK and Nobby spoke to the officials afterwards. Nobby said there were no worries and that they thought I was a tidy little boxer. Soon afterwards, I had a brain scan and an eye test. We used to go to a doctor in Handsworth, Dr Target. I'll never forget him. Real good doctor, he was. Nobby took me over there and he did my medical. Once I passed that, everything was done and I was ready to fight. Nobby used to call it the boxers' MOT.

* * *

Within a week of getting my medicals done, Nobby told me that I needed to get some boots and kit.

'What do you mean?' I said.

'You need to get some kit as you are fighting next week.'

'What, fighting?' I replied.

'Yeah,' he said.

I hadn't fought for five years. I got myself some boots and some shorts and had my first fight scheduled for October 1989.

* * *

When I first started boxing for Nobby, I wasn't really doing anything. I was doing a bit of labouring, a bit of painting and decorating. Anything to earn a few quid. But I was doing boxing more than anything. If I got a day's labour in, a bit of graft, then I would do it. But because I was fighting, that was my job basically. I was earning more by boxing every other week than I would earn doing a normal job for three or four weeks.

I was still getting into little bits of trouble but I was fighting, so I was earning money. I was occupied because I was going to the gym three, four times a week. I was running every day. I was always fit.

'It's just a fad. I'll have a few fights, keep myself out of trouble, earn a few quid.' All of this I was thinking when training with Nobby, and with my first fight coming up. I did not realise that the sport would not just be a job but a big part of my life over many years.

For my first professional fight, I went to Stafford Colosseum. Back then, you could still smoke at the shows as there wasn't a smoking ban.

I got there and weighed in. I was about 8st 13lbs. I shit myself. The man I was fighting had a rough beard, just a rough look about him. He looked about 30 and like a proper man. Alan Baldwin, his name was. I thought he looked tough. I was 20 and was still a boy.

At the time, I had only been out the nick three or four months. When I got into the ring, he would throw lots of shots and he was like a busy bee.

'He's going to kill me here,' I thought.

But in the end, I fucking battered him. I broke his nose in the first round and had him all over the place. But the referee gave it a draw. I didn't even know what a draw was in boxing at the time.

'What the fuck, it was never a draw,' said Nobby. 'But you can box him again next week.'

I didn't get this.

'What do you mean?' I asked.

He explained to me how it worked in the pros. But Baldwin never fought me in a rematch. He retired after our fight and never boxed again.

Instead of a rematch with Baldwin, for my second fight I boxed a man called Ronnie Stephenson. By the time I had fought him, he'd had 60-odd fights, was about 30 years of age and had been in the game many years. He was a pretty rough fighter and had man strength, whereas I was just a kid.

In the first round, I was jabbing him and doing alright. At the end of the second round, boom! He hit me with a right hand and put me on my arse. I'd never been put down before. I went on one knee, took the count, got up and boxed. At the end of the round, I went back to my corner.

'You done the right thing there,' Nobby said.

'But he put me over, man,' I said.

'Nah, it don't matter,' he replied.

I ended up losing to him on points. I was devastated as I was used to winning as an amateur. 'You did alright there,' Nobby said. 'You didn't panic, you took the count, you got up and smothered him.'

After the fight, Nobby asked me why I went on one knee after I was knocked down.

'To clear my head,' I said.

'You ain't a dummy, are you,' he replied. 'A lot of kids would have just jumped up. How are you now?'

'Eh, alright.' I said.

I boxed Ronnie four more times over the years. I got a draw with him the second time. The other three times, I boxed him out of sight. The last time I fought him was at the Grand Hotel. The fight was made at eight-twos, which means it was scheduled for eight rounds of two minutes each. I battered him. I had moved up a level. I'd improved. This was something that Nobby had also noticed.

'You've stepped up now, your game's come on. Those years out have done you good. You're still fresh. A lot of good amateurs get burned out by their trainers, thrown into championships bouts. You didn't and it saved you.'

* * *

My friendship with Nobby is very good. People used to get a bit jealous in the gym, saying things like, 'Are you Nobby's boyfriend?' I used to take fights that were available. He gave me the mentality to do that.

Don't forget, I was a thieving little bastard when I went to his gym.

'You don't have to do that,' he once said to me. 'You can earn. You're good enough to go and fight people who are better than you, who are champions. You can earn some good money without getting hurt.'

That's what his mentality was. Earn as much as you can without getting hurt. If I came out with a black eye, to him he wasn't doing his job. He would say to me, 'You shouldn't have had a black eye.' With certain opponents he would tell me, 'Make this fight easy tonight. This kid's a big puncher. Fuck him about. Do his head in. Tread on his foot. Hit him up the bollocks. Get through it.'

Nobby was a great believer in not fighting for three minutes of a round. 'Fight for a minute, hold them for 30 seconds. Tread on their toes for 20 seconds. Walk them back to the ropes...' Just loads of little tricks I did over the years. Some tricks you can't be taught. You just learn them as you go along. It's a craft like a builder who learns to build a certain wall because he gets experience. You get experience by doing everything. You don't know everything when you start a job. You learn to read situations better as you go on because of experience. You fight a kid who has been an ABA champion, Commonwealth Games champion, great amateur. It doesn't mean they are going to make a great pro. It has been proven over and over again. Audley Harrison, great amateur but never succeeded as a pro. Errol Christie, probably one of the best amateurs Britain's ever had, never made it as a pro. He was in some great fights but never got to the heights that he should have gotten to.

Nobby never boxed pro but he sparred boxers the calibre of Joe Bugner. He taught me certain skills, such as putting my head behind my left shoulder. If your head is right behind your left shoulder and your opponent throws a right hand, you imagine you're side on. You can slip that shot and you can come up with an uppercut and then finish with a left hook. It's a perfect angle. You just dip either side. You can see me do that in a lot of fights, especially after I had about 25 to 30 fights. I learned how to slip punches brilliantly. Sometimes, when I was on the ropes, people would throw a flurry of punches and I would move my head just a fraction and slip them. The shots would just miss me. You can ride the punches as well. If someone is throwing a big right hand and you're behind your shoulder, if they do catch you, you can ride it back and take the sting out of the punch. My left hand would be a bit low but I would be behind my shoulder.

With my right hand, Nobby taught me how to hold it up. He said to me that with the right hand, to make out that you're always on the telephone and that's where my hand had to be. If you slipped their right hand, they'll come back with a left hook. But you would be able to block that left hook as your right hand's up there. Then you can come back with a right hook, right uppercut or left hook all the time and it works. He was brilliant at picking things like that up.

* * *

Nobby likes horse betting. He's a real connoisseur when it comes to horse racing and is really good at knowing which horse to bet on. I have been to his house. He would have a phone line direct to the bookies. He used to ask me to pick out a horse when I didn't really know much about horse racing. I used to bet but not on his level.

He was also a very tongue-in-cheek geezer who always looked after his boxers. Some people say he didn't but he did. He always had their best interests at heart.

* * *

With Nobby, he used to work for all the big promoters and had good relationships with Mickey Duff, Frank Warren and Frank Maloney. He done them a lot of favours. He got them out of shit. Sometimes, there would be four pull-outs in a day. Who would they phone? Nobby.

'We need a ten stone [boxer], a nine stone and a 12 stone,' promoters would say.

'Yeah, don't worry about it,' Nobby would say.

They knew we would all be down there. None of us would fall over in a round.

He had a good reputation. You brought imports over and they would be knocked out in a round. The crowd would be angry. Especially if you had a show with only six fights on. You wanted the crowd to have four hours of boxing. You wouldn't want them to go down and have an hour's worth of boxing as they wouldn't be happy then. That's how it worked. Nobby would say to some managers that we would be a certain weight sometimes. But if we were taking the fight the day before, then when we got there we might be a little bit over that weight.

'Well, he only took the fight last night,' Nobby would say.

If the promoters complained, he would say that we were going home. He knew that promoters couldn't afford to let that happen, especially if their boxer was a ticket seller.

Nobby tried to earn you as much money as he could without you getting hurt. He would explain this by talking about when he worked on the doors for 20 years, which he used to do for £40 a night.

'I can do the doors, come out of there, not have a fight and earn 40 quid or I can have ten fights on the night, have a black eye, some cuts, and still get paid 40 quid. So, what do you do? You go to work, have no fights and earn £40.'

It's the same as in boxing. He always said that to me and it always stuck in my mind. Go in the ring, have a fight, make it as easy as you can, like a spar, and still get paid the same amount of money. Then fight again next week.

This was his motto.

I learned a lot from Nobby. He educated me. He kept me out of jail basically. He always spoke words of wisdom.

'You don't want to be sitting in a jail cell rotting,' he would say.

'Go in, earn the money. Come out and don't get a mark on you.'

When I got a black eye, I was mortified. It done my head in. I never really came out with black eyes but when I did, it pissed me off.

* * *

Nobby always used to look after me. Always.

Sometimes Nobby would say and do things that were off the cuff. Sometimes if a boxer was ready to spar, we would say to Nobby, 'Is he warmed up?'

'Yeah,' Nobby would reply. 'As long as he's sat next to the radiator!'

That was one of many mad things Nobby used to do and say.

What helped me learn the skills and tricks that Nobby would teach me were the other fighters in the gym. We had a lot of good fighters and we would learn off each other. Karl Taylor and Tony Hanna were other boxers in our gym who I learned from. We used to call him spanner. He's a firefighter now. He was a real tough fighter who had over 100 fights, including some with former British and world champions and was rarely stopped.

* * *

I was paid £180 for my first pro fight. The reason it was that little was because Nobby paid for all my medicals plus all my brain scans, which came to £400. Some people moaned about money taken out of their purse, to which Nobby would reply, 'Well, pay for your own brain scan.'

With a lot of boxing managers, when you turn pro, unless you're with a big promoter, you have to pay for your own medicals, such as your brain scan and your eye test. You have to get all the money for that yourself. If you can't get the money for the medicals, then you can't box. Nobby would always pay for it for you. He was good like that.

I've been in changing rooms and have seen boxers getting paid by their trainers and managers. Some fighters were getting the piss taken out of them in terms of how much they were paid after their fight. Nobby was straight with us. He would tell you how much you're getting paid before a fight. You either agreed to it or you didn't.

Now back in the day, most fighters would get £500 for doing a six-twos fight at a dinner show. Yet I would see kids in the changing rooms, after getting the bollocks knocked out of them in the ring, get paid £200 to £300. I have heard a manager say, 'Well, that's my money, that's the gym fees, that's for petrol.' Now every show a boxer goes to, you get your wages but your manager would also get expenses from that. What Nobby used to do with us is he would put the petrol in but would always buy us something to eat. Whereas I've been in changing rooms and heard trainers say that they and their fighter had a meal at the petrol station. But when they brought out the meal, the boxer's had a meal, the trainer's had a meal, the manager's had a meal and the kid's paid for it all. They've then classed it as expenses and taken the cost of the meal out of the boxer's wages. I used to think about how wrong that was.

Nobby would say to me sometimes, 'You see that there. That kid's getting £250 when he should have gotten £600.' When you look at it like that, you think of how bad that is. Their trainer is getting paid anyway. You're the one taking the punches. So literally, you're paying for the petrol there. You're paying for their meals and your own and they're taking it out of your money as expenses.

* * *

I was chuffed with the money I received for my first fight. But then my next fight, I got £250. The fight after that, I was paid £400. After that I was fighting every week, picking up between £400 and £500. I kept thinking that grown men weren't earning that going to work every week. I was making a good living. I wasn't getting hurt and I was doing it every week.

If it was a TV show then great, as it was more money. If I was fighting an unbeaten kid, I'd get more money. A fight with an ABA champion would be more money. A fight scheduled against a boxer who had won all his fights by knockout, more money.

The later you were offered a fight, the more money you could negotiate for. You got them by the bollocks really because the kid that you're boxing has probably sold a lot of tickets, and the last thing they want is to put a kid on the bill who has sold a lot of tickets and does not end up fighting. I saw it happen and the fans wouldn't be happy. Sometimes you can box a kid and they aren't getting any money. You're more or less on their purse. I boxed kids before who fought for nothing because I played hardball at the last minute. Say I was getting a grand, I have said that I want two grand. That probably goes into that kid's wages as well. It's a bit bad but that's what you can do. They've sold tickets to their mates and put coaches on for their fans, so you end up having their wages as they just want to fight. At the end of the day, they want to perform so they sometimes aren't really bothered about getting paid. They think they're superstars, that they're future world champions, so they aren't bothered.

I've had fights where I've counted my money and it's been short. Say I went to a show on my own and I'm getting £1,500 for a fight and they've given me the money. Nobby said to me from the start that I should always count my money in front of them when they give it to me. But once, I got the envelope with my money and I signed for it. I went back to the changing room, counted the money and it was about £200 light. So, I've gone back to Dean Powell and said 'Dean, this is light, mate.' He could have told me to fuck off, but instead he said, 'What do you mean?' I said, 'It's some money short.' Straight away without any hesitation he said, 'Don't worry. I'll give it to you in a minute.' He then called to someone, 'Give Pete some money there.' They didn't even question me because they knew I wasn't like that.

I told Nobby what happened and he said, 'I've told you before. You always count your money in front of them.' Don't forget, they are doing all of the wages on the night and at a big fight, you have about 20 boxers on the card.

Then you have the wages of the ten officials, then the doctors and the paramedics. They have to be done there and then. So sometimes they make mistakes. But as long as you count the money in front of them and tell him them your wages are light, then they'll give it to you straight away. But if you go back to your changing room, count your money and then go back and say, for example, that it's £500 light, they'll ask, 'How do I know you haven't taken £500 out?' That's why you always count it in front of them.

When I used to take some of Nobby's fighters to a fight, I always I always counted out their money in front of them and told them what I'm counting. Then when I'd counted out their pay, I would say, 'There's your wages. Count that money. Don't come back to me. Count your money in front of me.' That way, they couldn't say later that the fee was wrong.

But there was a kid, I won't say his name, I took him to a fight, not for Nobby but for someone else. Back in the changing room after the fight, I did the same as Nobby taught me to do. I counted his money in front of him and gave it to him. Later, when he got home, Errol Johnson, who was training him, phoned me up.

'So and so has phoned me. His money was light,' he said.

'No it wasn't,' I said. 'Let me tell you now. His money wasn't light 'cos I counted the money out in front of him.

Before I dropped him home, he went in the petrol station. He bought 40 fags and a bottle of whisky. Then I dropped him around the corner and he bought a bag of weed. That's where his money went.'

'Oh,' he said.

'Yeah, right,' I said. 'Phone him and say that to him.'

So, he's called him and he's called me back and said, 'Yeah, he forgot about that.'

'He didn't forget about it. He was trying to get some extra money out of you,' I replied.

I know every trick in the book with things like that as Nobby has taught me all of them. A trainer should always count their money before going back to the changing room and always count your fighter's money in front of them and get them to count it in front of you. That way, they can't come back to you and complain that it's short. There was no point a fighter calling me three hours later, saying that the money we didn't count is £300 light. I always covered my own back. Sometimes it's light because envelopes were mixed up. But trainers and fighters should always count their money there and then. That's a good trick of the trade.

I met a lot of boxers who were gullible. Some of them have boxed lads who I had already boxed. I would see them counting out their money and say how much they just got for their fights and I'd be sitting there thinking, 'Man, you just been ripped right off.' They have taken a beating or gotten stopped and can't box again for 28 days, yet you would hear their trainers telling them not to worry as they'll get them a nice easy fight for next time and I'm thinking, 'What a piece of shit.' But that's the boxing world for you. You see managers come and go in this game and promise their fighters the world but only fly-by-nights don't last long. Then you have the managers who have been in the sport forever, who know the game inside out and know every little trick in the book. Old school. I always liked boxing in Scotland, though I only got the one win up there. But Tommy Gilmour and Alex Morrison, who are the top two promoters in Scotland, always treated me well. They knew that I would always give their lads a good fight without adding a loss to their record. That is what they wanted.

* * *

After I had a draw with Alan Baldwin and lost to Ronnie Stephenson, I won four fights in a row before facing Wayne Taylor. Wayne was the brother of Karl Taylor and I knew them both as all three of us had boxed for Ladywood when we were kids. I remembered Wayne as he was a nice lad but Karl back then was a bit moody, though later we became good mates. Me and Karl both boxed for Nobby in the end but Karl boxed for Ernie Cashmore when he first turned pro. A few of my mates and family came to the fight and there was no way I was going to lose.

The fight took place in a leisure centre in Kings Heath, an area to the south of my hometown. We had a really good fight but I thought I would win as I used to get the better of our spars when we were kids. He was a tough lad and it was a good fight but I won on points. We had a pint in the bar afterwards and there were no hard feelings.

When Karl first came to Nobby's gym, he hadn't forgotten that fight and tried to rough me up in sparring. Yet I always stood my ground with him and he brought me on as a fighter.

Karl was a good pro and fought for the British lightweight title against Michael Ayers a few years later after holding him to a draw in their first fight. He lost the second time on cuts, I think. He was a tough lad out the ring and had a reputation for liking a fight after a few drinks. But me and him never had a cross word between us as he is a proper good lad.

* * *

The fight with Wayne was my seventh fight in just over two months. I won my next fight before losing the fight following that. I then had the first in a series of fights against Miguel Matthews.

At the time I fought Matthews he had fought about 20 times, though he would go on to have over 100 fights. He was a good journeyman. Nobby put me in with him as he felt that I would learn a lot from the fight. We boxed about four or five times in the end.

The first time, we fought to a draw. He came out of his corner and Nobby said, 'Watch him. He'll put your head down and he'll hit you on the blind side.' I learned a lot from our fights. He hit me in the bollocks and on the back of the head. He'd hold me, push me on to the ropes and use his elbows. He was a real dirty fighter but old school in his style. He would give anyone a fight. He was a real tough geezer, strong as an ox and probably had the best chin of any fighter I shared the ring with. You could hit him with the kitchen sink and he would just plough forward. He only got stopped a few times in his career, but never got knocked out. He fought some big punchers as well.

We all used to be on the circuit together. Me and him actually won a Services to Boxing award in London. I class him as one of my good friends in boxing.

I always say to him that he taught me a hell of a lot. He taught me these tricks that I wasn't aware of as I was still new to the pros. You would look at the ref and he wouldn't do anything. He wasn't a big puncher but was very strong. Nice geezer as well. After the fight he was sound but in the ring he was a fucking animal!

* * *

When I boxed as a professional, some of the mischief that I got up to during that time involved Ada. We weren't angels.

One night, we decided to rob a shop. We decided to try and get into the shop by going through the roof. This was different to the robberies I did when I was younger as we were dressed to the nines in designer clobber on our way out for the night. Outside the shop we cased the place, looking at how to get up on the roof. I went gung-ho on to an industrial skip.

'Hold on, son,' said Ada, but I got on to the roof in no time. No sooner had I got on to the roof than I slipped. I descended from the roof into the skip below. Luckily enough, the skip was full of old mouldy fruit and vegetables. I got myself out and walked back to the front of the shop, with rotten cabbage and apple peelings on my Armani jacket. Ada cried laughing at what happened and we pissed ourselves later in the pub!

We also used to train together. Ada would come to all of Nobby's gyms but we both used to use Stevie B's gym in Acocks Green. One time, we were due to go to the gym together. At the time Ada had bought a new car, a Mini GT, which cost him £100, from some geezer. He felt like splashing out! The car was a nail but it was his nail! He pulled up at my place and beeped the horn. When I came out and saw his car, shock doesn't even cover it!

'You're nuts, Ade!' I said laughing.

'Get in, you knob!' he said. 'I'm taking us to the gym.'

I got into the car with my training gear in my leather Head bag. I was clinging on for dear life as he was driving. Ada had only driven four times before. We were like *Starsky and Hutch* when in that car!

We got to the gym in one piece and I went straight to the loo after that car ride! We both had a wicked gym session. We got into the car and were just coming out of town when Ada noticed blue lights behind us. We tried to act cool but our arses were blowing louder than the broken exhaust. Ada parked the car and soon afterwards this big square-headed bloke has got me and Ada out of the car, into the police car and comes over to the road and starts booting Ada's pride and joy. His hard foot went through the footwell. Ada and the copper started going at it verbally as Ada was defending his beauty. As Ada is in the back of the police car and his Mini is on the recovery, I start to talk to the copper and pulled the latest edition of *Boxing News* out of my bag. I then trotted through town a free man. Little did I know that the police car would be behind him, side by side while he was walking through town, where Ada could shout obscenities at me and the police!

Another story about us occurred one stormy day when it was pissing down with rain and floods were everywhere. We had been training at the Queen's Head in Erdington. When me and Ada came out, the sky looked like it was about to be the end of the world.

While we were outside one of the boxers from the gym, a good lad and good fighter, offered us a lift back to my home.

It was great as it was three lads having a crack and we all got on. Drawing nearer to my flat at the time, the weather became worse.

I said to our mate to take a short cut. But unbeknown to us all, there was a flood separating us from my flat. Our mate drove through and his car was submerged like a sub. We had to make a sharp exit before we drowned. Each of us got on the roof of the car and got to safety. Our pal was standing there, gutted, looking at his car, scraping his head and pacing the ground.

'Oh fuck,' he said. 'What am I going to do?'

'I gotta go,' I replied. 'Me tea's done.'

Ada just stood there, laughing his head off.

Although I do get on with my mates and people in general, I can hold a grudge. There are people who I fell out with when I was 16 or 17 and I still don't speak to them now. If I don't like you, I don't like you for life. I've got a lot of friends but very few mates. I can count on one hand how many mates I've got. Proper mates. I don't have to see my mates for six months but I can phone them up and say, 'Look, I need a hand with something.' They don't ask what it's about. They'll come around to my house and help.

It's the same vice versa. If my mate phoned me now and said, 'Pete, I've got a problem,' I would go around to his house straight away. I wouldn't even ask what the problem was as I know he wouldn't be phoning me for nothing. I wouldn't really want to phone my mates unless it's a last resort. They are like brothers to me.

* * *

The first time I fought Matthews, it was my tenth fight. After that, I feel that I was probably overmatched as I was going into the ring with kids who had been area champions and who had had 60-odd fights, whereas I'd only had ten or 11. I was holding my own with them no problem but I was still losing. I was always boxing away from home, so even when I was winning I wasn't given the fight.

I came to Scotland once and boxed a Scottish champion. I beat him but didn't get the decision. At that point, I started thinking, 'Why am I trying as hard as I am?' Sometimes, if I was going up to Scotland, I'd try but I wouldn't try 100 per cent. I'd try 50 per cent and come out without a mark on me. I knew I wasn't going to get the decision. I could come out with two black eyes and a busted nose. I would still get the same money. That happened plenty of times in Scotland. You would just get into that mindset and think, 'Well, shall I try and have a go or shall I just have a move about?' It's being a professional. You're doing it without robbing the public. You can still put up a good fight but you're doing just enough to come second.

Mickey Duff used to say about me, 'He's a good fighter, that Peter. He does just enough to come second.' I don't come to win but I put up a good fight without really trying to win.

I loved getting hurt and as I said earlier, I could never say no to a fight. Never. In the gym, we used to have a noticeboard. My name would be on that board every time. Buckley vs so and so on this date with the number of scheduled rounds. Some of the lads in the gym would be jealous of this.

'Well, don't say no to a fight then,' Nobby would say in response.

The lads in the gym would look at the board and would ask, 'You on again?'

'Yeah,' I would say.

Nobby would say to the boxers that there would be a fight available and the lads in the gym would ask how much and who it was against. I didn't give a fuck who I was fighting. All I wanted to know was how much and how many rounds, as the more rounds the more money.

I always used to say, if you're a bricklayer, you don't say no to a job. I never said no to a fight. That was my mentality. Nobby loved that. He once said that the fan man that came into the arena during the second Riddick Bowe vs Evander Holyfield fight was me taking a fight at the last minute! He used to just come out with mad things like that.

* * *

I would buy *Boxing News* every single week and I'd read every page. When I left my flat, I left thousands of editions of that magazine. I used to just have them in the flat. It used to be a lot more detailed. It would tell you about the style of fighters. I would be there Friday, going around the shop at nine o'clock to buy my copy. Every undercard fight would be reported in quite good detail. I would read it from front to back and then back to front.

Even though my writing was crap, I had a notebook and would record who had fought who. Nobby would call me his boxing encyclopaedia. He would phone me up and say, for example, 'Brian Coleman has a fight against so and so. What's he like?'

'I'll phone you back in a bit,' I'd say.

I would look in my book and phone Nobby back and say something like, 'He's good. He's a southpaw, not a puncher. Brian will be alright.'

At other times Nobby would say to me, 'I have so and so for a fighter. What's he like?'

'Hold on. Let me have a look,' I'd reply and I would go and check my notebook. I'd come back to him and say, 'He's alright' or 'Yeah, he'll be OK for him.' Nobby would give me £50 for that info.

Lads in the gym would say that I was always getting matched. Nobby would tell them that I matched myself. For instance, I would read *Boxing News* and notice that someone would be scheduled to fight but that their opponent hadn't been confirmed. I'd phone Nobby and he would check it out.

'Eight threes, two and a half grand.' I'd say, 'Alright then.' Anytime I'd see a boxer with no opponent in *Boxing News*, I would say, 'Try and get me that fight.' Nobby would say, 'I wish I had ten of you.'

Then I got a second's licence. It meant that even when I wasn't boxing, I would still go to the shows and help Nobby do the corner. I would watch every bout on the bill, from fight one to the last fight. I would do this as I would be thinking that I could be boxing next week or Karl could be boxing next week and so on. Watching the fighters, I would wonder how I would do against them.

Nobby would say to me regularly, 'How would so and so get on against him?'

'No problem,' I'd say. He'd take my word for it. He would know himself but he knew I studied the game a lot more than him.

* * *

When I used to box at Solihull Sporting Club, it was dire. The crowd wasn't even allowed to clap or cheer. If I boxed at one of the shows held there and I was hitting the kid with a few punches, as soon as the crowd were about to cheer, the MC would go, 'Quiet please!' It was really weird.

But at some of the dinner shows I boxed at, there was quite a good atmosphere. The one thing I didn't like about after-dinner shows was that they started too late. Sometimes they wouldn't start until 9.30 or even 10.30, which was hard, especially if you'd been grafting earlier that day or had work the next morning. These shows would usually only have three fights on, four at the most. So if you were on last, you weren't fighting until 12 o'clock at night. They were a bit of a piss-take. I didn't really like them. The money wasn't bad but it was a shit event to box in as half the crowd didn't have a clue about the boxers. They were there to make deals with each other as they were all businessmen. So, they weren't really there to watch the boxing. But I remember boxing a kid called Chris Clarkson at the Mayfair in London at one such dinner show. Central Area champion, he was. He had double the amount of fights I had and he'd boxed some good kids. It was a good fight and I thought I beat him, but he got the decision.

After the fight, a geezer came into the changing room and gave me some money, and said that he'd won on me. I've had that a few times where someone has said, 'That was a good fight,' and given me money. But overall, I'd say only two per cent of the crowd were watching the boxing.

* * *

Around the time of my series of fights with Miguel Matthews, I was involved in another with a boxer named Drew Docherty. Drew had been a top amateur who had boxed for Scotland. I boxed him three times in total and our styles of fighting worked well together, which is why my fights with him were good. Out first fight took place at Solihull Civic Hall. He got the decision by half a point, though I thought I beat him. The second and third fights between us happened in Glasgow. At this stage of his career, he had become British champion at bantamweight. They were close fights but not in the referee's eyes in Scotland. Later on in his career, Drew went on to fight for European and world titles, and lost those fights. In each of my fights against him, I always held my own. That's why I know I could have fought for a British title.

Next thing, Nobby's said, 'Do you want to fight abroad?'

'Abroad?' I replied.

* * *

Not long after my fight with Clarkson, there was a fight happening in Denmark. I'd never been abroad in my life. I filled out the forms to get my passport and soon after, I flew to Denmark. I was due to fight a kid named Johnny Bredahl. This kid had been to the Olympics. Both him and his brother would become world champions and his brother fought Oscar De La Hoya for the world title.

We arrived in Denmark the day before the fight was due to take place. Our five-star hotel – I'd never stayed in one before – was out in the sticks and that's where we stayed for most of our time before the fight. We got up and had no breakfast, then went to the weigh-in. After that, we stayed at the venue all day, which was about half an hour from the hotel.

The venue was a massive arena. There were all Americans in my changing room, all loud saying they were going to do this and that. It felt a bit surreal, though Nobby used a good trick up his sleeve before the fight.

The fight was scheduled for six threes. Now abroad, they don't do two-minute rounds. So, when we landed in Denmark, Nobby asked a few people what Johnny was like as a fighter and he was told that he was a good kid. Soon before the fight was due to start, he went over to the timekeeper and told him that my fight was only six two-minute rounds. The timekeeper was Danish so didn't understand what Nobby had said. Nobby showed the timekeeper how long the fight was per round by demonstrating it on his watch. I didn't know any of this until after the fight.

The MC for the fight said in Danish and English who was boxing and that the fight was scheduled for six three-minute rounds. At that point, Nobby turned to the timekeeper and showed him two fingers to signal the length of each round and nodded at him. The timekeeper nodded back to show that he understood what Nobby said. The first round ended and I came back to the corner.

'I thought it was six-threes,' I said.

'No, it's six-twos,' said Nobby.

The fight ended and I lost on points in a good fight. Afterwards I said to Nobby, 'I thought they didn't do six two-minute rounds abroad.'

'That's what you pay for kid,' he laughed.

He knew it would have been a hard fight at six-threes but that I still would have done it. Yet Nobby pulled a masterstroke.

That is what he meant by saying that's what I paid him for. It was to look out for me as he knew I could do a six-twos fight against anyone really.

After the fight, there was a little after-party at the hotel. We had a few drinks and Nobby went to bed. I stayed up and was having a drink with an American boxer called Garing Lane, who'd fought on the undercard. Like me, he lost his fight on points, whereas all the other fighters had been knocked out. He was an OK guy and a journeyman in the making who went on to box some big names in the heavyweight division. Next morning, me and Nobby got the plane home.

I've since watched the fight on YouTube and I look 15! I did alright. An easy fight really. He beat me on points fairly, though I wasn't outclassed nor disgraced. A few years later, I saw him at The Point in Dublin when he challenged Wayne McCullough for the WBC title. I spoke to him and wished him good luck as he was a nice kid.

* * *

When I came back home from boxing Johnny Bredahl in Denmark, Tania told me that she was pregnant. Becoming a father when I was 21 made me grow up a bit as I never wanted my daughter to come and see me in a prison. Looking after a child motivated me more when I was boxing as whether I won, lost or drew a fight, I was still getting paid, meaning I was able to provide for her.

My daughter is a big part of my life. She was a proper daddy's girl when she was little, and me and my wife used to do everything with her. I would take her swimming every Sunday even if I had fought the night before, and me and Tania would take her to a dancing school twice a week. She used to enter dance competitions all the time and won a lot of medals. It was only when she went to senior school that she became disinterested in it.

She is my only child and I still spoil her now. When she was little, when I would come home after boxing, she would ask how much I had got paid. I would laugh as most of the time I would give her £50. She would think she was rich!

As new parents, at first we were living at her mom's place. Then we moved out and got a flat. It was nice up there. I just wanted our own place and to get some savings going while I was fighting all the time. Fighting every week kept me out of trouble, on the straight and narrow, as I wasn't robbing or getting into fights outside of the ring.

* * *

Nobby was chuffed and said that I did really well in the fight with Bredahl and didn't let the occasion get to me.

'Nob,' I told him, 'I've been fucking stabbed and had people chase me with machetes. I ain't scared of no one with a pair of gloves.'

At that point, Nobby said that the L plates were off and I could box anyone. My level of opposition went up. I boxed area champions, former British champions, former European champions, kids who had fought in the Olympics and I was holding my own with them.

One day, Nobby said that he was going to take me to York Hall, the famous boxing venue in London.

'Like the mecca of boxing?' I said.

'Yeah,' he replied.

So I fought there. Can't remember whether I won, drew or lost my fight but I do remember Nobby saying that I had done my apprenticeship.

'Once you can come out of Birmingham,' he said, 'you can earn money. Once you come down to London to box these kids, you're at a certain level, you can box anywhere.'

* * *

Nobby took me to the first fight between Nigel Benn and Chris Eubank. We were more or less seated ringside and you could tell that Benn hated him. It was no joke. We were also able to get backstage as Nobby used to be able to get wristbands, which meant we could walk all round the venue. We saw Benn, who was very fired up. He was ferocious. You could see the intensity in him. He wanted to rip Eubank's head off. Nobby said to me, 'He ain't playing here, he means it.' You could see the anger on Benn's face. Nobby had bet against Benn when he fought Michael Watson and won £600. He knew his boxing and was very good at reading fights. He said to me that at the Watson vs Benn fight, Benn was doing the same thing. He was pent up with rage, whereas Watson was nice and calm. Nobby said that he knew Watson would beat him as he had a good jab and was nice and calm. When Eubank came into the ring, he was cool, calm and collected. He didn't really let Benn get under his skin, whereas Benn did. That's what won Eubank the fight.

Benn wanted to destroy him and really wanted to hurt him. With Eubank, he was looking at it as his job and he didn't let Benn get to him. When Benn lost, you could see he was heartbroken.

* * *

I've been to weigh-ins where there was pushing and shoving. I never got into that as it doesn't win you a fight. You just burn up needless energy. You don't win a fight outside the ring. When people tried to and stare me out, I used to smirk. It didn't work as I thought them staring at me wasn't hurting me. It wasn't intimidating me. I've never been intimidated. When I boxed Michael Gomez, we came to the middle of the ring and he's put his head right in my face. I just pushed my head straight back into his. After the fight, he was as nice as pie.

* * *

Charlie Magri was my idol. He was a very good fighter in his day. He won the British title in only his third fight and later became a world champion. I've since met Charlie hundreds of times. When I was young, I used to love watching him and he used to have a pair of black and gold Title boots. When I first boxed as an amateur, my dad asked me what boots I wanted him to get for me. 'Black and gold,' I said, as Charlie Magri wore the same colours.

The first time I met Charlie was at Dennie Mancini's Lonsdale shop in London. Me and Paul Westley had a sponsor. The sponsorship came about as this person saw me box at the Grand Hotel and won a lot of money on me. This person gave Nobby £500, which Nobby then said he would use to take me down to London and get me kitted out in proper gear. I went to the shop and Magri happened to be in there at the time. I was in awe of him. Nobby spoke to him but I was starstruck. I was 21 or 22 at the time.

The boxing board used to put on a do in the Midlands. When it first started, it used to be really big. There used to be a lot of people that came from London. One year, it was at the Westley Arms Hotel in Acocks Green, which was down the road from me. It was packed. Charlie Magri was there. I knew him well enough by then to speak to him, so I said, 'Alright Charlie.' But I was speaking to one of my idols. It was like meeting a film star to me. He knew who I was. For him to know who I was seemed surreal. I grew up watching him and he was just brilliant. I've never told him that he was my idol growing up.

There was an article in *Boxing News* not long ago. He was a janitor at a school and they sacked him. If you sit down with Charlie Magri, you could listen to him all day long. I've met Michael Watson as well. I was at the same table as him at a dinner and what an inspiration that guy is. They are both lovely geezers to speak to.

And then who stopped him and retired him? Duke McKenzie. And I boxed Duke McKenzie in my next bout. It was a fight which was to change my boxing career.

CHAPTER 8

The Duke

Duke McKenzie wasn't my hero but I did respect him after he beat Charlie Magri. When it came to fighting him, I wasn't a journeyman at that time.

Nobby said to me one day in the gym, 'There's a fight going. Do you want to fight Duke McKenzie?'

'Wasn't he a world champion?' I said.

'Yeah,' he replied.

'Yeah, I'll fight him. How much?' I said.

Nobby told me how much I would be paid and that the fight would be scheduled for eight threes. I jumped at it.

At this stage of my career, I hadn't had many fights. Duke McKenzie had just lost his bantamweight world title, so he was a two-weight world champion. Then there was me. I hadn't even fought for an area title.

For my first fight with McKenzie, I had to be 8st 10lbs. At the weigh-in, when I jumped on the scales, I was 8st 10½lbs.

'Get that half a pound off,' said Mickey Duff, who was McKenzie's promoter.

I could have been 9st 10lbs, I still wasn't going to beat Duke McKenzie. Dennie Mancini, who was Mickey Duff's right-hand man, and Terry Lawless knew me and Nobby quite well. As explained earlier, it was Mancini's Lonsdale shop in London I used to go down to and buy boxing gear from before he sold it. He always used to look after us and get us a good deal. I was thinking when I got off the scales, 'Fucking hell, I've got to get off half a pound?' Dennie Mancini, I think if he didn't know me he wouldn't have given a fuck. But he was a nice person to me. He winked at me and then shook his head.

'Don't worry about that half a pound,' he said to Nobby.

'Cheers Den,' replied Nobby.

He knew the odds were against me. Half a pound wasn't going to do anything against Duke McKenzie. If Mickey Duff had known, he probably would have gone mad at Mancini as he wanted that half a pound off to drain me even more.

I thought that as he is only small, I would give him a good fight. I just thought that although he had been a world champion, that was at flyweight. He isn't going to be that bad, he isn't going to be that strong. He proved the complete opposite. He was bigger and better than anyone I'd boxed, amateur and pro. Our first fight was the first time I realised about levels in boxing. Boxing McKenzie opened my eyes to what boxing was truly about.

I got in there and his jab was awesome. It was like being hit with a broomstick. I was devastated when he beat me as I'd never been stopped before, amateur or pro.

In my second pro fight, when I boxed Ronnie Stephenson, he put me over in the second round. But he was a man, whereas

I was still a boy. He was 36 and had around 60 fights. Good journeyman. I took the count and lost on points. But I went on to beat him another four times when I boxed him. But when I lost to Duke McKenzie, it was like, 'Fucking hell.' He went on to win another world title and challenge for a third one. It puts it in perspective.

When I boxed him the first time, I went in with ambition. Even though I'd lost a couple of fights, I had more wins than losses. When I boxed him, I genuinely believed I was going there to win, not just for a payday. The second time I boxed him, it was a completely different story. Nobby phoned me up and said they wanted someone for Duke McKenzie and asked if I fancied it. All I wanted to know was what the money was. I can't remember how much I was paid. My approach to the rematch was completely different to the first fight. I'd grown up. I'd had a lot of fights since then.

I knew what my role was against him the second time round. That I was going in there as an opponent. The second fight I boxed him, my style was completely different. I was behind my left shoulder but the right shoulder was fucked. At the end of the second round, I was massaging my arm in the corner. His jab was like a broom handle hitting me in the face. It looked like he had nothing. But his jab was like snap, boom, snap, boom! There was so much power behind it but it was more the sharpness and the quickness of it. He had a first-class jab and a good right hand as well. Technically, he was the best boxer I ever faced.

I knew I wasn't going to win because of my bad shoulder. It fucked but I needed the money. I only done three rounds with him and my shoulder popped. I went to the corner and asked Nobby to pull me out and that was it. The second time was different to the first time. I was a lot more experienced. Having watched both fights on YouTube since that night, I could see how much experience I had in the second fight. But I shouldn't have fought him because of my shoulder. I had more ambition when I boxed him the first time. The second time, I knew the game.

* * *

I didn't think I'd fight again. I thought, 'Ah, fuck this. I'm never gonna box again. That's me done.' Like I say, I hadn't been stopped amateur or pro up to that point. It really hurt my pride. I just thought that was it. Not that I thought I was going to be a world champion or anything like that. It was just really disheartening. I'd never been hit like that in a boxing ring. Even at amateur level, I'd boxed top amateurs and no one had ever done that to me. I thought that was the end of me but it was the start of me. Nobby reassured me and said, 'Look, you lost to a geezer who was a world champion on two days' notice. If you got stopped by an idiot, then probably pack it in. But this geezer is world class.'

I also sat back and thought, 'You know, I fought five rounds with a former world champion.' If I'd gotten knocked out in a round that would be bad, but I fought five rounds with him, then I boxed him a second time with a bad shoulder but did it for the money. I fought a few more world champions who didn't stop me. People always ask me who was the best boxer I fought. Naseem Hamed? Acelino Freitas? Neither of them. It was Duke McKenzie. Three world titles in three different weight divisions. That's how good he was.

* * *

I realised my journeyman status after I lost to Duke McKenzie. As he was the first one to stop me, I thought, 'Fucking hell.' I wasn't at the level I thought I was at. Not that I thought I was going to be a world champion, but I thought a flyweight world champion done that to me. I started to take a lot of fights where I thought I won but I didn't get the decision. I would often take these fights on short notice, just for the money, and that's when I treated it more as a job than as a career. I thought this is a way to make money all the time.

That was my bread and butter. I wasn't looking at titles. I won Midlands titles but they were minor in my mind. I would love to have won the British title but it never happened. I fought loads of ex-European champions who just about beat me. There was nothing in it. The levels were miles apart.

A few years later I fought Fabrice Benichou, who was a former world champion. He later boxed Wayne McCullough and had previously held the IBF title at super bantamweight. I boxed him in an eight-rounder and lost on points. He said to me afterwards in his broken English that he couldn't hit me. The fight was easy. It wasn't as though there was a massive gulf in class. I held my own with him. I didn't become disgraced in there and I wasn't embarrassed in the fight. So, I knew I was good enough to compete at that level. Being a journeyman and being a good journeyman are two different things. You can be a journeyman and fight prospects all day long. When you're fighting former European and world champions as a journeyman, you've got to be a good journeyman to be able to go the distance with those geezers. I knew I was good enough to fight for a British title but in the end, money overcame the glory. I was looking to earn instead of winning a title.

* * *

My role as a journeyman was basically to get through one fight so I could fight next week. To come out without a mark on me, like having an easy spar. You don't want to come out of a fight with a cut eye, as even if you lose on points you're still out for 28 days. No journeyman wants to be out for 28 days as they're on the road every week. A good journeyman wants to be out every week. That is how you earn your money.

No journeyman I knew brought shame on the sport as if they were a journeyman, they knew their trade. These so-called journeymen from abroad weren't journeymen because as soon as they got hit, they would fall over. We still have a handful of decent journeymen now but with Covid-19, they are not getting any work.

Sometimes, if I knew it was going to be a hard fight, I'd have a go at them in the first round just to let them know I was there, so they can't walk over me. Sometimes my opponent would know themselves that they weren't going to stop me, so they would box differently to how they would box other people. They would take half a step back instead of going full on at me all the time.

Even though I was short-tempered outside the ring, I was always a bit of a thinker when boxing as an amateur and I took that to the pros. I was never in a rush when in the ring and was always taking my time, thinking about what the other fighter was going to do. I was good at reading fighters and working them out quite quickly.

Weird as it sounds, there are ways to lose as a journeyman. One way is that you don't try too hard and the other way is that you let your opponents overwhelm you. You can't just stay on the ropes. Anyone can be tough and take shots. But you have to be clever. You've got to tuck your head behind your left shoulder and move side on, so there is less of a target for your opponent. Instead of fighting three-minute rounds, you fight one-and-a-half-minute rounds. You fight for 30 seconds, have a little breather, tie them up, then have a walk around. A great thing to do when a journeyman is boxing is instead of you coming out, just stand your ground. All I used to do is literally move my foot to the left and just pivot. I would go back and forth like that. Meanwhile, your opponent is bouncing round and using loads of energy. All I'm doing is using the least amount of energy I can. I'm just moving one foot here, one foot there. Then I just have a walk around with my hands by my side. Opponents would look at me and think, 'What are you doing?' Then they would set themselves to throw a shot while I was standing there, and I would just walk off!

Another thing I used to do was talk to my opponents. I used to do their heads in with my constant chatter. When I was in with big punchers, after two or three rounds I would say to them, 'Thought you were a big puncher,' and grin at them. Sometimes I'd even take a shot on purpose. When you get that rush in the ring, you feel invincible.

On one occasion, me and another journeyman named Kristian Laight were talking to Jon Pegg before a show. Jon asked us, 'How do you guys do what you do?' Kristian looked at me, I looked at him and we both knew what the other was thinking. You can't teach it, really. It's just inside you. You know how to do it. I've taken Kristian to a few of his fights and talking to him was like talking to myself at times as he knew exactly what I was on about. As I say, you just break up the rounds. You hold them, you walk them back to the ropes, you lock their arms, push them off, walk off again. You could turn a fight that is eight three-minute rounds into a 12-minute fight over the distance of those eight rounds, as you just fight for a minute of each round. It's hard to fight for three minutes of a round. You have to be super fit.

For example, someone like Paul Ingle could do it. When I was in the ring with him, I had to try and break his concentration, otherwise he would have really gone to town on me. The second time I boxed him, he was beating me up throughout the first three rounds. Throwing shots at me all the time. Brilliant workrate. But, as in the first fight, I started breaking his concentration and was tying him up more and more. That's what you have to do. Like I said, it's not something that you can teach. It's like being a bricklayer. The longer you do it, the better you get. With being a journeyman, the more fights you have, the more tricks you pick up. It's an art and not everyone can do it.

There are only a handful of journeymen in this country that can do it. That's why they keep bringing in people from abroad as you can't get the journeymen that you used to be able to get. About 15 or 20 years ago, you had a lot of good journeymen. Nobby had a stable full of them. We all learned off each other. You would learn new tricks, like standing on someone's foot. That's a brilliant trick. You're boxing someone and you just stand on their foot. When me and Naseem were boxing each other, he used to do that. All of Brendan Ingle's fighters used to do that. When you're boxing someone and you stand on their foot, they automatically look down. You'd then hit them with an uppercut, a jab or any shot you could hit them with. It's a brilliant trick if you could get away with it. Sometimes, the referee doesn't see it. If they do see it, they will give you a bit of a bollocking and tell you to not do it. But sometimes the ref doesn't see it as they're not looking down at the feet. They're mainly looking from the head to the waist, as that's where the scoring punches are. If you can step on their foot three or four times in a round, it really does their head in. It really pisses them off. Their corner knows as they will say to the ref, 'Ref, he's trod on his foot!' But the ref wouldn't notice and I would be like, 'I don't know what he's on about.' Especially if you're boxing a southpaw, that's a brilliant trick as you can stand on their feet all day long.

Sometimes if I went into a fight and had been on the piss, I would hold more than I normally would as I wouldn't be feeling great. As I'm holding my opponent, the ref would go, 'Put the hold down now, Pete. I'm not warning you again.' You could make it look like they were holding you instead. If you're on the blind side of the ref and you lock your opponent's arm underneath you and they're trying to pull away, you could say to the ref, 'Ref, he's holding, he's holding!' Then they would argue back that I'm holding them and you can blag the referee. It's just years of learning and doing tricks like that. Sometimes, I would go into a really hard fight and I would definitely have to try and break their concentration. You'd hold him, walk them back to the ropes, hit them in the bollocks, hit them low on the blind side of the ref. Sometimes you just have to do what you have to do. The fights with Miguel Matthews taught me that. When I first boxed him, he was hitting me low about five to ten times. I'd be looking at the ref and he hadn't done anything because he hadn't seen it. But I learned how to do it on the sly in that fight.

* * *

Say you're taking the fight on short notice at eight-threes, which is a long time in the ring. If you're not 100 per cent fit, you've got to learn how to walk around and switch off. What it is, these kids have been training for three months for an eight-rounder. All they've been concentrating on for the last three months is this fight against their opponent. When these prospects are training, and their original opponent pulls out, they have not got a fighter who is of a higher level than me who they are going to fight at the last minute. We're not as fit as them, so when you go in there they come out their corner at 100mph. Therefore, you have to learn to slow them down. Tread on their feet, hold them, hit them low, hit them on the back of their head, then tie them up. When they are standing there posing, I would just look at them and walk off. When a fighter sets their feet, that's when they throw their power shots. As soon as they set their feet, you just need to walk off. Take a few steps back. It's a really hard thing to teach someone. You have got to know how to do it. There are only a few fighters who can really do it. Good journeymen. If you try and fight for three minutes of every round, you're fucked. You can't do it unless you're a machine. Little tricks you learn, like holding them and hitting them on the blind side when the ref isn't looking. Walk, push them off, have a walk round. You have to learn to slip and block punches. Everyone can be a tough guy. But I didn't have 300 fights through being tough. People used to say to me that I was tough. I would say I was smart. You learn how to be smart from years of experience, going down to gyms to spar with good fighters. When you're paid to spar, that's like a fight. They're down there to take your fucking head off.

If I saw one of my opponents warming up beforehand, I half knew how they would come out to box me. There were times when a lad would see me while they were warming up and they'd be on the pads trying to impress me and be all like, 'Look mate, this is me.' It used to make me laugh sometimes. Nobby would chip in and say some witty remark like, 'You're not fighting him, are you? Who made that match?' He would always say it tongue in cheek because I was used to it, and I would just laugh.

* * *

Even though I was a journeyman, I could still bang a bit. If you look at a lot of journeymen, many of them hardly have any stoppages or have put people over. I did put quite a few people over and I stopped a few boxers as well. An example of this was when I boxed Dean Pithie, who was an ABA champion. He was the last man to beat Naseem Hamed as an amateur. When he turned pro, there were big expectations of him. He did alright in his career, fighting for the British title and becoming Commonwealth champion. When I boxed him, he was just up and coming. He was like a little bulldog that came flying out at the start of the fight. I hit him with an uppercut and a left hook and I stopped him in his tracks. I could see it in his face, him thinking, 'Fucking hell. This ain't supposed to happen.'

He then just boxed behind his jab. He was still coming forward but he was thinking more. He knew he couldn't just rush in.

Journeymen are hard-working pros who too often don't get the rub of the green. One instance of this was when I boxed at Norwich City's football ground, Carrow Road, against a local lad called Jackson Williams. He had boxed Amir Khan in Khan's sixth fight, so he had a good number of fans there. It was a really easy fight in which I didn't get out of second gear. On the same bill, my gym mate Arv Mitto was having his 100th fight. He won it easily but the fight was declared a draw. That still pisses me off as Arv was a really nice man. You wouldn't have thought he was a boxer. He was a really laid-back lad from the Black Country. I mean, it was his 100th fight and he really tried and won easily in lots of people's eyes. That's what boxing is like for a journeyman. The lad he boxed was going nowhere in boxing but they robbed a hard-working pro of a win – and in his last fight.

CHAPTER 9

Hard spars and my first title fight

After my loss to McKenzie, it was just over a month before I got into the ring again. My opponent was Jamie McBride and the fight took place in Scotland. Despite what had happened in the McKenzie fight, I wasn't nervous. If anything, the fight was a piece of piss. McBride seemed ten levels down from my last fight and I taught him a lesson.

He was easy to hit, he didn't move his head and came in straight lines. When I backed him up, he would go back to the ropes in straight lines as well. But he was a tough lad who took my punches well. I thought I won but in Scotland you were two rounds down before you even got in the ring. I had no chance of getting the decision.

* * *

I fought a lot in Scotland and it was also the place where I was given my nickname.

There's a geezer called Craig Stevenson who is an MC and was doing a lot of the ring announcements for the Sky Sports shows. One time when I was due to fight someone in

Scotland, he said to me, 'I'm going to introduce you as The Professor tonight.'

'Nah, don't do that,' I said. But he introduced me by that name. It never really stuck and I never went by that name myself. I never used to tell an MC to introduce me as The Professor in the ring as The Professor to me was Azumah Nelson. For me to have that nickname, I thought it was a bit of a piss-take.

* * *

Once, there was a show at St Andrews in Scotland and I decided I was going up on my own and would just ask someone to do my corner when I got there. So I phoned the train station and asked them what time the first train was due and if it was a direct train, meaning that it only stopped twice. They told me the first train was due at eight o'clock. I thought, 'Fuck it, I'll get that train and sleep throughout the ride.' I got to the train station in the morning and caught the train on time. While on the train, the inspector comes on to check everybody's tickets. When he got to me, I asked him if the train we were on was going direct to Glasgow.

'Nah pal. It stops at every station to Glasgow,' said the inspector.

'You're fucking joking!' I replied.

I was well fucked off but couldn't do anything about it. It was mind-blowing. The train journey was long, about four and a half hours. My phone had no signal while I was in the train and I only got a signal once I got off at Glasgow. As soon as I got off last train and was on the platform, the voicemail on my mobile came on. It was a message from Tommy Gilmour apologising as the show had been cancelled. I was fucking pissed. I called Nobby and he was like, 'OK, don't worry. Tommy will sort you out.' At that point, I phoned up Tommy Gilmour. Tommy always looked after me and was a good promoter.

'Fucking hell Tom,' I said to him. 'I just got your message.'

'Yeah, sorry about that,' he replied. I can't even remember why the show was cancelled. I think a few fighters had pulled out and there were only two fights left on the bill.

'Don't worry,' he said. 'I'll look after you. I'll sort you out.' So, he phoned up Nobby and explained to him what had happened and told me to jump back on the train. Luckily, I had my bank card on me, so I was able to go to the cashpoint and get some money out to buy another train ticket back to Birmingham. Obviously, I would have got paid after I fought.

On the way back home on the train, I was fucking pissed. Fair play to Tommy, he was true to his word as a few days later he sent me about £500 down. So, he looked after me in that way.

From that point on, Tommy would pay for my ticket to fly up there. It was sometimes cheaper to fly anyway. Half the time, I would go up on my own.

Bennie King was a real good bloke. He's dead now. He used to box up in Scotland. He was very nice to me and I always got on with him. If I used to box in Scotland and Bennie was there, I would ask him to do my corner. I always offered him some money after the fight but he would never have any money off me. But if I saw him at the bar, I'd buy him a whisky. Although I still fought in Scotland despite what happened with the late cancellation of that one fight, I never caught the train nor drove up there again.

I also went up to Scotland to box Donnie Hood. I used to watch him on TV when he was fighting for WBC International titles. I wasn't bothered about fighting him and was really excited for the fight. The fight was top of the bill as part of a dinner show in a hotel in Glasgow. It was set for eight-threes. I came out of my corner and I boxed really well. I beat him up. Boxed his head off. Come the eighth round, Donnie had two black eyes. There was no way whatsoever that he beat me. Yet as I say, Scotland back then was a hard place to win on points.

At the end of the fight, the referee lifts up the hand of the winner. As soon as the bell has rung to end the fight, I've walked to the referee and he's walked straight past me.

'Nah, not again, man! Even this, you can't rob me this much.'

This is what I was thinking as soon as he walked past me.

The ref put Donnie Hood's hand up. He looked fucking battered. I just thought, 'Fuck this, man!' It really pissed me off. Even the Scottish crowd was booing.

As soon as I came out of the ring, some in the crowd were saying, 'You won that, son, you got ripped off.' Scottish people don't really say that. If I had really lost, I would accept the loss. Normally when I went up to Scotland, I wouldn't try as much. But I really fancied this fight. I thought I could beat him as I didn't really rate him that much. He was very basic.

There was a video guy there who used to record all the fights. I asked him if I could order a video of the fight.

'Yeah,' he said. 'I'm going to have to send it to you.'

It was 15 or 20 quid at the time. I paid my money and gave him my address. I never got the video. I would love to have it so I could show people that I beat him.

Donnie actually fought for the European title and boxed Johnny Bredahl, who I had fought in Denmark. Maybe if I had got the verdict over Donnie Hood, I could have fought for that title. I'm not saying I would have beat Bredahl as he was a really good fighter. But the Donnie Hood fight, I was ripped off to fuck. I didn't take my loss personally against Hood himself as he wasn't the referee. He was just fighting his fight. But he should never have beat me there. Never.

Another time I went up to Scotland to box a kid who was a noted puncher. I can't remember his name but he went on to fight for the Masters title. He had an unbeaten record yet I dropped him in the first round. He just about beat me on points. I probably should have got the win but, again, you don't get a win in Scotland. It's fucking hard up there. I fought in Scotland loads of times. I beat Scottish champions but never got the decision. Worst place to box. Worse than Germany.

I would say that I lost quite a lot of my fights that I knew I had won because I was the away fighter. I also lost these fights because I had refs come to me and say that if Nobby hadn't been working my corner, then I would have won that fight. They did not like Nobby because he would give the refs shit if he felt his fighters were treated unfairly. They would probably say it didn't happen but the refs have said that to me. Nobby would speak to the refs but in the next breath he'd call them all sorts of names. He had a real mad sense of humour. You either knew his sense of humour or thought he was off the wall. You had to understand him to know him. If the referee would give a bad decision against any of our fighters, Nobby would go to the changing room to see the ref, get an eye test out of his bag and give him an eye test! This wasn't just a one-off and it wasn't just with me. He used to do it with all our fighters if he felt he got a raw deal.

As I've mentioned before, Nobby's a tongue-in-cheek character. It would have been lovely to interview him but he wouldn't do it. He's that type of person. A very private man. Someone who used to box with me phoned me, a South African guy called Billy McDougal. He was trying to open a gym and he said to me that he would like to speak to Nobby to get some advice but that he didn't have his number.

'You haven't got his number?' I said.

'Nah,' he replied.

When Nobby sold his house and moved, he didn't tell no one his new address. He still lives in the same area but I don't know where. Nobby would come and take me out for meals. I still don't know where he lives. I wouldn't ask him as he would have told me if he wanted me to know. He doesn't give anyone his phone number.

'Listen,' I said to Billy. 'I don't know his number. You know what he's like. He's a very private person.'

He wasn't one to mince words. He would call it as he saw it. That's how he was. He didn't give a fuck. He was a big bloke and looked quite intimidating.

* * *

From fighting a few times in Scotland, I was in Dublin fighting another opponent. While I was in the city, Oliver Harrison, who has trained boxers such as Amir Khan and Jamie Moore, happened to be there. He came over to me and offered me a fight for a few weeks away.

'The kid's fuck all,' he said. 'I'll give you a few extra quid and just have a walk around with him.'

'Yeah, alright,' I said.

A few weeks later, on the day before the fight, which was a Saturday, I went out all day. I went to the bookies and bumped into a few of my mates. Then I arrived at the pub and started drinking. I was getting wrecked and my brother was there with his mate. I didn't really know his mate but he was a cheeky bastard. He was going on about this and that and thought he knew something about boxing. He got cheeky, so I gave him a dig. My brother then started going mad at me. We started fighting then I fucked off and came back to the pub with a hammer, but they were gone. I went back home and carried on drinking.

The next day, Andy Mayers phoned me up about half ten in the morning.

'I'm picking you up.'

'What you on about?' I said. I'd forgotten that I was fighting. I went to the show still pissed. How I passed the medical that day I'll never know.

I can't remember who I was fighting but he was green as grass. During the fight, I hit the kid with a left hook and his legs went. Oliver was like, 'Peter, Peter! Come on, come on!' I just had a move around with him for the rest of the fight. I think he gave me an extra 500 quid on top. It didn't even feel like sparring to me. It was easy money.

* * *

Because our gym was in Aston, the last gym Nobby owned, we used to have quite a few kids who came off the street. Nobby never turned any of them away. They would come in and ask if they could do a bit of training.

Once, there were these two guys who came into the gym. One of them seemed sound but the other was very arrogant and talked about how he had done kickboxing and this and that.

'Oh yeah?' Nobby said.

The next thing, this guy said, 'Can I spar him?' and pointed me out. He must have thought that because I was small it would be easy. Nobby turned to me and asked me if I wanted to spar. I jumped at the chance.

'Yeah, I'll spar with him. Come on then.'

I saw this guy looking at his mates as if to say, 'I'm gonna fuck this guy up.' I got into the ring and absolutely knocked the bollocks out of him. Normally I wouldn't take the piss in sparring when in with a new kid. But he came out of his corner swinging and I fucked him up. I don't even think he lasted one round with me.

In our gym, no one really used to take the piss. You would have the odd fighter who would try and do that, if they were in a bad mood.

I classed 99 per cent of the fighters in my gym as friends. But there were the odd one or two who I didn't have the time of day for. I'd see them spar with someone who was lighter than them or not as experienced and I would see them take the piss. It would do my head in as I never used to like people being bullied in the gym. I'd say, 'Next time, I'll spar him. The fucking bully boy.'

'Yeah, go on then,' Nobby would reply.

I wouldn't say I battered them but I'd let them know that they couldn't take liberties with me.

When new kids used to come to our gym, Nobby would approach me, Tony Hanna and Brian Coleman and say, 'Have a move around with them lads.' Now in a move around, Nobby wants to see what the other kid has got. He knows what we are capable of, so he doesn't have to see what we got. But we would let the kids tee off with some shots, just to give them a bit of confidence and see how they would cope with the spar. But over the weeks when they kept sparring, we would turn up the pressure bit by bit each round. It's alright giving it out. You've got to be able to take it as well.

One day, I was sparring Brian Coleman, a real good mate of mine. I had an off day in sparring. Brian gave me a left hook to the body and a left hook to the head and it fucking hurt me. Really hurt me.

'Fuck this,' I said as I turned to Nobby and just got out of the ring.

'You alright, Pete?' said Brian.

'Nah,' I said. 'Brian, it ain't you. It's me.'

My head wasn't right for sparring that day. Brian was a good sparring partner. He wasn't taking the piss out of me. We never took the piss with each other. But after those left hooks to the body and head, he basically bent me in half. Brian was like, 'Pete, Pete.' He couldn't apologise enough.

'Brian, it's not you,' I said.

He felt bad as we were good mates. Even when we sparred, we used to let shots go. But he just caught me on an off day. Some days I hit him with some good shots but we never really went over the top in sparring.

After I sparred Brian, Nobby didn't say anything to me after I left the gym in a huff as he didn't really know how I felt. I supposed he had seen it happen loads of times in the gym with his fighters. Back home, I was moody for a few days. I said to Tania, 'That's it, I've had it with boxing.' She just listened as she knew I'd be back training again.

After about a week, Nobby phoned me up. He cracked a joke, something along the lines of asking if I had left the country or words to that effect.

'There's a fight happening in about a week. You want it?'

I asked who the fighter was, how many rounds and so on. The next day, I went to the gym and sparred with a few of the lads and felt sharp. I came home buzzing again. The passion for boxing was still there. I think I just needed a week off as sometimes you just have to have a little break and not think about boxing for a bit.

When you're doing it week after week, day in and day out, you can get bored of things. I would never turn a fight down. Sometimes I would have three fights booked up, which I liked at times, as I was thinking about the money. But there were times when I did think, 'Fuckin' hell, I wanted to go out this weekend but I'm fighting. And I'm fighting next weekend also, so I can't go out on the piss.' Yet when I arrived at the venue to fight, if I boxed well, I would look forward to the next week. If I boxed like shit, then sometimes I would dread the following week's fight. It's just how my mood was sometimes, especially when I was cutting weight. In the early days, I had to be a certain weight, otherwise they'd take dough off you. So, sometimes I'd be pissed off with the dieting, especially in the summer. Some days, I'd just be sucking ice lollies or tip tops all day long. It did make me fucking grumpy and a bit of a nightmare to live with. But once I weighed in and got some food in me, I felt OK. It's like if I had an argument with my missus in the morning and I'm fighting that night. Sometimes I wouldn't box as well as I could. But no matter what, she would always say, 'Good luck tonight' and I'd say, 'Yeah yeah.' I'd always ring her after I boxed to let her know I was OK. In the early days, I used to phone my mom as well as she always wanted to know how I got on. She wasn't bothered whether I won, lost or had a draw, as long as I was OK.

* * *

Me and Karl Taylor always used to have a good spar as we knew each other as kids from Ladywood. Karl had a reputation as a tough kid and for good reason. Karl was a hard spar. He would spar anyone. When I was getting ready for the Midlands title fight against Brian Robb, Karl was the ideal sparring partner. Pressure, pressure, pressure. Me and Karl used to have some great fights. But we were always good mates after. But he knew how to push me and vice versa. Nobby would say that people would pay to watch our spars. Sometimes when you're sparring, as soon as you get the upper hand all of a sudden they get the grip. You're still a fighter and you've still got your pride.

'You ain't pushing me back,' we would say to each other.

Me and Tony Hanna used to have some fierce spars as well, but we were mates straight after. The better the spars we had, the more it got the adrenaline going. We got a buzz off it.

* * *

My match against Paul Lloyd was a really hard fight. He hurt me to the body and my face was marked up. His punches were really sharp and the gloves were small as well. I wore Reyes gloves for the fight, which were like mitts for the bag. He gave me two black eyes and put me down. He was a great body puncher and every punch felt hard, even though on paper he wasn't a massive puncher. The fight was stopped after five rounds.

The fight had taken place on a Saturday. The following Tuesday, I had my driving test in Shirley and failed it. I got in the car and the examiner saw my licence and realised that I should have had the test in Yardley. So, I took this test and I thought I drove really well. I hadn't been nervous at all while driving. The examiner asked a couple of questions and then smirked as he said, 'Sorry, but you've failed.'

'You're fucking joking,' I said. I got out of the car, slammed the door and spat on the car and said, 'You fucking prick.' I had two big black eyes from the Paul Lloyd fight when I did my test and I think the guy saw me, knew from my licence that I'd come from Acocks Green and thought that I was a thug. He didn't know that I was a boxer, so he probably looked at me and thought I was scum. I was put straight back in for my driving test two weeks later, drove like crap and passed!

Soon after I fought Paul Lloyd, I was asked to spar him. At the time, he was training in Birmingham with the Lynch brothers, Paddy and Tommy. I'd been out on the piss the night before and thought I would just have a move around with him. I arrived at the gym in Digbeth and got the gloves on while having a chat with Paul. The bell rang for the start of the spar and Paul went straight on me. He threw body shots, uppercuts and hooks to the body. I'm thinking, 'Alright mate, slow down a bit.' Anyway, four rounds later I was really feeling it. I had beer coming out of me as well.

Boom!

He threw a left hook to my rib area. I turned away hurt from the shot and grabbed my side.

'You OK, Pete?' Paul asked.

'Nah Paul. I think you broke my fucking rib.' The pain was fucking killing me. It was a hard spar but that's how you learn.

Ada and one of my other mates said that they would take me to the hospital to check if my rib was broken. But in the car on the way there, Ada and my other mate were making me laugh, and it was killing my side.

We got to the hospital and were sitting in A&E and some bloke in there was being all loud. So, Ada got out a clipper, which gives you a little electric shock, put it on the bloke's neck and shocked him. He fell off his chair and everyone was laughing at him as he was being a prick to everyone who was there. He went to jump up and face Ada but when he realised that there were three of us, he just started shouting and fucked off out of the hospital. I was checked by a doctor, who said that I hadn't broken my rib, just badly bruised it. It did hurt for a few weeks, though.

I got paid about £80 for those four rounds. That's why I never did paid sparring again. I thought, 'Fuck that.' I was out for about three weeks with no training after the rib incident.

I used to get offers to go to London for sparring. It's like a job. You go down, you get put up in a hotel, you stay there for a week and you get paid every day for sparring. But I never fancied it. I decided against being used as a sparring partner.

Plenty of people I know have been sparring partners. You get paid but it's not a lot. And they're getting their money's worth out of you. You probably have four sparring partners and they would each do at least a couple of rounds of sparring a day. But in those couple of rounds, they're trying to take your head off. I've seen it. So, I never really fancied being a sparring partner for hire. I know Karl Taylor used to go up to Newcastle and spar Billy Hardy and John Davison. Karl's a tough kid. He would go up there and get on really well. He would hold his own with them. But going down to London was different. You would go to the gym, do your sparring and then you would get dropped off back at the hotel. Once there, you were just stuck in there on your own for the rest of the day. That wasn't for me.

It has been known to happen that if you do too well as a sparring partner, they wouldn't call you back. Don't try and get a sparring partner who is similar to the fighter you're fighting. Say you're a fighter who is going to fight for a world title. You want your fighter to feel great in sparring, getting the best of all their sparring partners. It's like when Mike Tyson lost to Buster Douglas. He was apparently dropped in sparring. So, you don't want to be going into a fight when something like that has happened.

It's like when I had area title fights, I would spar Karl Taylor and Gary Peynado. Gary Peynado was an ABA champion, a good pro fighter who used to box for Nechells. When I first started sparring him, he was all over me. Body shots, head shots, he was like a busy bee. But over the coming weeks, when I got used to his style, I started to get the better of him. So, when I went into a Midlands title fight, I knew that Gary Peynado was better than Brian Robb for workrate, so that side of my game was sound. Because I did so many rounds with Gary and Karl, it stood me in good stead. A boxer wants to be going into a fight feeling confident, due to getting the better of your sparring partners. As a boxer, you don't want your sparring partners knocking the bollocks out of you as then you'll be thinking, 'Ah, I've been sparring like shit this time.' I've never done it but I know people who have been hired for sparring and because they have been doing very well, the boxer who hired them decides to fuck them off.

At my gym, I used to spar middleweights. We had good fighters and I would learn some things from them. For instance, Paul Wesley was a really good fighter. Really underrated and fought fighters such as Steve Collins and Crisanto Espana, both future world champions. I learned so much from him. When I sparred him, he would teach me little things as he was ring smart. He had quite a lot of losses but just look at the losses of those he fought. He knocked out both Neville Brown, who became British champion, and Ian Strudwick, who challenged for the British title, in one round. We'd learn from each other at the gym. They would say that Nobby's fighters were tough but we weren't. We were smart and Nobby taught us how to be smart. As soon as you were in Nobby's gym, he taught you how to slip shots and always move your head. That's why my nose is OK.

* * *

After my fight with McBride, I was scheduled to fight Brian Robb. He was a good amateur from Telford and a real tough kid. He wasn't a bad fighter, though he fought with his face. Our first fight was scheduled for eight-twos. I stopped him on a cut eye in the seventh round. Brian used to cut quite badly. He was screaming that the result was a robbery but I was winning the fight anyway.

For the rematch, we were both put up for the vacant Midlands Area super featherweight title. It was my first title fight and it was due to take place at Wolverhampton Civic Hall. This was the first time that I had sold tickets for a fight. I had two coachloads of people come over from Acocks Green and they brought down a load of their fans. It was scheduled for ten three-minute rounds and it was a real good fight. A ten-round war. And I beat him quite comfortably on points.

Not long after that, his promoter offered me good money to defend my title in Telford, at their town hall. I accepted his offer and took a lot of fans down there.

As I was fighting, the fans were shouting, 'Fucking Irish scumbag.' They were just giving me loads of abuse.

In the first round, I was jabbing his head off. In the second round I threw a right hand, just missed him and my shoulder went. At the time, I didn't know that I had torn a muscle in my shoulder, so I went back to the corner and told my team that I'd hurt it. They massaged it and sent me out for the next round, at which point he started beating me. He was outhustling me as he had a good workrate and I didn't throw my right hand for the next few rounds. At the end of the ninth round, my corner told me that I needed to stop him or I was going to lose. I came out of my corner for the final round and hit him with a right hand that knocked him spark out. He was gone. By landing that knockout punch, I tore my shoulder even more. The next time I saw Brian after that, he told me that when I knocked him out that night he had to go to the hospital due to a concussion. When he came back to the venue to get his car, it had been robbed. Then when he went to work, he had been made redundant. He said it was the worse fucking week of his life. I never defended my Midlands Area title again. I still have the belt now. At the time, there was talk of me fighting Hugh Forde for the British title but it never came about.

When I boxed Brian at the Civic Hall for the vacant title, the money was crap for the ten rounds we boxed. But when I boxed him in the rematch, that took place in Telford, which was his hometown. There was this promoter who was new on the scene named Ken Purchase. Nobby had him over a barrel when it came to how much we were getting paid. He said to me that Brian wanted to fight me again, so how much did I want to get paid for the rematch? I said some silly amount.

'He ain't going to give you that,' said Nobby.

'Try 'em,' I said.

When Ken first started out in the game, he would be phoning Nobby up for fights and Nobby would be asking for silly money. Ken would never question it. Back in the day, if you were in a fight that was set for six-twos, you would probably get £500 to £600.

'He's only gone and paid you over the odds for six-twos,' Nobby said.

'You're joking!' I replied.

'Yeah, against a crap kid as well!' Nobby said to me. 'He ain't gonna last long in this game. So, we better get everything out of it while we can.'

He was new to the game, so Nobby got the best deals out of him. Ken would phone up at the last minute and say that someone has pulled out. Nobby would be like, 'I think that's gonna cost you x amount, Ken.' And Ken would say, 'Yeah yeah.' He never questioned it. He just thought that what Nobby said was gospel. So, I got a nice little earner for an area title fight on someone else's turf. The amount I was paid to fight Brian for a Midland Area title, you don't really get that much for an area title fight.

I like Brian. We got on really well. When I saw him, he told me what he was being paid for our fight. He didn't even get half of what I got. To make him feel good, I must have made out that I got the same money because I wouldn't have rubbed it in his face as I knocked the kid out. They had to pay for me to go to his hometown and defend my title against him. The crowd were calling me an Irish bastard as I had green and white shorts on. I took a coachload of people there and his fans sold the place out. But he didn't earn two bob. He must have thought I got the usual amount for the fight at that level, but I did very well in that fight. It was good money as I was able to go on holiday the next week.

I should have stopped fighting after the shoulder injury. Greed was probably the reason I carried on fighting. I basically learned to fight with one arm. I was a bit scared of letting my right hand go because the pain put me in agony.

When I went to see the doctor due to the injury, he said to me that I needed to have a good six months out of the ring. Instead of resting it for six months like a normal person would do, I left it for about six weeks. I couldn't afford to have six months off as I wasn't working, just boxing. I had a physio look at the shoulder and even had heat treatment. But none of it worked. Someone recommended an acupuncturist. So I went there, saw the woman and told her what the problem was. She put a needle in my arm, twiddled it about and I could feel the muscle in my arm moving.

'Yeah, I can sort that,' she said.

So I was having acupuncture on my shoulder twice a week. While I was having treatment, I was still boxing, so I never let it fully heal. It would heal for a bit then I would fight for a few weeks. I wouldn't really spar, I would just go running. Then I would have a bit of treatment on it two days before a fight.

'You really need to rest your arm,' she insisted. 'You shouldn't be fighting. You've got ligament damage.'

I could feel it wasn't right sometimes. I would be warming up in the changing rooms on the pads, throw a right hand and overstretch it a bit and the muscle would pop. It was like a little gap between my shoulder and up my armpit and the muscle would pop between there a little bit. I would literally just push it back in. I could feel the muscle come out the joint. It really killed me, so I learned to box with one hand, as I mentioned before. Paul Westley used to do a lot of cross-arm defence and I picked it up from him. I muddled along like this for a for a couple of years. It's why my record isn't what it should have been. If I would have taken six months off and had the operation on it, I probably wouldn't have had 300 fights but I would have had better results. I had trouble with it for years.

* * *

After my title fight, I fought a kid called Mark Bates from Essex, who was with Matchroom, so was a Barry Hearn fighter. They were expecting big things from him. They were saying that he was going to fight for the British title. His record was eight wins and two losses but he had beaten a few good lads such as Steve Robinson, who went on to win the WBO world featherweight title. He also knocked out Elvis Parsley, who would later challenge for the British featherweight title. His team thought he was going to be the bollocks but I really fancied the fight. I had seen him fight and thought I could beat him.

We fought at Basildon in Essex. When I got in the ring, I looked over to his corner and he seemed nervous. He wouldn't really look me in the eye when we were called to the middle of the ring. As the ref gave his little talk, he still wouldn't make eye contact with me. After the first round, I felt stronger than him and was pushing him back. I was moving my head as I came in and so making myself a harder target to hit clean. As the fight was going into the next few rounds, I was catching him with the cleaner shots. I could tell just from his face that he didn't like it. I won't say he didn't have heart as if he didn't have heart, he wouldn't have been a boxer. But he didn't like it and I had him on the back foot. I kept backing him up and every time I hit him, there was a little whine here and there. He kept looking at the ref, looking at his corner.

That fight is on YouTube with Jim McDonnell and someone else commentating. All they're going on about is, 'Mark Bates might be doing this, might be doing that.' All of a sudden, I push Bates back and they then say, 'Oh, Buckley's a good fighter,' and they start giving me a bit of praise.

Going into the fifth round, I still felt a lot stronger than him. I hit him with a left hook to the body and I heard him grunt. I knew at that moment that I'd hurt him and I started to back him up. I hit him with a screw shot right hand on the chin and it dropped him. He got up but was hurt, so I jumped straight on him and hit him with a few uppercuts as he tried to hold me. I stepped back and hit him with a cracking overhand right and down he went again. Just before the bell rang to end the round, I looked in his eyes and could tell that he didn't want it any more. As he went back to his corner, I looked over and he was shaking his head to his trainer. His corner pulled him out. You could see he was devastated as he thought he was going to be a British champion. I think he carried on boxing but he was never at that level again.

I received some good exposure from the fight as it was on Eurosport the next day. I went to the pub and a few people had seen the fight, congratulated me and remarked on what a good fight it was.

I next fought a southpaw called Johnny Armour. We were scheduled to meet at the Royal Albert Hall. The fight should have been stopped as he was cut to bits. He beat me but if the fight happened now, it would have got stopped. Mickey Duff was his manager, so they were not going to stop it. He went on to win the WBU title and also became European and Commonwealth champion. He wasn't a big puncher but his workrate was brilliant.

* * *

There were certain fighters I fought who I rated highly. One such fighter was Craig Dermody. He was a brilliant fighter.

He trained out of a gym called Collyhurst in Manchester. Brian Hughes used to train him. Hughes was a very good trainer and was also Craig's manager. He trained boxers such as Pat Barrett, Robin Reid and Michael Gomez, amongst others. I remember going down to Collyhurst and sparring with Michael Gomez when he was younger and I heard about Dermody. People were talking about him quite a bit. I think he was an ABA champion.

I boxed him at a week's notice down in Manchester. It was a really good fight. Craig wasn't a big puncher but he had every move in the book. He was brilliant. The first time we fought, he beat me by about half a point. The second time I boxed him, I noticed improvements in his style. The kid should have gone far. What happened with him is that he boxed a kid from my gym called Karl Taylor. He beat Karl to be fair but the person who was refereeing the fight was green as grass. At the end of every round, Nobby being Nobby, he would say to Karl so the referee could hear, 'You won that round, Karl! You won that round!' The referee didn't know what was going on, so all he was hearing at the end of each round was, 'You won that round!' The referee started to side with Karl, as he was inexperienced. At the end of the fight, Karl was given the decision. Karl swears he won it but he didn't win it. Craig Dermody never boxed again. He just went off the scene. He would have gone far. If you watch one of his fights on YouTube in black and white, it's like watching a fighter from years ago like Harry Greb. He was amazing. He had every punch in the book. Uppercuts, bolo punches, everything. And I remember Brian Hughes saying that he was going to go all the way. After I boxed him, Brian asked me what I thought.

'That kid is the bollocks. He's really good,' I responded.

But he got one bad decision and just drifted away. He was such a wasted talent. He was a really good kid and it was a shame. But some kids can't handle it when too much pressure is put on them. Everyone thinks if you haven't got a 0 at the end of your record that you're not good enough. That doesn't mean fuck all. Nearly all the great fighters have lost. You don't have to have an unbeaten record to be good. It isn't about how you start the game, it's about how you finish it. In my opinion, if he had stuck around, he would have definitely gone on to world honours.

There were a few fighters who were quite highly rated but who I didn't see as anything special. Fighters like Dean Pithie, who I mentioned before, did alright as a pro and won the British title, but people were raving about him when we fought.

Paul Griffin was another boxer in that category. He was Irish and had won a European gold medal. I boxed Paul in Cork on the undercard of Steve Collins versus Neville Brown. Nice kid and a lovely boxer. But I thought, 'I don't know why they are raving about him. He's going nowhere.' And he ended up going nowhere. He didn't win any major titles. But he was classed as the best thing since sliced bread. After our fight, we had a pint together. Real nice down-to-earth kid. But I didn't see what all the excitement was about. Before the fight when I was in Cork, people were saying to me, 'You're boxing Paul Griffin. Oh, he's a brilliant boxer.' Good boxer but he couldn't crack an egg.

Another prospect I fought was Alan McKay. I boxed him at the Royal Albert Hall. He had just beaten Colin McMillan on a cut eye. He was due to fight for the British and Commonwealth titles, so they had me as a warm-up fight. I fucked that up as our fight was a draw. I actually thought I beat him. Yet for me to get a draw away from home says it all. There was talk of me getting the British title shot instead but it never happened. I boxed three times at that same venue and got a win, a draw and a loss.

There were a lot of fighters who I watched and thought, 'I could beat them.' There was talk of me having a British title fight at one time against Hugh Forde. He was a really good fighter and I fancied the fight. He probably would have beat me but I really fancied it.

* * *

For my next fight, I boxed in Germany against a kid called Ruben Condori, who had 108 fights. At the time, I had not yet had even 40 fights but I was top of the bill there. It says on BoxRec it was an eight-rounder but it was really a ten-rounder. He had fought for the WBC flyweight title. I don't know what he was doing based in Germany but he was only a little geezer. I thought the fight would be a piece of piss. But Nobby warned me, 'Look, he's going to come out and hit you in the bollocks and try and rough you up any way he can.' And he did exactly what Nobby said he would do. He hit me in the bollocks, hit me in the back of the head and just roughed me up. It went the distance and I lost. But I had a great time in Germany. Paul Westley was out there and the fight was promoted by a bloke called Olaf, who was a really good guy.

Paul Westley was in Germany because he was supposed to be boxing a lad called Horace Fleary, who was from Bradford but was based in Germany. When we got there, the British boxing board got in touch with Nobby and said Horace had boxed in Britain five days before and if Paul boxed him then he would be in trouble as you had to have seven clear days before boxing again. Because Horace was on a German licence he would be allowed to fight but despite this the boxing board still said no to the fight. Nobby managed to get Paul some money off the German promoter. So in the end, Paul was not fussed that he wasn't fighting.

After I fought Condori, I went to the bar in the venue and had a few drinks. I had a good reception at the bar and some of the people there were asking for photos. This wasn't the first time that people had asked for photos or my autograph.

* * *

I've had people ask for my autograph loads of times. I had people emailing and writing to me from the UK and other countries, asking if I would send them an autograph or a signed picture. Now and again if I was in the right mood, I would send them an autograph back. But I didn't do this all the time. The letters would always go to my mom's house. They must have found out where I lived, maybe through my boxing licence. My mom used to say, 'Oh, you have a letter here.' It would be someone from America, Germany or Spain.

Once I was on holiday in Spain when a lad from Liverpool came up to me on a day out and said he had seen me box a few times. A few months later, I was boxing at Everton Park Sports Centre when the same lad came up to me and asked if I remembered him from the holiday. I said, 'Of course I do.' He laughed and told his mate they would be cheering me on that night. He was a top lad. But for years, there was this one fan from Germany asking me if I could send signed photos. To tell the truth, I just blanked him. When I got to the venue for my fight with Condori, this same bloke introduced himself and said that he had been writing to me loads and so on. He seemed really chuffed to meet me. Really knew his boxing. He said he had loads of photos of me fighting, which was a bit weird. He asked why I had not replied as the letters used to go to my mom's place. I blagged it and said that I didn't live there, even though I did visit my mom's house often. He then asked if he could take some photos. I said yeah. Man, he must have taken about 100 photos of me. I don't know if he was a bit of a stalker or a big boxing fan, but he just took loads and loads of photos of me. After the fight, he wanted more photos. I had to say to him, 'OK mate, I think you've had enough.' He wouldn't leave me alone and in the end I had to be a bit stern and say, 'Listen mate, you've had your money's worth. Fucking do one.' He followed me around all night. It was a bit weird.

I never heard from him again after that fight. He probably could have decorated his house with the number of photos he had of me.

After we left the venue of the Condori fight, we all went into town and went out on the piss. We went to one club, then another one, before waiting in the queue outside to go into yet another club. When I say we, I mean me, Paul Westley and another German fighter. There were a few Turkish guys in the queue, along with a load of American soldiers. We were waiting patiently when suddenly it's kicked off between the Turks and the Americans. Knives were coming out and I was like, 'Whoa! Fuck this, I'm out of here.' They were just tearing up each other, fighting on the road. I said, 'I ain't going in there,' and we went somewhere else.

When we got back to the hotel, we saw Olaf smoking hash.

'Hey Olaf. Give us some draw,' Paul said.

'Come to my room,' Olaf replied.

We went to his room and he pulled out a half ounce of solids.

'Take a draw,' Olaf said to Paul. So, Paul bit Olaf's solid in half and took the piss basically.

'Nice one,' Paul said and fucked off.

He went out and had a few beers as well as smoking the draw he just had. We were in Germany for two nights. The following night, we went out and we came back to the hotel about five o'clock in the morning. In the hotel, there was a bar that was closed. We booted the door off this bar, went in and started helping ourselves to drinks. We then went back to the room and got fucking pissed. About seven o'clock in the morning, Nobby's come to our room and banged on our door as it was time to leave. Both me and Paul were still pissed at this point and had very little sleep, if any at all. We jumped into either a bus or taxi, I can't remember which, but we got to the airport and were not sober. Me and Paul arrived at the airport, got checked in and we went into this room. I didn't know what this room was but we ended up falling asleep in there. We just crashed. We could have been there for ten minutes or half an hour, I don't know. The next thing I remember, we were getting woken up by the airport security with guns pointed at our faces. My head was banging. The security asked us what we were doing and marched us out. I can't remember whether we were going to get arrested. Nobby came over and defused the situation straight away. He was a good talker. He told them that we were boxers and that we had boxed on this big bill. The cops weren't happy, though they did let us go. As soon as they left, Nobby gave us a bollocking. He said that he'd been looking around for us and that we shouldn't have been in that room. We felt like shit. We got on the plane on time and crashed, though we did laugh about it after.

* * *

I fought Donnie Hood and faced Duke McKenzie in the rematch after my adventure in Germany. I then was offered a fight against a boxer who, at this point, was my most high-profile opponent.

CHAPTER 10

The Prince

I knew Prince Naseem, or just Naz as I called him, before he turned pro as he used to go to a lot of the shows with Brendan Ingle. What you saw is what you got. He had an entourage and was a brilliant bloke. When he turned pro, he was knocking everyone out.

Nobby asked me if I wanted to fight him. I didn't need to think twice and said yes to the fight.

Now, a good friend of mine from school is an ex-boxer called Norman Dhalie, or Storming Norman as he was known in the boxing world. He was mad as fuck but was a good mate for years. We both used to box for Nobby and would often go out drinking together.

A few weeks before I was due to fight Prince Naseem, Norman was fighting a Wincobank fighter and knocked him out at a show in Newcastle. Afterwards, he was talking to Naz as his family, like Naseem's, are from Yemen. Naz was trying to find out anything about me that could prove useful in our fight.

'What's Buckley like?' he would ask Norman.

'Ah fuck off,' Norman replied. 'I'm not telling you nothing about Buckley. He's my mate. He won't be scared of you. You're not knocking Peter out. He's tough as fuck.'

'We'll see,' said Naseem. Later, Norman told me about meeting Naseem.

'Naseem was trying to get info on you. I told him to fuck off.'

Naseem was rated but I didn't think he was going to be a unified world champion and best fighter in the world in the featherweight division. He was good but I didn't think he was going to go to the heights that he did. I really didn't. They were all raving about him. They said that he was a good amateur but he had only fought as a junior. He didn't fight as a senior, I don't think. He was only a kid.

I boxed Naz the first time at Everton Park Sports Centre in Liverpool. During the fight, he was trying to bomb me out. I knew it wasn't going to happen as I wouldn't let him knock me out. He was hard to hit and had the best defence of anyone I fought. You couldn't get near the fucker. When he hit me on the chin, I never saw stars or anything like that.

Overall, I thought the fight was easy and I think I nicked a couple of rounds, though I lost on points. Norman was at the fight with Naz and after the fight Norman was like, 'Told you Naz, told you.' Norman was like that. He didn't give a fuck. I think Naz liked Norman because Norman was nuts, very loud and both of their parents were from Yemen.

* * *

In between the two fights with Naz, I was in Belfast with a kid called Gary Flear. He was a good fighter, who was around years ago with the late Wally Swift. He knocked the sport on the head for a few years. When he decided to come back, he went to Nobby's gym. He was a real tough kid and a lot better than his record suggested. He beat some good kids in his first year of boxing. He was a southpaw and tough as fuck. The only thing about Gary was that he used to cut easily. But I remember taking him down to Manchester, where he boxed Jamie McKeever, who later fought for the British title. He gave Jamie a boxing lesson.

We were in Belfast as he was due to be fighting an unbeaten kid. After the weigh-in, we decided to go get something to eat. There was a big Orange parade going on and I didn't think anything of it.

Later on, we were back at the hotel and someone said to me, 'You know you're staying at the Europa, don't you?'

'Yeah,' I said.

'It's the most bombed hotel in Belfast.'

'You're fucking joking,' I said, shocked.

'Yeah,' the guy said.

Don't know how true that is but that is what we were told.

Where we were eating in the daytime was about a mile away from our hotel. Me and Gary were at the hotel and we could hear a boom sound in the distance. We didn't think anything of it. We then heard that where we had been eating earlier in the day, there was a café and restaurant a couple of doors down that had been blown up after we had left that street. I did shit myself a bit thinking if we had been eating there a bit later, we could have been caught up in it.

Gary's fight was on the undercard of the Eamonn Magee vs Shea Neary fight for the Commonwealth title. I'm not blowing my own trumpet but I could read a fighter really well. I knew what to say and Gary was a good listener. I told Gary exactly what he needed to do to win the fight. He stuck the kid on his head. Beat him easy.

Gary went up to his room drunk. I went up later to what I thought was his room but I couldn't unlock it. I was steaming drunk and started banging on the door in the early hours. Then, this big geezer answered and looked annoyed.

'What you doing knocking on my door?' I said that I was looking for Gary.

'You're on the wrong fucking floor,' he said. His missus came over and started moaning.

'Fuck off,' I said, as I was drunk.

Before I knew it, others in the hotel heard the commotion and came up and out of their room to see what the matter was.

I didn't know who they were but I was a bit weary then. The hotel manager came and said that if I was causing problems I'd be thrown out, so I stumbled away and eventually found my room.

It was the next morning when I came down for breakfast that the hotel manager had a word with me.

'You didn't give him any mouth, did you?' they asked.

'No,' I said. 'I don't think so. I just woke him up.'

'Good,' said the manager. 'He is a very respected man around here.' Meaning he was either from the IRA or an Orangeman.

On another occasion, after a fight, me and Tony Hanna were back at the hotel, drinking until late. Two of these geezers were there having a drink and asked us if we wanted to come with them to a party. I told them that we couldn't go as we had a flight to catch in the morning.

Tony didn't really know the score about Belfast. He asked me why we couldn't go to the party.

'Cos we're fucking English,' I said. 'They'll take us off somewhere, man. We're fucking English to them at the end of the day. Don't trust them. We ain't going nowhere.' We decided to stay in the hotel and we ended up getting wrecked.

Those were a couple of several memorable experiences I had when visiting Belfast. The first time I went there was with Nobby. Nobby is a big bloke who looks like he's in the army. Then there was me with short, cropped hair. We were picked up by a taxi soon after our plane landed.

'If we get stopped, don't speak,' were the first words the taxi driver said to us. During the taxi ride, we just saw soldiers and road blocks. I shit myself.

Another time I went there, this geezer said to me, 'You Catholic or Protestant?' 'Catholic,' I said. Next thing I know, he's driving down the Shankhill Road, pointing and saying what happened on each part of the road.

The following day, another taxi driver dropped me off at the airport. Now, there are two airports in Belfast and he dropped me at the wrong one. The driver took me to Belfast City instead of Belfast International. Luckily, he gave me his number. As soon and I went to check in and found out I was at the wrong airport, I phoned him even though my mobile phone battery had very little power.

'Mate, you gotta come back and pick me up,' I said. 'I'm at the wrong fucking airport!' Thankfully, he came and took me to the right airport. Over the years going there, Belfast has lightened up a bit, especially compared to what it was.

* * *

Before I fought Naz the second time, the gym in the back of the old Central Library was used by Carl 'The Truth' Williams for his fight with Frank Bruno at the NEC. He was in our gym for about a week preparing for his fight.

Now, our gym was basically a shithole. It had no hot water. It was like a ghetto in many ways, though Carl loved it. He would say, 'Now this is what you call a proper gym!' He entered the gym with this old bloke, who looked in his 70s and was his trainer. While Carl trained at Nobby's gym, I used to chat with him. He was a really interesting man and told me all about the ghetto he was brought up in. Growing up, he had lived in proper rundown streets. He would tell stories about the gyms back home and how they were worse than the one in the back of the library. He also said something to me which I've always remembered.

'Kid, you're just a piece of meat and when you're done, you're done.'

'What do you mean?' I said.

'Once you've passed your sell-by date, you're forgotten about.'

On the night of his fight with Bruno, he asked if Nobby and I could do his corner along with his trainer. Well, I passed the spit bucket up in his corner. Nobby more or less did his corner and was giving instructions as Carl didn't seem to have any respect for his trainer. It was mad to me really that I was in the opposite corner to Bruno. It was surreal.

Carl was a good fighter but he was taking shots off Bruno all night long. I don't know if it was the ninth or tenth round, but he got stopped. I always thought, 'Nah man, he could have carried on, he could have.' He done so many rounds with him and I feel he could have done a couple more, but he didn't. After that, Bruno got his world title fight with Lennox Lewis. But Carl was a real down-to-earth geezer.

Carl said to Nobby when he found out he was gay, 'You're a cool dude but you're flying the wrong way, man.' Even Nobby laughed.

* * *

When they asked me to fight Naseem the second time in Cardiff, they all thought that I would turn it down. But instead, I decided to fight him again.

I could tell when he came out of his corner for the first round that he wanted to do a number on me. I knew that would be the case as I don't think he liked the fact that I stood up to his punches in the first fight. He wanted to prove that he could knock me out.

He was beating me but I was taking his shots well. He was talking to me throughout the fight and I was responding to him in kind.

When the end came, I thought the ref was warning me for an elbow but then I realised that he was stopping the fight. I was angry and began storming around the ring muttering, 'Fucking joke,' to myself.

'That fight shouldn't have been stopped,' I said to Naz

'Yeah,' he replied, 'but I was beating you anyway.'

'I know,' I said. 'But you wouldn't have stopped me.'

The stoppage pissed me off as because the official result was a knockout, I wasn't allowed to fight for 28 days.

I was the only fighter to face him twice and a few months after our rematch, he fought for the European title. People knocked him but he was a brilliant fighter.

* * *

Although I was fighting on a regular basis, I was still getting up to mischief between fights. Not long after my rematch with Naseem, I was in a pub and David came in with his mate. I never really used to drink with my brother as when we were younger, we used to fight a lot. This particular mate of his was being cheeky. I ended up chinning him and then me and my brother ended up fighting. But that's happened more than once.

Another time, when I was 25, my brother was in a pub. I came into this pub and I noticed David, who was in there with a mate from work. His mate knew that I was a boxer but he was cheeky.

'You better tell your mate to shut his mouth, unless he wants a dig,' I said to David.

My brother was telling me to calm down. But I kept on telling him that I didn't like his mate. Straight away, I knew I was going to have a fight with this kid. Then he said something else, at which point I just got up from my seat and chinned him. His mate fell off his chair and me and my brother ended up having a scrap.

'I'll fuckin' do him, I tell ya!' I screamed.

About three months later, I was driving somewhere in Acocks Green. My brother was on this job and I saw him drive off. 'I wonder if that kid's in there,' I thought. So, I went around the back of this house and sure enough, the guy was there by himself.

'Oi! Remember me, do ya?!' I said to him.

'Look,' he replied, 'I don't want any trouble.'

'Listen alright,' I said as I grabbed him. 'You want to fuck with me? I'll fucking knock you out.'

'Oh, I've already forgotten it,' was his reply.

'Yeah, alright then,' I said and fucked off out of there.

Later that day, my brother phoned me.

'What are you doing going to my fucking job? Just stay out of the way!'

Another eventful time between fights happened when I was in the Hummingbird in Birmingham for a rave. I was with a couple of mates of mine and while there, we decided to take some acid.

As we came out of the venue, we kept walking and ended up by the Rag Market. The Rag Market is a building in the city centre which has different stalls selling all sorts of stuff. It's also where Nobby happened to work as a driver for the market. At about half four, five in the morning, Nobby saw us and beeped us over.

'Fucking hell,' I said to my mates as I turned and noticed Nobby. We walked towards him, though I was off my fucking head.

'What you doin'?' Nobby asked.

'I'm walking home,' I replied.

'Well, jump in and I'll give you both a lift.'

During the ride, one of my mates was sitting in the back and just laughing his head off.

'What the fuck's wrong with him?' Nobby said. I was trying to keep a straight face but I couldn't as I was tripping.

Nobby had just arrived at the top of Sparkhill and at this point my mate in the back is still just crying with laughter.

'Just drop us here,' I said to Nobby. 'My mate only lives there.' But my mate actually lived in Hall Green.

So, after Nobby dropped us off, me and my two mates walked from Sparkhill to Hall Green. As we were walking, the police spotted us, stopped us and asked for our names. One mate gave them this mad, made-up name. I also gave them a mad name but my other mate gave them his real name. Even though he gave them his real name, the police thought he was lying and asked him what his proper name was! Me and my mate were in bits as our other mate was trying to convince the police that he had given them his actual name. In the end, the police just fucked us off. We continued to walk to Hall Green off our tree!

* * *

Next, I fought back at Civic Hall in Wolverhampton against Matt Harris. The night before, I was out on the piss and got into a scuffle inside a KFC. They said that I'd pushed in the queue, which led to me punching out a guy, and I fucked my hand up. My hand was fucking swollen.

Now for this fight, Nobby wasn't with me. He didn't even know I got into a fight the night before. He was at another show somewhere. By this stage of my career, there were times when I used to go to fights on my own.

Nobby had a lot of fighters. There were times when he'd say that there was a fight going but that I would have to go on my own. But by then, I'd had 100-odd fights. So it wasn't like I was new to the game.

I knew all the trainers. I'd go to a boxing show and everyone, from the officials to the timekeepers to the refs, knew who I was. Because of that, I was never fazed when I went to a boxing show. It didn't matter where I was as a ring is always just a ring. I would fight anywhere.

How it would work is that I would always know a trainer at a show and I would just say to them, 'Be in my corner and I'll give you 50 quid.' And they would be like, 'Yeah, no problem Pete.'

All they had to do was put Vaseline over my eyes and wash my gumshield. They would give me a bit of advice but really, that's all they had to do. You couldn't just have anyone in your corner, it would always be a BBB of C [British Boxing Board of Control] trainer or manager. Sometimes, Nobby would say that he couldn't come with me but he would arrange for someone else to accompany me. If this had started happening when I'd only had ten or so fights, then that would have been a bit naughty. But as I say, I'd had 100-odd fights by then, so it wasn't a big deal.

With the first fight against Harris, I was in the changing room talking to this Canadian trainer. Richie Woodhall was top of the bill fighting Jacques LeBlanc for the Commonwealth title.

'Fucking hell, man,' I said to this Canadian geezer. 'I've fucked my hand up, mate.'

'Do you want me to tape you up?' he asked.

'Yeah,' I replied.

Anyway, he taped me up before I saw a doctor. Nowadays, you can't get away with that. You have to have your hands clear before the doctor can see you. I knew all the doctors as well, you see. Anyway, the doctor came into the changing room and said, 'Alright Pete, how you doing?'

'Alright doc. Sound,' I replied.

'Let's check that your hands are OK,' he said. 'Can you squeeze them and make a fist?' It was fucking killing me to do it, but I managed it. I passed the doctor's exam and boxed Harris basically with one hand. Though he was not a puncher, he was a good boxer. Because of my hand, I just had a move about with him and I lost the fight on points.

CHAPTER 11

Trouble after the bell

I had a few more fights before I was put forward to fight Matt Harris for another Midlands Area title. I was fighting at featherweight and this fight was at super bantamweight, which is 8st 10lbs. When the officials asked me if I could do super bantamweight, I was like, 'Yeah, no problem.' We agreed to the fight and we fought at the Aston Villa Leisure Centre on the undercard of the Rob McCracken vs Paul Wesley British title fight.

When Harris fought me the first time round, he thought that's how I was going to be for this rematch. Yet boxing him for the Midlands super bantamweight title, it was a completely different story.

If I had a week's notice for a fight, that was quite good for me as I was always in the gym and running anyway. I wouldn't go on the piss, I'd pack in the fags and would just watch what I would eat that week. As soon as I had a couple of weeks' notice, it was game over. I always fancied winning a fight when I had a few weeks' notice. As I had plenty of notice, I never went there to lose. I always went there to win.

The second time I boxed him for the Midlands Area super bantamweight title, I had six weeks' notice. I had a training camp like a professional. Coming into the fight, I was in really good shape. It showed as I stopped him in six rounds. I absolutely destroyed him. I smashed him to bits.

Sometime after that, I can't remember exactly how long after, there was a show on which I defended my title against him. It would be the third time we would meet. But I wasn't able to get down to 8st 10lbs. This is how bent boxing could be. The officials said to me, 'Listen, what can you get down to?'

'Nine stone,' I said. They said 'alright then'. I got down to nine stone.

1. I had taken the fight on a few days' notice. Normally, you have a brain scan for a ten-rounder but as I had a brain scan not long before, it covered me for this fight. So, I boxed him and thought I beat him.

2. At the weigh-in, I basically jumped on the scales. My trainer put his hand on my arse and lifted me up as he's leaning over. According to the scales, I was 8st 10lbs. But I wasn't 8st 10lbs. They knew I couldn't make the weight but they turned a blind eye. The fight was scheduled for ten rounds. I boxed him over the distance and I thought I beat him, but they gave him the decision by half a point.

I boxed him a final time after that on short notice. My trainer said to just have a move about with him. I hit him with a left hook and his legs were going all over the place. I still lost to him on points.

* * *

Although I was still boxing, I now had a trainer's licence. Because of this, I was able to take Karl Taylor over to Dublin to fight PJ Gallagher. Gallagher had been an amateur and I think he was with Frank Warren. I loved going to Dublin as that's where my family is from. As far as how the fight went, in short, he lost on points. He was basically ripped off as regards the result.

Afterwards, we went on the piss back at the hotel with the late Dean Powell. We were up all night. I'll always remember it because my niece did Irish dancing and the World Irish Dancing Championships were taking place right at the hotel we were staying at. Karl went to bed at about four or five o'clock in the morning and I stayed up drinking all night with some Irish lads. I didn't get to bed until about seven, eight o'clock in the morning. I was steaming, so I got back to my room and crashed out knowing that we had to get the plane about one in the afternoon. When I got up, I was fucking struggling but still managed to get ready to leave the hotel. When we got to the airport, Karl saw a bar and right away asked, 'You having a drink, Pete?' I replied, 'I am fucked, can't handle it man.' But Karl sure liked to drink, so he went ahead and started drinking without a care.

My head was still banging. All I wanted to do was sleep. Sitting at the bar at the airport, Karl was drinking his pint of lager and I was just sat there, having a cup of tea while feeling like death warmed up. That's how much I was struggling. I got to the plane and just waited for it to get into Birmingham. That wouldn't be the last time I would get into trouble the day after a fight.

I also was in Paul Wesley's corner a few times and he boxed in some big fights. He fought on the undercard of the rematch between Nigel Benn and Chris Eubank at Old Trafford in Manchester. He boxed a kid called Warren Stowe in an eliminator fight for the British title and I was in his corner for that. That was some atmosphere. Paul Wesley beat him to get his shot at Rob McCracken for the British title.

I've been at all the big fights such as Bruno vs Lewis and Benn vs Eubank because Nobby always had someone on the card. We used to get a wristband so you could access all areas. If I wasn't fighting on the undercard of a big fight but still wanted to go, I'd ask Nobby if I could work the corner. He'd say, 'Yeah, no problem,' and I'd go down and work with him. Then I would stay and watch the main fight. I could always get a pass for backstage.

When I boxed on the undercard of the Mike Tyson fight in Manchester when he fought Julius Francis, I was outside my changing room and I could see Mike Tyson going fucking nuts. He looked scary as fuck and was going mad. He was raging. I kept thinking, 'I don't want to get in the way of him!' I also boxed on quite a few Ricky Hatton and Prince Naseem undercards. I just used to love going to the big fights.

* * *

Around this time, I went abroad again for a fight with Nobby. I moved back down to super bantamweight and fought for a WBA Intercontinental title against Harald Geier. I was given about six weeks' notice for the fight, which was one of the longest notices I had. I trained like fuck as I had to be really fit. I needed to be 8st 10lbs but I weighed in at 8st 7½lbs. I was ripped. My missus thought I looked too skinny. Geier was world ranked at the time and had won all of his 17 fights, with 14 of those wins coming by way of knockout.

The fight took place in Austria and I stayed at a big health resort, which was a really nice place. Geier's dad had something to do with the promotion of the event. On the night of the fight, he picked us up and took us to this venue. It was in Vienna but right out in the sticks, in the countryside. I got in the ring and the national anthems were played and all that bollocks. This kid was world ranked yet there was nothing in the fight. I boxed really well and I dropped him in the ninth round with a body shot. He was out on his arse and struggling to breathe. The referee gave him a long count then took him back to his corner and wiped his gloves, giving him about 30 seconds to recover. I battered him for the last three rounds yet they gave him the decision win by a wide distance on the scorecards. I'm not saying I beat him but if the fight had been over here, it might have been a different result. I was never going to get a decision there. He fought for the world title the next year and was knocked out in the first round. He also fought Johnny Bredahl, who was a good fighter, for the European title and was knocked out again.

I stayed in Austria for a couple of days. After the fight, they had a bit of an after-party. The next day, me and Nobby went into Vienna on the train, going through the mountains and looking around the city, though I became a bit bored. When we went back, as I say, it was right in the sticks. So I walked out on my own to try and find a pub. I found this bar. I went in there and asked for a beer. Next thing, some people came up to me.

'You boxed last night?' they asked.

'Yeah,' I said.

'Yeah, we saw you. Good fight.'

I was a hit with all these Austrians. I couldn't understand what they were on about but they were all buying me drinks.

The fight in Austria had a real good build-up. It was treated like a world title fight over there. The place was sold out. I was treated like a superstar. After the fight, people were coming to me and asking for my autograph.

* * *

Although I was trying to keep my head down and not get into trouble when I was boxing as a pro, I was nicked a few times on things. One time, Tania's sister was with a lad that I know. I got on with him as we used to drink in the same pubs. But one night, Tania's sister phoned the house to say that her boyfriend was kicking off down there. I had not long come home pissed up. Yet I jumped in my car and drove down to the house but left the car around the corner. All I could hear when walking to the house was shouting and just kicking off. The doors to the house were open, so I went in and saw her boyfriend there. I punched him in the mouth and the next thing you know, we are fighting on the floor. As we were fighting in the living room, the police entered the room and pulled us apart. At this point, we were both trying to fight the police but I was still trying to get at him. We were eventually taken to the police station in Solihull. We were two cells away from each other and I was shouting at him for about an hour, telling him that I was going to fuck him up. We both got charged with affray but the next day I went to the pub to see what he had to say. Both him and Tania's sister always had a few rows when he was pissed. Yet he was an OK lad. I went to him and said, 'What you saying? Want to carry on, then?' He was like, 'Pete, I was pissed. Can we leave it, mate?' 'Yeah,' I said, 'but I've been charged now with affray.' He replied, 'I'll say I started it. Sound OK?' We went to court the week after and he said that he started the fight, that we were pissed up and that we are mates. He just got a fine. We were lucky the police didn't do us for assault on them as they got a few shots off both of us. But we became better mates after that and we still have a drink if I see him now as he's a good lad.

* * *

One day, I boxed a kid called Vinny Feeney. I'd been out on the piss. He was a good Irish kid. We boxed at York Hall, the fight was on Sky Sports and it was scheduled for eight-threes. He couldn't crack an egg but was a nice boxer. I took the fight at short notice and was overweight, but still chose to box him. Although I lost, it was an easy fight. He became WBC International bantamweight champion later on in his career.

Now there was this pub in my own area I would drink in. It used to be called Beagles but now it's called Inn on the Green and it was my main pub. The day after I fought Feeney, I went in there with my mate Curly. There were a group of lads there who I knew. Some of them were sound and some were OK.

This one cocky bloke (who I still see sometimes but he never says fuck all to me) said:

'I saw your fight last night. I tell ya, I could have beat that kid.'

He was taking the piss. He had never boxed in his life. My mate looked at me as he knew I had a short temper when I was drunk.

I said, 'You fuckin' what? Could ya?'

Bang! I gave him a shot to the jaw. Sparked him out.

He fell off the chair. Geezer had a broken leg. His legs were in the air.

Then I said to the others, 'Anyone else want to try to beat me or want to say anything?'

His mates were all like, 'Nah Pete!'

At that moment, I thought that they were a bunch of fucking mugs. A few of his pals laughed. But I always got a lot of respect in my area. Still do.

* * *

I was watching *Coronation Street* in my flat when I heard a car horn beeping. I opened the window and Nobby was there in his car.

'Come on,' he said. 'There's a show in London.'

'How many rounds?' I asked.

'Six-threes.'

'Sound.'

I came down and got in the car.

'Who am I boxing?' I said to Nobby.

'Ah. The ABA champion,' he replied.

'Yeah, alright, sound.'

The ABA champion in question was Marlon Ward and the fight was taking place in London. I went into the ring and boxed him without a problem, though again I lost on points.

It was a dinner show, so it didn't start until ten o'clock. I used to always have my kit ready in the bag. As soon as I boxed and came home, my missus would wash and iron my kit and it would be back in the bag. I had my training bag and my boxing bag.

* * *

Andy Mayers was a boxer, though he never boxed for Nobby. Nobby knew him from when he used to work the doors at the clubs and also through the boxing scene as Andy was a good pro fighter himself. He got Andy some money when he lost his sight in one eye due to a sparring session in Denmark. He was insured somehow by the boxing board and Nobby told him that and explained to him how to sort it out. Because of Nobby's help, Andy was able to get some compensation for the injury. After that, Andy started popping in the gym. At first, he was training until Nobby told him to get a grip. 'You're never fighting again. Grab the pads and give some of the boxers a few rounds.' That's how Nobby spoke. He didn't beat about the bush. Andy started helping out at the gym in Aston and was a very good pad man. Yet he liked a drink, whisky in particular.

I got on with Andy really well. I knew him from years back as he boxed for Nechells ABC and was a few years older than me. I used to go to many fights with him. He is really laid back and everyone in the gym liked him. If Nobby couldn't take me to a fight, Andy sometimes would. Andy doesn't train fighters any more. He stopped training fighters when Nobby did. They were was a good team together but it was Nobby's gym and he called the shots.

One day me and Andy went up to Glasgow, as we had done many times. After I boxed, we went back to the hotel and started drinking in the room we were sharing. I had a few spliffs and the next thing, I'd fallen asleep. Some time after, I don't know how long it was, I was woken up by some banging on the door and someone shouting my name.

'Pete! Pete! Open the door!'

Getting up half pissed and stoned, I opened the door. Andy was standing there, no shoes, just wearing a t-shirt and jeans.

'Where you been?' I said.

'Pete, I've been up the road.'

'What do you mean?' I replied.

He sleepwalked into the lift and before he knew it, he had woken up about a ten-minute walk from the hotel.

'I had no shoes and socks on, though I had my jeans on, and I found myself 200 yards down the road,' he said. 'Don't tell Nobby, will ya?'

'Nah, no way,' I replied.

I don't think I ever did. I still stay in touch with him to this day. He was well liked on the boxing circuit and never thought he knew it all. He is an easy-going guy.

* * *

I fought a number of boxers who would later become world champions. One such boxer, who I mentioned earlier, was Paul Ingle. We fought twice. The first time I boxed him, it was about two weeks after I was in a ten-rounder in which I won my Midlands title. I was able to give him a really good fight despite losing on points.

Yet the second time we fought, on the day of the fight I had the flu. For three rounds, he just beat me up and was really close to stopping me.

'Fucking hell,' I thought. 'Why did I take this fight?' To be fair, it was for good money. For those first three rounds, he threw so many punches. But after that, he must have thought he couldn't get me out of there and he eased off the gas. I managed to fiddle my way through the rest of the fight and he beat me on points. But he is a really nice guy. Sound geezer.

When I boxed Colin McMillan, he stopped me but came in a lot heavier than me. But before McMillan fought Ingle, Ingle asked me how I thought he would do against him.

'You'll beat him,' I said. 'You'll stop him on workrate.' And that's exactly what Ingle did as McMillan was killing himself to get to nine stone.

After my fight with Paul, we had a pint together.

'I really wanted to stop you, Pete,' he said to me. 'I was trying my best as Naz couldn't do it. It would have looked great on my record.'

I was actually close to sitting it out after the third round as I felt like shit. Yet something inside me wouldn't quit. I think Paul thought the same and he said to me afterwards, 'Pete, I thought I had you, mate.'

'You nearly did, pal,' I said. Yet for the rest of the fight, I just gritted my teeth and bit down on my gumshield.

From the fourth round on, it became a bit easier. In my head, I just kept ticking off the rounds. Four to go, three to go, and so on. It was a built-in thing in my head that I would never allow myself to get stopped in the last round after going all the previous rounds.

* * *

I boxed Ady Lewis. He was a little pint-sized rocket man. He was like a mini Mike Tyson. When I boxed him, he'd had about seven fights and knocked out all his opponents. The kid was a puncher. He looked about 12 but the kid could fight. He went on to win the British and Commonwealth titles and fought for the European belt.

I was the first one to take him the distance. I was a lot heavier than him to tell you the truth. I was probably nine stone on the night I fought him and probably half a stone heavier than him. That half stone kept me in it. It was an easy fight really. They had to get him a featherweight like me because he was too powerful for everybody at his weight. He was a strong fucker. And a good kid.

* * *

When I boxed Spencer Oliver, he was the main event but it was only a four-round fight. I came out and thought, 'Fucking hell, this kid has sold some tickets here.' The MC introduced him as Commonwealth Games medallist, ABA champion and so on. He was a busy fighter, threw wicked combinations and a nice guy outside the ring. He dropped me in about the third round. I was on the floor thinking, 'What the fuck?' I got up, smothered him and came back into the fight. It was a real toe to toe. A real good fight. He beat me but I showed what I was about as a boxer. I boxed Naseem before I fought Oliver. As soon as I took Naz the distance, everyone I fought then were prospects. They were all trying to trump Naseem.

* * *

Considering the number of fights I had, it's no surprise that I saw some weird things happen during and after the fights, especially when it came to the fans. There was a traveller called Ernie Loveridge who used to box for Nobby. When Ernie first started boxing, he was a welterweight and a real tough kid. Once, he was boxing a kid called Darren Dorrington in Bristol. While he was fighting Dorrington, some of the crowd were calling him a 'fat bastard' as he did look a bit out of shape. At the venue, there was a balcony where some of the crowd were standing and someone actually threw a beefburger from the balcony at him while he was boxing. He went mad. He was trying to get out of the ring to chin them.

A similar incident occurred before a fight with Patrick Mullings. He was a boxer I had fought a few times. He was a good fighter and a southpaw. A nice kid as well. He was a former ABA champion and had two wicked fights with Spencer Oliver.

Every time we fought, it was a good fight. We had faced each other three times and I was supposed to box him a fourth time in Peterborough. We were top of the bill. It was set for eight-threes and I was getting good money for it. I was all gloved up and ready to walk down into the ring. Just as I was ready to leave the changing room, I could hear loads of shouting. I didn't know who had been fighting before me but when I opened the door to look into the hall, it was kicking off big style. A full-scale riot. Chairs were being thrown and loads of fans from different groups were fighting each other. There were loads of police there with dogs and CS gas trying to break up the melee. The promoter of the show, Frank Maloney, came into the changing room.

'Fucking hell,' he said. 'That's it. Shows done.' We were the last fight of the night.

I still got paid about £2,000 for not fighting! I wouldn't have beat him anyway. It was a win-win for me as I was free to box again straight away, which I did a week later. I basically got paid for a fight that did not take place. That happened a few times when I got paid for not fighting as the show had run over its deadline of 12 o'clock.

Sometimes incidents would happen with fans after the fight.

I was in Stoke at Trentham Gardens for a fight against a kid called Gary Marston. He was a local kid. They gave it a draw but I beat him basically.

After the fight me and my mate, who came up to Stoke with me, were on the drink. As we were drinking, this fool came up to us and said,

'I've lost fucking money on you.'

'What you on about, mate?' I said. 'Just fuck off.'

'I lost a bet on you to win,' he replied.

At this point, I was just trying to pacify him. But he kept going on, so I once again told him to just fuck off. Then Nobby came up and asked what was going on.

'Oh this prat,' I said. At that point, this guy turned to Nobby.

'I lost money on him and he should've won,' he shouted.

The bloke kept going on and on and became a bit aggressive. Nobby quickly grabbed him around the throat, pinned him to the wall and literally lifted him off the floor.

'Look,' he said to this guy's face. 'You don't mess around with my lads. You don't speak to them like that.'

Me and my mate were just laughing at this prat. His face was as white as a ghost. Nobby just put him back on his feet and told him to fuck off.

* * *

On one occasion, me and some of the lads were in a car going to Scotland. One of the boxers in the car was called Howard Clarke.

During the journey, the car pulled into a service station. We got out of the car to get some fish and chips. Howard had brown sauce and red sauce in his hands.

'What the fuck you doing?' I said.

'I don't know which one to have,' he replied.

'You know what? I'm going to have both,' he said. And he squirted both brown and red sauce all over me. We were laughing our heads off, though in hindsight I think that was one of the early signs of the dementia he now has.

A few years later, a fundraiser was organised for him in Dudley. He had started to slur his words and would say the maddest things. It was seen as funny at the time but not now. At one time, he was as sharp as a razor.

We used to have some good laughs when we were boxing. One night, we were in Scotland and a promoter said, 'Here you are.' It was some tickets to a nightclub. 'Just mention my name to get in.' There was me, the Ramsey brothers, Andy Meyers and this kid called Pedro, who I remember was a good fighter for his young age. At the club, the kid would not have a dance. He wouldn't spend the pennies. He didn't drink either. He just sat there all night drinking coke. We were just ripping the piss out of him. He said his missus knew what money he had and would want to know what he spent it on.

My mom and dad before they got married. After my dad died my mom never married or was with anyone again.

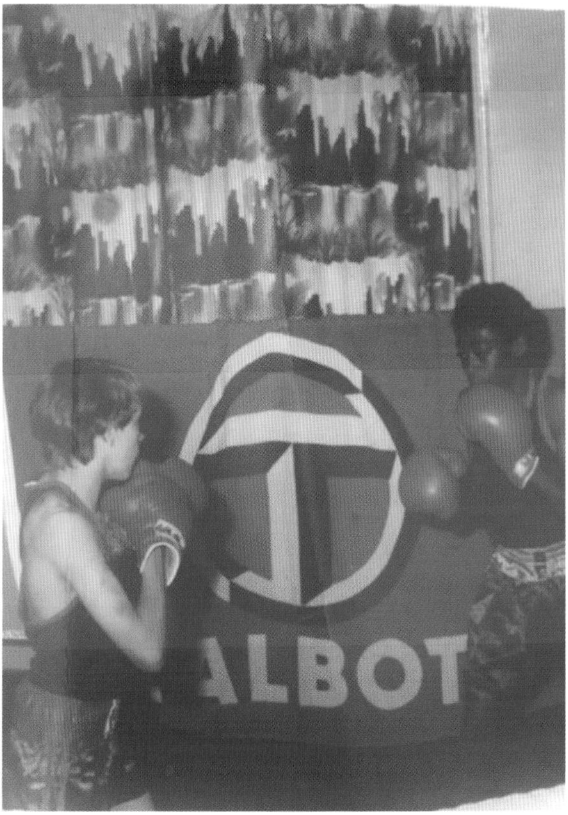

Me and Ernie Locke doing the pads at Talbot. I was about 12.

Me training at Talbot.

Me, Ernie and Les Barnett after I lost in the quarter-finals of the NABC championships.

Me facing Miguel Matthews. Don't know what fight this was, as we boxed five times. I learnt a lot from this man. Very tough guy in the ring. Lovely man outside it.

Me and Nobby are at the gym in Thomas Street, Aston.

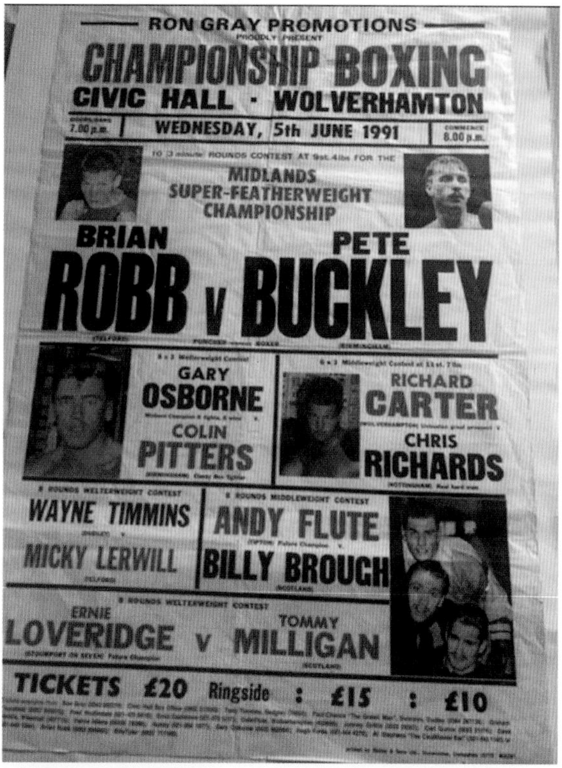

The poster of me and Brian Robb for my first Midland Area title fight.

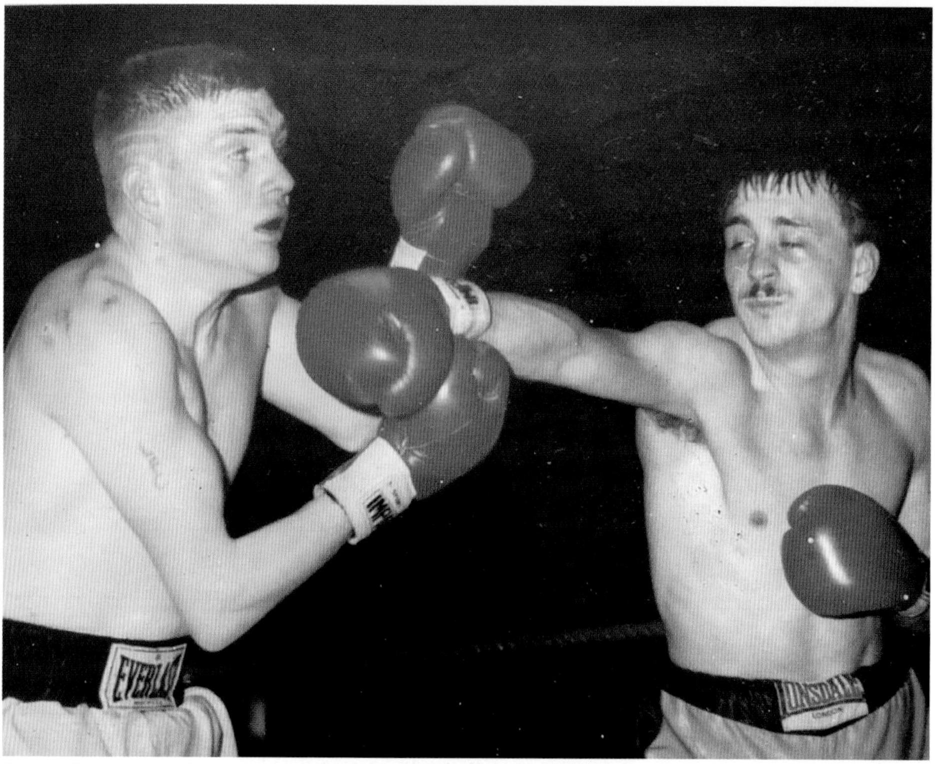

Boxing Brian Robb for the Midland Area super featherweight title, which I won over ten rounds.

Me and my mom who was my world. Loved her to bits and I was broken-hearted when she died.

Me getting picked up to go Manchester for my 200th fight.

Me with a big black eye after my 200th fight, two weeks after my brother John died.

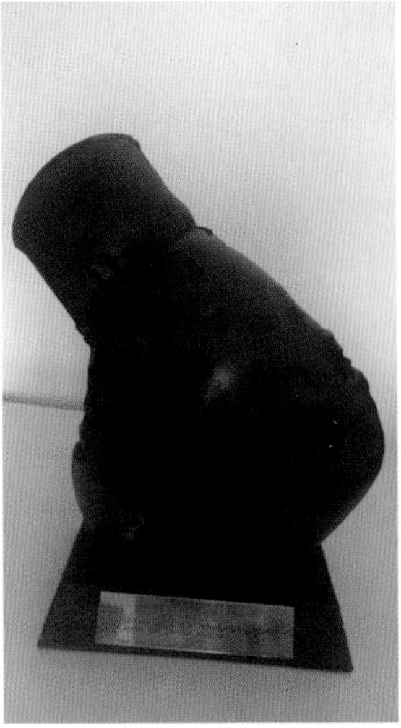

The glove I got in the ring after my 200th.

The day I married Tania and that's my daughter Sinead.

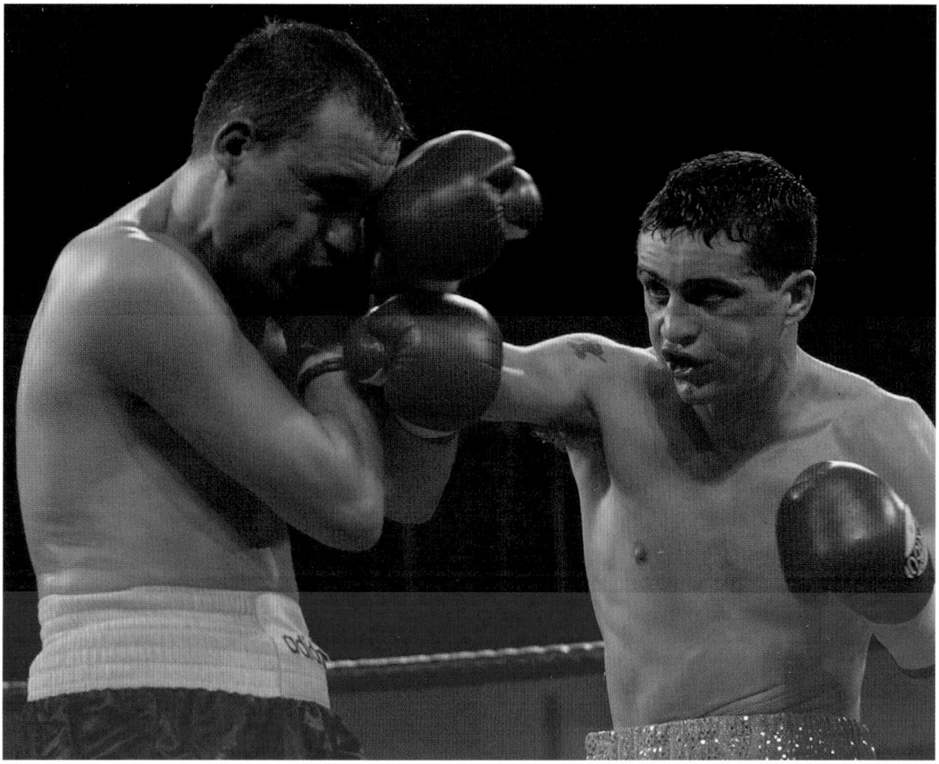

Billy Corcoran lands a right hook on Pete Buckley during the super-featherweight fight, 5 March 2003, at the York Hall in Bethnal Green, London.

Peter Buckley in his 300th fight lands a punch on countryman Martin Mohammed on his way to winning on points during their light welterweight boxing match at the Aston Villa Events Centre, Birmingham, 31 October 2008.

Peter Buckley celebrates winning in his 300th fight.

CHAPTER 12

Paid without throwing a punch

I never got angry going into a fight as it doesn't help you. Apart from that, I got on with every fighter I fought. Before fights, sometimes I would speak to them. After fights, I had a drink with them. For example, I could see Kell Brook today and he would ask, 'Hi Mr Buckley. How are you?' I was in Sheffield a few years after I packed it in, taking a fighter up there to fight. He had seen me and come out of his way to speak to me. Yet there was one boxer who annoyed me. His name was Matt Brown.

Matt Brown was a cocky kid. Too cocky. He thought he was better than what he was because he was unbeaten. After the weigh-in, he was giving it the big 'un, saying that he was going to do this, that and the other. 'Oh fuck off,' I said.

'I've never been knocked out,' he replied. 'Who are you to think you can knock me out?' He thought he was going to walk straight through me.

We were supposed to be the fourth or fifth fight on the bill that night, but they put us on third. First round, I had him all over the place. His eye was cut. Eventually, the ref had to jump in as he was out on his feet. A first-round stoppage. It was probably my best performance on paper as he fought for the British title at super featherweight and lightweight after I beat him. He lost both those title shots on points but I was the only one who stopped him in his career.

He was still giving it the big 'un after the fight, saying that he hadn't warmed up properly. I said to him that I wasn't warmed up properly either and just told him to fuck off. That happens sometimes and you have to be switched on at all times.

* * *

In this game, you string up the wins and the phone goes quiet. When I knocked out Matt Brown in a round, I don't think I fought for over a month after that. Managers don't want to put you in with their kid if you've just come off a win as they think that you would fancy the fight. They want you to get back into the losing role again before they match you. To combat that, you match yourself hard. You take a hard fight and you have a loss in your column. Any journeyman will tell you. You string two or three wins together and your phone's going quiet for a bit. You aren't fighting as promoters don't want you in there with any bit of ambition.

* * *

Sometimes Nobby would hire a minibus as we would have that many fighters on a show. We were all good mates, there was a camaraderie there and we would all wish the best for each other. After weighing in for the show, we would all get fish and chips and just have a good laugh. As mad as it sounds, some of the boxers would be in the shops doing some shoplifting. They would come out of the shops with a pair of gloves, for example. You wouldn't expect it from professional boxers. But to us, it was like being on a school trip and we would revert back to being kids. We would just be silly.

Once, there was a marquee down in London. It was at a market somewhere. We had gone there and there were five of us due to be boxing. After we boxed and had been paid, we went to a bar. On the way back, some of the fighters were smoking weed. There was also a man who is now dead but was a mate of one of the boxers. He had been to prison but was not a boxer himself. He was smoking a spliff and passed it round the minibus. 'Fucking hell, what you doing?' Nobby said. 'You call yourself professional athletes? All smoking drugs in the fucking back!' I used to smoke weed but I never smoked on the day of a fight.

* * *

Sometimes when I was boxing on a big show, such as one headlined by Ricky Hatton or Prince Naseem, I didn't always know what time I would be fighting. It's called being a floater. If a fight ended quickly, then I could be on straight away with just two minutes to warm up. But sometimes if I was having a fight that was set for eight-threes, I could be on last when all the crowd have gone and the only people left in their seats are just the fighters' fans. Because the venue would be empty, you could hear every word the trainers were shouting. The good thing sometimes was that the fight would be cut to four-threes instead, yet I still got the same money. This was sound as most of the time on those types of shows, it would be a good kid I would be boxing. So, in my mind I had already won as I didn't have to be switched on for eight rounds. Doing four rounds instead was easy. In my mind, I was thinking that when a fight was eight-threes, at some point it was going to be hard. When the fight dropped to four-threes, I got a buzz. But I knew a lot of boxers who didn't always get that lucky. Nobby told me that he had seen managers say to their lads that the rounds in their fight had been cut, so he would only pay them for the rounds they had done.

After Patrick Mullings, I was supposed to box Toncho Tonchev at York Hall. He was an Olympic silver medallist who had lost to Oscar De La Hoya in the finals. Like Mullings, he was being promoted by Frank Maloney at the time and was based in Britain. He probably would have stopped me as he was a lot bigger than me. I'd seen him fight and thought he was a real good fighter. I took that fight for the money but was wary about taking it as I was thinking, 'Fuck me. This geezer could knock me out.'

On the night of the fight, I was really nervous. There were a lot of fights on the bill and I was a floater, so I didn't know when I was going to be in the ring. There was a deadline at shows as regards when the bill had to be completed by. If the event went past 12 o'clock, they would pull the remaining fights. It was a new rule that the board put in as I remember boxing on a Naseem Hamed bill in Manchester once and didn't get in the ring until 12.45am. It wasn't good as I felt fucked boxing at that time of night. Anyway, it was late and getting close to the deadline. Dean Powell, God rest him, was the matchmaker that night. He turned to me and another fighter and said, 'Look, it's your fight or his fight that can get pulled. Give me £50 and I'll pull your fight.' I gave him £50 but still got a nice payday for not fighting. After five minutes, he returned and gave me my money and said, 'That OK, Pete?' I was chuffed as I still got paid and to be truthful, I was glad the fight was pulled because it would have been a hard fight as Tonchev was class.

Sometimes the schedule on a bill would change at the last minute. It could be that the order of the fights on the lower end of the undercard would change, or that the length of a fight would be different. A perfect example of this is a fight I had with Paul Halpin, who was a Southern Area champion at featherweight. I boxed him on the undercard of the Vitali Klitschko vs Herbie Hide world title fight in London. It was supposed to be a six-rounder. Yet while I was getting changed, the officials came into the changing room and asked:

'You want to fight now? We'll cut it to four rounds. Still get paid the same money.' I didn't even get the chance to warm up.

On the way to the ring, you could see Nobby in the video of the fight saying, 'Fucking hell! Not even a minute warm-up. Straight into the ring. I bet he's had a fucking warm-up!' They probably had ten minutes' notice before me. They likely had a good warm-up but I didn't. At the end of that fight, I came back into the changing room and a brand new pair of Air Max trainers I had worn had been robbed. I only bought them the day before. I came back to the changing room, had a shower and I couldn't find my trainers. I was having an argument with security as I was looking for them. You needed wrist bands to get into the changing rooms.

'Oi!' I said to the security guard who had been posted outside the changing rooms. 'Someone's had my fucking trainers away!'

'Uh, I don't know, I don't know,' the security guard said.

'Well, there's someone running in here without a band on then.' He said this wasn't the case, so I started arguing with him. By this point, Nobby had come into the changing room.

'What's going on?' he asked.

'My fucking trainers have been robbed. Brand new trainers cost me £120. He's a fucking prick, he is. He either knows someone and he's let them in here or he ain't doing his job and let someone in without a pass.'

With no other footwear to hand, I had to come home in my boxing boots, which took the piss. It was obvious that a boxer had robbed my trainers. I don't know who it was and I've never found out who took them. You don't do that. It's an unwritten rule. You don't rob out of changing rooms. I remember when we were kids as amateurs, there were people who robbed out of the changing rooms. But I'd never known it to happen when I was pro. Yet the same thing happened when I boxed Rob Hunt in Dudley. I came back and my phone had been robbed out of my changing room. Boxers don't rob off each other but someone robbed my phone that night. I had an idea who it was, I'm never going to say, but it was possibly someone from my own gym. Put it this way, when I had a spar with them, I went a bit harder than I normally do.

For my next scheduled fight after my non-fight with Tonchev, I was boxing on a Naseem show scheduled for one o'clock in the morning. But as the fight didn't start before the deadline, I still got paid £3,500. Three nice paydays in a row for fuck all! Others at the gym thought I was lucky but I was there to fight. I was chuffed and it meant I could fight again straight away. Good times!

* * *

My next fight was against a Mexican called Gregorio Medina. In truth, I shouldn't have taken the fight. I wasn't fit as I'd hardly been in training. I had been out on the piss and was going through some personal shit. Money was tight, so I took the fight for the money. He came over as a sparring partner with another Mexican fighter who was fighting for a world title, though I can't remember who that was. Can't remember how many rounds it was for, but Nobby pulled me out. Throughout the fight I was thinking, 'Fuck this.' My head wasn't right. The only genuine stoppages I had were against Colin McMillan, Duke McKenzie the first time and a fight with Acelino Freitas that was to come later. I think I'd been hard with my missus at the time, going through a bad year. I just shouldn't have had the fight.

* * *

Richard Evatt was one of many fights in my career that I feel shouldn't have been stopped. I got stopped on my feet. He was a big puncher, though, and enough respect to him. Real good kid. Used to be called The Tiger. He fought Junior Jones. Beat Jones up, then was stopped in the 11th round. He was found dead a few years ago. I used to message his dad on Facebook. A real tough kid who was an ABA champion and was with Matchroom. He would come in the ring with leopard scalp in his hair and leopard shorts. Three times I boxed him and he stopped me once. The ref who stopped the fight was Paul Thomas. I don't think it should have been stopped. He did hit me with some good shots but he didn't put me over and I saw the fight fine. I know I would have gone the distance with him as I'd gone the distance with him before. But the rest is history as they say.

When I saw the fight on YouTube years later, he did hit me with some bombs but I still got through them. I still think it shouldn't have been stopped. But the referee is in a better place to say it than me.

* * *

Following on from Evatt, I fought Scott Harrison. It was only Scott's second pro fight. He was quite straightforward in how he fought. He had real big shoulders. It was quite an easy fight to tell the truth. I boxed him twice. He was basic but was very strong. When he shoved you off in the clinches, you could feel his strength. He was a good fighter and a nice kid. People used to say he was crazy but I got on with him.

I had four fights in a couple of months between facing Scott Harrison and fighting Tony Mulholland for the first time. My first fight with Tony was on the Naseem Hamed vs Wilfredo Vazquez undercard at the Nynex Arena in Manchester. It was set for six rounds. Although I lost, it was an easy fight. Tony was just a boxer without power and easy to read. I didn't have to get out of second gear for that fight. I boxed him again a couple of months later in Liverpool. I had about five more fights in that two-month period.

I loved boxing in Liverpool as they know their boxing up there and I always got a lot of respect. I enjoyed boxing at the

Nynex Arena as it was always on a world title card of some kind. I liked Glasgow but knew that I wouldn't get a win up there, though I was always treated well by the promoters. York Hall was a venue I loved as the fans were always proper boxing people. They would tell you straight if you put up a good fight. Plus, I had wins and draws down there a few times. The changing rooms were crap but the history of fighters who box there is special. I was due to fight another future world champion in my next fight. But something took place the day of the fight that put paid to that.

CHAPTER 13

Mugged

I was in the city centre in Birmingham and there is a shop there called Oasis. Back then, Oasis was in a different location to where it is now. It was next to an underpass. On this day, I was meeting Nobby in town and he was late. Nobby was never late. I had this green leather coat on, a bit like Robin Hood. I went down the underpass to use the phone box at the bottom of it. As I came out, there were two guys there. When I used to go certain places, I always used to have a truncheon in my kit bag. Anyway, I came out of the phone box and these two guys were standing there and one of them was in my way.

'Yo,' the guy said. 'Take your jacket off.'

'What?' I replied.

'Take your jacket off,' he repeated.

'You fucking havin' a laugh, mate?'

I thought I knew what was going to go on. All of a sudden, I banged him and gave him a few digs on the floor. His mate shit himself and ran off. Me and the other bloke got up from the floor and he fucked off. But my hand was busted up as I smashed him on the head. I got to the other side of town and was thinking, 'If they come back, I'm going to do them.' I phoned Nobby up.

'Where the fuck are ya?' he answered.

'Nob,' I said. 'I can't fight. Two fucking geezers tried to mug me in town and I've busted my hand up.'

'What you talking about?' Nob asked.

'Nob, two guys tried to mug me in town. I hit one and my hand is busted up.' My hand was swollen as fuck.

'Ah, fucking hell,' he said. He then asked where I was.

'I've got to get out of town as I busted this kid up, man. I can't fight, mate.'

'Alright, don't worry about it,' he said.

I went home and my missus was wondering what was going on. I told her that two guys tried to mug me in town and that I thought I'd broken my hand. But I was flapping a bit as I thought I'd proper battered this guy in town.

It was a good earner, this fight, a good money fight. It was against Lehlo Ledwaba. He ended up boxing a guy called Ricky Beard. It was a few weeks before I fought again. I hadn't broken my hand, though it was badly swollen. I packed it with ice and it went down after a few days. I used to always go running but I didn't go to the gym and hit the bags for about two or three weeks. I always kept in shape. I didn't hear from those two guys again and I heard nothing from the police. I could be fighting ten geezers. I wouldn't give no one anything. You'd have to fucking kill me. My missus would tell you, I'd have to be killed.

I watched the fight on Sky later that night. Ledwaba stopped Ricky Beard in about two or three rounds. He was only a flyweight, a bantamweight at most. But he was a tough kid and he knocked the bollocks out of Ricky Beard. I thought, 'Fucking hell. I was supposed to box that kid!' He was a South African and WBU champion who later became a legitimate world champion. When he was the IBF super bantamweight champion, he was supposed to be fighting an American in one of his title defences, but the American pulled out. Manny Pacquiao came in at short notice and his trainer Freddie Roach fancied the fight. Pacquiao stepped in and beat Ledwaba. Pacquiao was only a flyweight at the time but he took the fight at super bantamweight and knocked him out. It was because of that fight that he became known in America.

I ended up boxing Ledwaba six months later. He had something to do with Frank Warren and Sky. I boxed him down in Bristol and the fight was easy. A piece of piss. I was jabbing him and I boxed good. He didn't beat me in every round.

Ernie Fossey, who was Frank Warren's matchmaker, came up to me after the fight.

'The fight was fuck all. But you got a nice payday, yeah?' he asked.

'Yeah,' I said.

The fight was easy. I couldn't believe the guy was in line for a world title as I thought he was pretty basic. I spoke to him on Facebook later on and he was a real nice geezer. As for Ernie Fossey, I got on with him too. He used to look after me and I had enormous respect for him. Proper lovely geezer. I went to his funeral when he died.

The first time I was due to fight Ledwaba, it was supposed to take place in Glasgow. The dough I got for the re-arranged fight was better than the first time we were due to meet as the second fight was an eight-rounder, whereas the first fight was due to be a six-rounder. Plus, he'd knocked Ricky Beard out, so I got a few more quid out of it. It was a nice earner.

* * *

When I was going to fight Steve Murray, he was rated at the time. He stopped two kids from my gym, including Karl Taylor. He was blowing them away. But he was a lightweight and I was only a super featherweight. Just before I boxed him, I spoke to Glenn McCrory about the fight.

'You fighting that Steve Murray?' he asked.

'Yeah,' I replied.

'Oh, be careful, son,' he said. I told him that I'd be alright.

The fight was a piece of piss. He was very busy coming towards me but it was my strategy to have them come at me. It was a good fight. He then fought Bobby Vanzie and then Graham Earl for the British title and was knocked out in both fights. He was a big ticket seller, though as I say my fight with him was easy.

I boxed a fighter called David Burke twice. He was a big lad who won the WBU title. He also fought for the European title and beat Colin Dunne. The first fight took place in Liverpool. He was a southpaw who had a long reach. He beat me. The second time I boxed him, it was an eight-rounder. He put me down three times in the first round. I thought, 'Fucking hell, man!' But I got up and went the distance with him. I gritted my teeth. He was looking at me and saying, 'I've got you, Buckley.' I thought, 'You fucking ain't, man!' One of the knockdowns was a straight jab, which caught me square and dropped me. I got up. He dropped me again. I got up again.

I wasn't hurt. He just overwhelmed me in the first round, but I got through it.

'What you fucking doing on the floor three times?' Nobby said when I went back to the corner.

'I don't know, man,' I said back to him.

'You going down again?'

'Nah,' I said.

I went the distance with him, just fucked him about. He beat me easily enough. Normally a ref would stop it but I wasn't really hurt. But he was a real good kid. That's one style I didn't like fighting, big, tall southpaws. I hated them. If they were tall and orthodox, I could get close to them. But with southpaws, they would just fight horrible.

In between my fights with David Burke, I went over to Ireland after a late phone call to box Martin O'Malley. He was supposed to have beaten Floyd Mayweather as an amateur. He had about 16 fights and had won them all before facing me. To bring him over from America, they must have rated him.

I had no trainer with me, which was a bit bad, but still took the fight. Basically, Nobby said that he was unable to come with me to the fight, so I said that I would go over on my own. Once I got there, I asked a trainer called Mike Shinfield from Derby if he could second me, which he agreed to do. As Mike took me in, someone said, 'Give him a drink.' I'd been on the piss and I accepted the fight for the money.

O'Malley was hitting me with shots and after three or four rounds, the referee stopped the fight. I remember going mad at the ref. He wasn't even hurting me. He was just pushing me on the gloves. Not saying that I was going to win but it shouldn't have been stopped. A lot of English referees knew who I was, so they knew how much I could take and they knew how I could come back. The referees in Ireland are very inexperienced and weren't used to having many pro shows. As the ref had never done one of my fights before, he didn't know how much I could take. He probably thought I was getting a hiding but I would have gone the distance with him.

* * *

When I boxed Acelino Freitas in Liverpool, I didn't even know who he was. Nobby offered me the fight. He said that there was a Brazilian fighter who had just signed with Frank Warren. I didn't really know anything about him. Normally I used to look up fighters but I didn't look Freitas up. I hadn't heard of him.

When I got down to Liverpool that day, I bumped into Gary Thornhill. I'd boxed Gary twice. He was boxing at the same event and was British champion at the time.

'You're boxing that Brazilian, aren't you, Pete?' he asked. I said, 'Yeah.'

'He's fucking big, mate.'

I didn't really think anything of it. I just said 'yeah' to him. I didn't see Freitas at the weigh-in as it was the day before and I'd only accepted the fight a few hours after the weigh-in had taken place.

I warmed up as usual, then got in the ring first. I turned around and I swear to God, I genuinely thought the wrong geezer had come into the ring.

'I'm not fighting him, am I?' I said to Nobby.

'Yeah you are,' replied Nobby.

'Fucking hell, he's big!'

He was maybe a stone heavier than me on the night of the fight. The fight was made at super featherweight. I was about 9st 6lbs and he was the biggest geezer I ever faced in the ring. His chest was big, his arms were big. He was just *big*! When he got into the ring, I really thought it was the wrong kid. He was that big. He didn't even have skinny legs; he was just big.

Then they introduced us. He had 18 fights, 18 wins and 18 knockouts. I walked back to my corner and said to Nobby, 'Fucking hell. That's a nice one I got here, isn't it!' Nobby just laughed.

'Oh, you'll be alright.' he said.

I came out for the first round, tucked up and stayed tight. He hit me with a body shot which didn't really hurt me but literally knocked me off my feet before I punched him. It was just strength. He put me down with that body shot. I beat the count and fiddled my way through the round with a cross-arm defence. I even tried to push him back but he was just solid. Scott Harrison was a strong fighter but Freitas was like trying to push a fucking house. I came back to my corner at the end of the round and Nobby asked if I was alright.

'He's fucking strong,' I said.

'Just do your thing, just fiddle him about,' instructed Nobby.

I came back out and all I did was keep really close to him as he liked to wing his punches in that first round. I was doing alright but he was just too big for me. The second round, I was doing OK, reading his shots better and with my cross-arm defence he's wasn't getting his punches through. I was frustrating him but he was still pushing me back. He would push me back just by pushing his shoulder against me. He was bullying me around the ring. He didn't hit me on the chin. He didn't shake me again. But his physical strength was just too much for me. It was like going in with a middleweight. I've sparred light-middleweights and middleweights, yet he felt super strong.

In round three, he came out of his corner and just started throwing these bombs at me. It became hard in there but I got through the round. When I returned to my corner, Nobby pulled me out. I didn't complain when he said it. Even Nobby said he'd dropped a bollock.

'Soz kid,' he added. 'Didn't know he was that good.'

The fight wasn't going nowhere and I wasn't going to fiddle my way through eight rounds with him. I probably could have gotten hurt and the money for the fight wasn't great for what it was.

Nobby knew he'd fucked up because he hadn't looked him up. I didn't even know his name at the time or I would have done a bit of research on him. I would still have said yes to the fight if I knew more about him beforehand as I didn't know how to turn down a fight.

Afterwards, I found out that he was a superstar in Brazil. They loved him over there. They were saying how he was the next big thing in boxing. He won the WBO world title eight months later, knocking out Anatoly Alexandrov in 89 seconds. I didn't feel that bad after that. Later on in his career, this geezer fought some great fighters like Diego Corrales and Joel Casamayor. Barry Jones fought him later. Jones was a lovely boxer but wasn't really a puncher. Yet he put Freitas down in the first round. It was a big shock as nobody gave Barry Jones a chance. I fought Jones three times, lovely boxer but not a lot of power. Despite the knockdown, Freitas got up to stop Jones in the tenth round.

He actually came back a few years ago at light-middleweight and then retired again. But I didn't know he was in politics until recently.

* * *

Losers Limited. I didn't like the name. Nobby had done it as a tongue-in-cheek thing. None of the boxers liked it. What Nobby did is he allowed a documentary to be made about his stable of fighters. I was never on it. I said I wasn't going on it. What he was doing was basically taking the piss out of himself. People used to say that Nobby's gym was full of losers. But he used to say to us, 'Look, you're not losers. You're all earning money every week. How can you be losers? You're not out robbing people. You're not hitting old ladies over the head and robbing their handbags. You're not doing this and that. You're winners, lads. Don't think you are losers or I'll call you losers. You're winners in life.'

He always stuck with that. But with regards to this documentary, I said to him, 'I ain't doing this. I ain't being classed as a loser.'

'Why not?' he said.

'Nah,' I replied. 'I'm more than that.'

'Fuck them!' he replied. 'Fuck what they think. They ain't paying your bills. They ain't buying your cars. They ain't buying your holidays.'

Brian Coleman took part in the documentary. So did the Ramsey brothers Mark and Paul. A few of the other lads done it but I wouldn't do it as I thought it was taking a bit of the piss out of the lads and the gym. I had a bit more pride. OK, I was boxing and I was losing nearly every week. But I had more pride than to say, 'Yeah, I'm a professional loser.' I was a professional loser in a way. But sometimes I won and I didn't always go there to lose. Sometimes I went into the ring and thought, 'Fuck it. I'll have a move about.' Other times, I'd go to win and didn't get the decision. Mainly, that was down to Nobby as even though he got on a lot with them and they respected him, he fucked the referees off. Nobby didn't give a fuck. He was like, 'Fuck them. It'll be forgotten about next week. You lost this week. You'll be boxing again next week.'

Warriors Gym or something like that would have been a better name. We were all warriors. We would fight at the drop of a hat. We didn't give a fuck. Not just me. Brian Coleman, Karl Taylor, Tony Hanna, Paul Wesley, Pedro Thompson, the Ramsey brothers and so on. We'd all fight anyone. World-class fighters, European-class fighters, British title challengers. Some of the boxers had their latest fights included in the documentary. All of the fights went the distance, which proved Nobby's point that this is how his lads earned money, that they didn't have to be a champion to make a decent living. We proved that boxers can earn money by knowing their boxing and knowing what they are taught. We weren't disgracing ourselves. We didn't fall out over the name Limited name but I just didn't like it.

Although the fighters in Nobby's gym didn't just fall over and always gave their all, I heard stories of fighters who dived for money. Once I was in Denmark (I won't say the boxer's name) and there was this British boxer who had won titles. He was offered a good amount of money to go the distance.

When he came back, he said to me, 'I could have boxed him all night long. But I got sorted.'

'Fucking hell,' I thought.

I was never asked to take a dive. I would never let anyone stop me but I'd have a move about with them. If someone said to me, 'Pete, let them stop you in four rounds,' I would have told them to fuck off. But there is a difference between that and having a move about with someone. When I have a move about with someone, I still get paid. But I wouldn't let someone stop me. No chance. I wouldn't have had a stoppage on someone's record for someone to say, 'Oh, I'll give up some extra money for you.' But to have a move about with someone is a different thing because for one, I probably ain't going to get the decision and two, it's an easy night's work. So, you just play them at their own game. I could be offered to fight someone who's had four fights, four wins, all on points, sold £2,000 worth of tickets, but you just have a move about with him. And I'd say to their manager, 'Well, what's it worth?' They'd offer me an extra £500 and I'd say, 'OK then.' I would basically have a spar with them and as soon as they got a little bit cheeky, I'd give them a little dig just to remind them. Don't forget, the kid never knew that I was having a move about. Their trainer would never say to them that they were giving me an extra £500 to have a move about. The kid would never know about it.

* * *

My first fight with Bradley Pryce was on the Mike Tyson vs Julius Francis undercard in Manchester. It was quite an easy fight as he was a lightweight and wasn't a banger. He had long arms and had a bit of a funny style. He was from the Calzaghe gym, so I knew he was going to be a good fighter as Enzo didn't work with idiots. After my fight, I was getting changed and all I could hear was someone shouting and kicking off, saying, 'Fuck this shit!' It was Tyson. He was going mad and I thought that he wasn't going to fight. He looked mad as fuck. Leaving the changing room, I walked past him and as I looked at him, I said, 'Good luck Mike.' He gave me a little nod of his head. Not that he needed it as he knocked Francis out in the second round. I remember thinking no wonder he beat boxers before the bell as he scared the shit out of me. He looked like a right mad bastard.

When I boxed Bradley Pryce the second time, I wasn't up for the fight. It shouldn't have taken place. It was one of only a few times I felt like I had cheated myself for not even trying. I was not mentally present for the fight but there were reasons for this. The journey to the venue was very long. I'd been in the car six hours and the traffic was terrible all the way up there. I was also starving and had been on the piss the night before. When I arrived at the venue and got out of the car, I felt like shit. I was told straight away that I had to go to the weigh-in as I was on first. I initially weighed in, saw the doctor and got bandaged up. Very quickly I was being called into the ring and I was doing eight-threes. I didn't have any time to warm up.

He was so much heavier than me the second time around. Heavier than I had been told he would be. The first shot that hit me was a big, straight jab. It caught me square on and put me on my arse. I got up and he caught me again, this time with a right hand that dropped me.

'Fuck it,' I thought and the ref counted me out on my feet. It was the first time I'd ever been stopped in the first round. I think the referee knew that I wasn't up for the fight. No excuses. I wasn't myself and felt like shit. Bradley was a lot heavier than me. He'd been weighed the day before. So, I knew that on the night he would be a lot heavier than me. He looked like a big welterweight. I thought that they were having me over, so I thought that I was robbing the money off them. That's what I did in my mind as I didn't try. It did my head in to do that as I am a proud person. For me to do that pissed me off big time. My reputation in boxing was that I was a tough lad who would fight anyone. Yet in my head for this fight I quit in the ring, and that was a hard pill to swallow. He did what he had to do. Fair play to him as I took the fight, and he was better than me. I was a bit greedy for the money.

CHAPTER 14

Weight issues

As already shown by some of the stories that have been told, it wasn't just inside the ring where things would happen. Some of the more memorable things that happened during my career happened after my fights.

When some of us from the gym were in Scotland (me, Brian Coleman and Andy Meyers, who was my trainer for the fight I was having there), we would all go out on the piss. Alex Morrison was a good promoter who always looked after you. I have a lot of respect for the man. Tommy Gilmour was another promoter I respected. I was always treated well by the promoters in Scotland. Not by the referees but the promoters were always 100 per cent. Alex would always say, 'Hey lads, if you want to go to so and so nightclub, mention my name at the door and go straight in.' Alex was well respected in Scotland. That's just who he is. One night after a fight, we went out and we had not long come out of this club and were by Glasgow train station. I remember seeing two geezers there having a fight. One of the guys just pulled out a blade and slashed it against the other guy's face. I thought, 'Fucking hell.' I did think that we shouldn't be drinking up there but we had no trouble really.

I went up to Scotland on my own to attend one of Alex's shows. The kid I was due to box failed his medical. Then Alex asked me, 'Pete, would you do me a favour?'

'Yeah, what?' I said.

'Will you box Brian Carr?'

I'd boxed Brian Carr a couple of times before. Top amateur. He had fought for the Commonwealth title. He was actually having dinner at the place where I was boxing. Because my fight fell through, I could have just gotten paid. But Alex said to me, 'There's only two fights on. Will you fight Brian Carr? I'll sort you out.'

'Yeah, no problem,' I said.

Brian Carr went home, got his kit and I ended up boxing him. It was a bit mad but Alex said to me afterwards, 'Thanks for that, Pete. You didn't have to do that. I appreciate it as there was only a couple of fights for the show.' Also, if the two fights he had on were stopped in the first round, you aren't going to get your money's worth. But Alex knew that me and Brian would have a good fight. He always looked after me like that.

* * *

I remember taking a fight on one day's notice when I boxed Carl Greaves from Nottingham. I think it was for the Masters super featherweight title. I couldn't make the weight but as he sold a load of tickets, they needed someone who they thought would give him some rounds. Yet I had seen Carl box a few times and one of my gym mates, a traveller named Jon Jones who fought under the name of Benny Jones, had knocked Carl clean out before. I jumped at the chance when the fight was offered.

I think Carl thought he was in for an easy night but I was well up for the fight. If I had been 100 per cent fit, I think I would have beaten him. But I gave him a really hard fight and he just nicked it on points. He said to me afterwards that I had pushed him all the way. I then boxed him a second time a few months later. Once again, it was on late notice but I still gave him a hard fight, which he just won again on points. I said to Nobby that I'd love to fight him again with at least four weeks' notice and said that I would beat him.

'That's not going to happen, Pete. They are not going to risk it.'

I would have loved to have had more notice for the Masters title fight and had the chance to add it to the Midlands titles I had won.

* * *

Early in my career, I used to walk around at about nine stone when I wasn't fighting. But really, I was a super bantamweight. I could even do bantamweight at a push. One of the ways I used to get my weight down is I would put bin bags plus layers of clothes on and I would turn the oven and the hobs on in the kitchen. I would do this the night before the fight.

Say if I had accepted a fight in which the weight limit was 8st 10lbs and I only accepted the fight the day before. Don't forget back then boxers weighed in on the same day as the fight. The first thing I would do is go home and weigh myself. I would be weighing myself all week anyway as if it was a good fight that was set for eight-threes, for example, then I'd be on the ball with my weight. If I was a couple of pounds over, then I would go for a big run and probably lose a pound. The less weight a fighter has to lose, the harder it is to lose it. Once I lost that one pound, I would then dry out. Drying out means that I wouldn't drink anything for 24 hours. Say I had some fish for dinner at six o'clock. Before I went to bed, I would cut a lemon in half or in quarters and suck it dry. It would taste bitter as fuck. But when you woke up the next morning, you would check your weight and you could lose a pound. It's a brilliant trick. Old-school fighters used to use it and it worked, but it's dangerous. These days, because weigh-ins are the day before, you can still lose the weight while you're taking in liquids. But when I was doing it, you would just cut out all the liquids, especially in the summer. But it was very hard.

That week, I'd be moody as fuck in the house as I was trying to get the weight down. When I fought Harold Geier in Austria, the fight was made at 8st 10lbs. But I had a number of weeks to train for that fight. As soon as it was first announced, I was doing ten-mile runs then dropping it down to five-mile runs and doing sprints. In the morning, I would only have a boiled egg for breakfast. In the afternoon, I'd just eat fish, salad or chicken. The day before a fight, I would have nothing. My last drink would be at ten in the morning and I wouldn't have a drink again until after the weigh-in at three o'clock the next day. You know how you see fighters jump on the scales and then as soon as they are off, they have a drink straight away? That's how I was.

If I took a fight on late notice, it didn't really matter as I was doing them a favour. I boxed Tony Silkstone in York once. Again, I had to be 8st 10lbs. I would be 8st 10lbs but he was 8st

10 1/2lbs. So Nobby said that Silkstone would have to take off the extra weight. But a deal was struck whereby they gave me an extra £100 on top on my wages. Half a pound was fuck all.

'He can either get it off or you get £100 on top,' said Nobby.

'Yeah alright, I'll have the extra £100,' I told Nobby.

I boxed Jon Jo Irwin in Solihull. He had boxed for England and won everything as an amateur. We were supposed to be nine stone for our fight and he came in two pounds heavier. So that two pounds meant he had to pay me £200 out of his wages. That's how it used to work back then. Nowadays, I don't think it does so much. Towards the end of my boxing career, I'd turn up at a certain weight and it wasn't really spoken about as I was doing them a favour. When you were top of the bill and the fight was set for eight-threes, you had to make the weight. If you didn't, you had to get the weight off or forfeit some money. Most of the time, I'd rather forfeit the money than try to get the weight off.

If Mickey Duff's fighters didn't come in on weight, he fucking went mad. He did not like it. Mickey Duff always wanted the edge on you. He was a brilliant manager who knew when his fighters were ready. Like when Lloyd Honeyghan beat Don Curry. No one gave Honeyghan a chance. Mickey Duff said he would beat him and he did.

When I was training a few fighters, I would help them on the scales myself. You just have to keep talking to the officials. Some of them don't think you can see. Say the kid's standing on the scales and I'm next to him. As I'm talking to the official, I just lift the kid up and tell him to keep on talking to them. You can drop half a stone off by doing that trick. It's a great trick and it evens up the fight.

See, with Sid Razak for instance, I knew he'd be heavy. I would just put my hands up behind his back and lift him while they were looking at him and the scale. You weren't going to win the fight. I remember when Sid fought Tommy Coyle and I took him down to Hull for the fight. He was ten stone and he was supposed to be 9st 5lbs.

'I'm a bit heavy, Pete,' he said.

'Keep your hands behind your back,' I told him. He knew what I was going to do.

'Yeah, 9st 4lbs,' the official announced. 'Get off the scale.'

If I ever took a fight on a couple of hours' notice, these tricks could even things out.

'Their fitness is there [raises his hand], your fitness is there [lowers his hand], so it levels it out. Your weight keeps you in the fight,' Nobby would say.

Once you're off and they put it down, it's done. I learned all that from Nobby.

Something else that would affect my weight involved the Midlands Area boxing board secretary. His name was Alec Kirby. What you could do back in the day is, if a boxer had a fight with someone on the Saturday, you could go to his house and he would weigh them in.

He would then give a certificate to the boxer, which would state their weight and he would sign and stamp it. When the boxer went down to London and presented the certificate, that would be their weight. He would weigh me but I wouldn't be 8st 10lbs as stated on the certificate. I would be 9st 3lbs, which I probably was the day before.

As he knew you were up against it, he would turn a blind eye if you were a couple of pounds over the limit.

If you were the home fighter back in the day, you could tell the inspectors that were due to be at the fight what weight you'd be and they would write that down. You can't do that now. Back in the day, they used to fiddle the weights, believe me. It was a bit bent like that. People don't really speak about that side of the game. I boxed fighters who were a lot heavier than me and vice versa. But because all involved wanted the fight, it went ahead. Sometimes I would come in on one day's notice, would weigh about 9st 12lbs but the announcement on the night would be 9st 4lbs. At the end of the day, they had been training for six or seven weeks, their opponents had pulled out and if someone comes on short notice, they're going to be heavier, simple as that. So that little bit of weight you have on them evens things out. You got to know the game. That's how it works.

When I boxed Colin McMillan, I knew he wasn't the same weight as me. I knew he was a lot heavier. Don't tell me he was 9st 2lbs the day before, because he wasn't. He was bigger than he looked and had big, thick legs. So, it was little things like that.

When I boxed Carl Greaves in a ten-rounder, the fight was made at 9st 4lbs but I was about 9st 8lbs. At the weigh-in, Nobby lifted me when I stepped on to the scales. They knew I was unable to make the weight. They would turn a blind eye as Carl Greaves was top of the bill. They wouldn't have a top of the bill if I was unable to fight him. They knew I could do ten rounds with him. So, what were they going to do? Get me in the ring and do a good ten rounds with him or bring in an import who Carl would blow away in a round. No one would be happy then. Carl said to me after the fight, 'You were never fucking 9st 4lbs.'

'I know I wasn't,' I laughed. 'But I fucking saved your show!'

I boxed Carl a few times and we always had a good fight. It was little tricks like that. Four pounds isn't anything really, so it evened itself out. He would have been training six, seven weeks for a ten-rounder. I hadn't. I had been ticking over. I still did the ten rounds, which were a piece of piss, but it was a good fight.

Fighters don't fight in their weight class any more. They boil themselves down. I never really did. If I wanted to, I could have fought at bantamweight all my career. But I wasn't into boiling myself down. I think it's dangerous. Say a fighter has been training six, eight weeks solid for a six- or eight-rounder. I take the fight on one day's notice. So, if I'm half a stone heavier, it evens it out a bit, as he is fitter than me and I'm a bit heavier than him. It keeps a bit of balance. My extra weight has kept me in the fight. That's how it worked. The kid would usually be better and fitter than me, but as I'm a little bit overweight it evens things out.

When you drain yourself, your fitness goes quick. You can be a little bit overweight. Sometimes you can be too fit. I've boxed before when I've been too fit and after two rounds you have fuck all. Your sharpness is gone, everything. But you can be a little bit unfit and always have your reserve tank.

I shouldn't have done it but sometimes if I was quite a bit overweight and had a fight that night, what I'd do in the morning is I would go for a run. Then I would go to a sauna for an hour, just get a good few pounds off me. I was in London once to see the Billy Schwer vs Colin Dunne fight and a geezer came over from America. Robert Smith asked him if he had done the weight alright.

'Yeah,' he said. 'I was in the sauna this morning.'

'Were you?' Smith replied. 'You ain't fighting then, mate.'

'What?' he said, looking surprised, possibly because it's acceptable in the States. Here you can't do it. If he hadn't said anything, no one would have known.

'You fucking div,' I thought.

I always used it say to fighters, 'Don't say you've been in a fucking sauna.' I knew not to say it. It's a stupid thing to do but it's money.

* * *

I remember once we boxed up in Liverpool at a show that was being shown live on Sky Sports. There was me on, the Ramsey brothers, Paul Denton, Brian Coleman, Karl Taylor and Paul Wesley. Say if there were eight fights on the bill, six of Nobby's fighters were in the away corner. They could have eight fights on the show and could have eight first-round stoppages. That's no good for TV. They knew that if they had six of Nobby's fighters, at least five of us were going the distance. They knew we were tough. We didn't go there just to grab the money and fall over. Sometimes, some of the lads had been on the piss the night before and they didn't fancy it, and they would rob the money by letting themselves get stopped. But they didn't like doing it. It didn't reflect well on our gym. Losing by decision and not by knockout made a difference as to whether we would fight next week and the week after. It was about earning money.

* * *

It was either a Friday or a Saturday. At the time, I had this little shit car and I was parked near a bridge. Nobby phoned me on my mobile, telling me that there was a fight going on that night. But I was underneath my car as it kept coming out of gear. I had to get underneath it to bang it and then knock it back into the gearstick. As I was working on it, I burned my arm on the exhaust pipe.

'Fucking hell, Nob,' I said. 'I'm stuck under my car in Balsall Heath. Ring me back.'

I phoned my brother David and told him the crack. He came and picked me up. I dropped him back to his house and borrowed his car to get to Nottingham.

I drove to Nottingham on my own. I arrived at the venue with an hour to spare before the fight. I asked someone if they could bandage me, then I saw the doctor for the medical. As I had my top on, he couldn't see the burn. It was only a slight burn but painful.

I boxed Alex Moon, who was Commonwealth champion at the time, for six rounds. Piece of piss. An easy fight, though he won. I got paid well for it. I came back home and gave my brother back his car. The next day, I went to the auctions to buy a new car.

On another occasion I had been on holiday in Mallorca for a week, came back on Sunday and Nobby phoned me to ask if I wanted to box the following Thursday.

'I'm a little bit heavy,' I said.

'Well, you've got four days to lose a few pounds.'

'Yeah alright,' I replied.

Once, I came back from holiday on Friday morning and I phoned Nobby as I had some cigars for him.

'Alright Nobby, I've some cigars for ya.'

'How are you?' he said. 'You have a good time?'

'Yeah.'

'You drink much?'

'Every night. Why?'

'There's a fight going on tomorrow.'

'Who against?' He told me the name of the opponent.

'What's the money?' He told me how much.

'Phone them back and tell them I'll have it,' I replied.

Even though I'd been on the piss, I would be active on holiday by doing swimming and going on long walks. I did that a few times. The way I looked at it is that the fight was paying for my holiday.

I accepted a fight on two hours' notice against Rob Hunt, who was from Staffordshire. He was a big lad, six feet, a former kickboxing champion and known as a big puncher. I was actually having my dinner in the house when at five o'clock the phone rang and it was Nobby.

'I might have a fight for you in Dudley,' he said.

What happened is that Jason Nesbitt was supposed to fight Hunt and he was getting a set amount of money. He phoned Nobby and said that he wanted more money. He took the piss basically, as Hunt was a big ticket seller and Jason knew it. They had to put the kid on that night as he'd sold a bundle of tickets. So, Nobby's phoned me in response.

'You might have a fight. Nesbitt's fucking me about. He wants more money. I've offered him more money. See how it goes.'

Half an hour went by and he rang me back.

'The fight's yours if you want it.'

I was getting good money for it. The fight was set for either four or six rounds. I grabbed my kit (which, as I mentioned before, was always done anyway), jumped in the car and drove up to Dudley. I even did some training that day.

Arriving there, I had to weigh in right away and I was a bit heavier than I normally am as I'd eaten. My weight was 9st 10lbs whereas Hunt's was about 10st 4lbs.

Hunt had knocked both of his previous opponents out, yet my fight with him was a piece of piss. It was easy. I hit him with a nice right hand in the first round. It didn't make him wobble but it did make him step back a little and have a think. After that, he just boxed me. He had a very long reach. I just got behind my guard, messed him about and tied him up. It was an easy night's work. The fight was on a Friday night. I went into the gym the next Monday without a mark on me. Nobby was taking the piss out of Jason Nesbitt.

'You earned good money the other night, didn't you Pete, for that spar?' he yelled.

'Yeah, easy pay day,' I replied.

We were just having banter really.

* * *

I once boxed a Kosovan kid who called himself Tony Montana, who was based out in Sheffield from the Brendan Ingle camp. He used to box like a typical Ingle fighter but he wasn't as good as any of them. We boxed once in London. He wasn't a bad kid but he was an awkward bastard. He was holding me, pushing my head down and the ref gave him a warning. He then actually pushed me and I just flipped backwards over the top rope and landed on the timekeeper's table. I fucking hurt myself. As I was getting back into the ring, the crowd were all laughing. The referee gave him a right bollocking. I got back in under the bottom rope and carried on boxing. I then grabbed him in a headlock and whispered, 'You dirty bastard.' He won on points, though I thought I beat him.

My next opponent was Terry Fletcher, who was a mate of Matthew Macklin's. He stood about 6ft 1in and was a good amateur who had boxed for England. The fight was at Wembley Conference Centre and he sold a few tickets. During the fight, I could hear Macklin shouting, 'Go on Terry. Watch him now. He's going to do this and that.' Because he was Macklin's pal, I didn't think anything of it. If that had been my mate fighting one of Macklin's pals, I would have done exactly the same thing.

During the fight, I was throwing feints and using loads of tricks that I learned as a pro. I stood on his foot, backed him up to the ropes and pushed his head down. I was just fucking him about. I was never going to outbox him as he was tall and had a good jab.

Though he was a good fighter, Fletcher never fulfilled his potential. He had a few fights and then faded out.

After that, I fought Henry Castle, who was another former ABA champion. Nobby phoned me.

'There's a fight going on. I'm going to pick you up in half an hour to 45 minutes.'

'Alright, sound.' We went down to London and the fight was at a dinner show. The venue was a posh hotel.

Like other dinner boxing shows, there wasn't any atmosphere. All they could do was clap. It was similar to when I boxed in Germany. It's a bit different there now, though smoking was still allowed then. It felt really weird.

When I first started boxing in the pros, there was boxing in nightclubs. The ring would be full of smoke as the smoking ban indoors hadn't happened yet. It was a good thing they did stop it in the end. It was hard boxing like that.

CHAPTER 15

My 200th fight

I wasn't going to go through with my 200th fight, which was against Baz Carey, because my brother John had died two weeks before. I was home one night and my missus's brother, who was mates with my brother, knocked on the door. As soon as I opened the door, he said to me, 'You better get up to Heartlands Hospital, something's happened to John.'

'What?' I said, surprised.

He didn't really know what to say to me. I thought he said that John had been in a car crash because my head was racing all over the place. I was the first member of the family to arrive at the hospital. Soon after I arrived, I was told that my brother had had a heart attack and died. When I went to John's room, he was just lying there. He died shortly after his 40th birthday.

We'd had a party for his 40th the week before. Me and my brother were really close. There was about a two-week gap between my brother's death and the Baz Carey fight. I told Nobby that I wasn't fighting. He was like, 'Alright, whatever.' He didn't talk me into it but someone from Frank Warren's office phoned me and said that I was going to be making history and that we would try and get me a win. In the end, I just agreed to it as they were paying me good money. I needed the money at the time as we hadn't paid for my brother's funeral and bought quite a few bits for it. Ernie Fossey, who was Frank Warren's matchmaker, sorted me out. He knew the circumstances. It was supposed to be a six-rounder but was cut to four.

'I've sorted you now, got you a few quid for a four-rounder,' said Ernie.

Frank Warren sent a limo down to pick me up and I had about five of my mates with me, and we all went to Manchester for my fight. I was on before Ricky Hatton, so the place was rammed and it was a good atmosphere. I think it was Jimmy Lennon Jr who introduced me.

I just went through the motions. I hit him with some good shots but he gave me a fucking big black eye. I'd never had a black eye that big in my life. No disrespect as he was a tough kid, but I should have beaten him to tell the truth. He beat me by a point or something like that. My head wasn't there and I was just deflated afterwards.

After the fight we got a few drinks from an off licence, went back to the limo and started drinking. I wasn't feeling it. It had been a good occasion as it was the first time that 200 fights had been done. Plus, people had come from all over the world to watch the fight. I should have gotten a win but my brother's death took the shine away. I probably shouldn't have fought but as I say I was paid good money. Money that I needed at the time.

I thought after that fight that would be it. I'd finished. But I was back in the gym two weeks later, after my brother's funeral. I was down and moping around the house. I went to the gym and I began feeling a bit better, and then I was fighting again. My 200th was a big deal, though it wasn't as big as my 300th would be.

* * *

Jane Couch, who I was friends with, said to me one day, 'Pete, do you want to box next week?'

'Yeah,' I said.

'I'll get you a win.'

'What you on about?'

'I'll let you box that kid from your gym, Mike Harrington.'

'Yeah?'

'Yeah.'

Mike Harrington was a guy who boxed at our gym. He wasn't very good.

So, I went down to Bristol. Me and Mike went down in the car together and we actually boxed each other. We both knew that I was going to beat him. The only thing I didn't do was stop him. Every time I used to see Jane, she would say to me, 'Pete, I got you that win, didn't I?'

'Yeah,' I would reply.

With Jane, there's no messing about. What you see is what you get. She is one of the soundest people you will ever meet.

* * *

Chas Symonds was a decent boxer. I boxed him down in Bethnal Green. He used to come down the ring dressed like Michael Katsidis, like a gladiator. He sold a load of tickets. He fought Ross Minter for the Southern Area title. He was a nice kid but he thought he was better than what he actually was. We had a move around and he hit me with some good shots. His fans were shouting his name during the fight. I could tell that he thought he was going to knock me out. After I boxed him, I think he went to live in Cyprus soon afterwards, and I remember seeing him at a show down in London. He had flown over from Cyprus to box. I spoke to him and I think he knew then that he wasn't as good as he thought he was. But when he started, he was unbeaten throughout many fights. He was a strong little kid but he didn't have much boxing skill. He would come forward and he was game. But he really believed his own hype. So, in his fight in London, he stepped up and met Minter, got stopped and then I think he knew his role in the game. He didn't have many more fights after that. He won one, then lost one regularly after that fight. And to think that he was unbeaten when I met him.

* * *

My fight with Ceri Hall meant a return to Ireland. The fight was at a golf resort, about an hour's drive from Dublin. Ceri was trained by former world welterweight title challenger Colin Jones. Once again, I was offered the fight at the last minute. I got the phone call the night before and another lad from the gym named Dean was already fighting on the bill. Anyway, I got there, weighed in and then had a bite to eat. I was top of the bill, so was the last fight on.

Coming out of my corner for the first round, I had a look at him for the first 20 to 30 seconds, like I normally do. He was quite sharp, so I was just doing my thing, covering up but letting him know I'm not just there for him to look good. I knew after a few rounds that he wasn't the biggest puncher, so I started letting my shots go and was doing OK. Like most of my fights, in the last couple of rounds I started to put a bit more meat on my shots. I hit him with a few good hooks and uppercuts. I won the last round easy and I think that shocked him a bit. Despite this, he did enough in the early rounds to win on points.

* * *

Nine times out of ten, I'd meet up with my opponents afterwards. I boxed Ryan Brawley on his debut at the St Andrew's Sporting Club in Glasgow. He was a good Scottish boxer who had won the *Prizefighter* tournament. Before the fight at the hotel, I was smoking a fag outside and this kid walked past me, giving me a funny look. I remember looking at him and I think I even nodded at him.

I spoke to Ryan recently and he said that he walked to the venue and thought, 'Fuck me, there's the lad! I'm boxing him and he doesn't even give a fuck!' He saw that I was just standing there without a care in the world! He thought that I hadn't weighed in as I was also eating right outside where we were fighting. I always used to have a fag before I fought as that is how I was. We ended up having a good fight.

* * *

I'd heard of Kell Brook before I fought him on his debut. As I used to get *Boxing News*, I had read about how good he was as an amateur. Kell trained at the Wincobank gym, the same gym as Naseem Hamed. When I boxed him, I got to the weigh-in and even though I'd been on the piss the night before, I was still lighter than he was. But when he stood next to me, he looked massive. In the first round, he was trying to take me out but I just tied him up and messed him about by walking him to the ropes and pulling his arm down. I kept talking to him while we boxed, saying, 'Come on, Kell, you're a big puncher.' After three rounds he knew he wasn't going to stop me, so I opened up every now and again just to keep him in check. He beat me on points and every time I used to see him at shows after I packed the sport in, he always came over and shook my hand. 'You never forget who you boxed in your first fight,' he said to me. He is the nicest man.

What happened next was vindication for all the years that I had fought, despite having a losing record.

* * *

Nobby said to me that he was invited to the British Boxing Awards dinner and that I could go as his guest. I had been to this awards show once before. It was either at the Savoy or the Ritz the second time I went. I was sitting at the table and the event programme had the nominations for certain awards, but it didn't say who was to get the Joe Bromley Award. It was a surprise award, though awards like services to boxing and fight of the year were on the programme.

During the ceremony, Amir Khan got up on stage. He started talking about the award he was giving out. He then said,

'The Joe Bromley Award goes to Peter Buckley.'

I was really shocked as I thought I had just been invited as a guest at this event. I knew how big this award was and was really honoured to get it. It gave me a bit of a lump in my throat. I was really proud of myself as I thought, 'Man, I'm on this list now forever.'

To think of all the people who have won this award, and to see my name, Peter Buckley from Acocks Green, on the award was surreal. I never thought when I started boxing that I'd be nominated for, never mind win, an award of that type. Out of all the boxers in the country, hundreds and hundreds of boxers from journeymen to champions, getting the Joe Bromley Award was a real big thing for me, so I was taken aback. I had to make a speech. I don't know what I said but I was in a state of shock when I accepted the award.

I won the Midlands Services to Boxing Award a few times but this was something else. I looked through the programme to see who had won it. People like Lennox Lewis, Brendan Ingle and Alan Minter. You go through the list of people who have won it and it was a real big honour to be a part of that list. I just never thought I would win an award like that one.

At the awards, I was on a table with Michael Watson and his carer. Chris Eubank came over to say hi. He had so much respect for Michael and you could tell that he really cared about him. It was a surreal moment and I felt chuffed to be around so many great fighters.

* * *

Dublin was one city I enjoyed boxing in, especially as I had relatives who were living there. During my career, I boxed there a few times but I remember going over there on my own once. Nobby couldn't come as he was working. I got a phone call on the Thursday and was asked if I could box that Saturday. A flight from Birmingham was arranged on my behalf and I stayed in a big suite in the Hilton while there. Matthew Macklin was boxing on the bill as he used to box for Brian Peters, who was his manager. I lost my fight on points against James Gorman. All the lads who boxed on the bill that night had a drink together on Saturday, and then most went back to England on Sunday, but I stayed until Monday. Where the hotel was located, Dublin City Centre is a five-minute walk. I walked up into the town, went to a bar and started having a drink. Very soon, I was talking to these blokes in there. I was on the piss with them all day and night. Told them I was Pete from Birmingham and that my family was Irish. I was just having a crack with them. It was a lot of fun.

The Patrick Hyland fight was a different fight. I got the call the night before. I got on the plane at Birmingham airport about nine o'clock in the morning because I had to get to the weigh-in for about 12 o'clock that day. I was a bit heavier than him but it didn't matter as I had only taken the fight the night before. It's an unwritten rule that I could be heavier than him as I was doing them a favour. He was a good lad. Hyland was a top Irish amateur who won everything. He was from a famous boxing family back in Dublin. Three of his brothers all boxed and their father Paddy Hyland was a boxing man through and through. Paddy knew the score, so he didn't mind that I weighed a bit more than his son. I knew I would take him the four rounds. He came out fast with a good, sharp jab and he could mix up his shots well. I had to be switched on as I knew he wanted to knock me out. I wasn't going to let that happen. Tucking up tight, I just kept moving side to side, using the whole ring. As soon as he came close, I would tie him up. It was a good fight from my point of view as I didn't get hurt. I didn't win a round that night but had a good time in Dublin. There was an after-party at the hotel and I had two more days in Dublin before catching a flight back to Birmingham. I was out on the piss while there and met some local lads and ended up on the drink with them. It was a good weekend.

* * *

I set my goal of 300 fights when I had fought 292 times. But without announcing, in a way I had packed the sport in. I'd had enough. But I went to watch my mate Tony Hanna fight for a British Masters title up in Scotland. I was sitting on the top table with Tommy Gilmour and had a few pints. Someone on the table asked why I had decided to retire.

'I've had enough,' I said.

Then Tommy Gilmour said to me, 'You should do another eight. Do your 300.'

A few drinks later, I thought, 'Fuck it, I'll have another eight fights.'

I said to Nobby later that night that I wanted to reach 300 fights, but I think he thought it was the alcohol talking.

That was on the Monday night. A couple of days later, I didn't have a gym as Nobby had knocked it on the head. So I phoned up Errol Johnson, who I knew well, and told him that I wanted eight more fights.

I thought that if I got to 300 that I would have done alright in my career. So I started going to Wednesbury gym. I had seven fights in about eight, nine weeks to get to 299. There was talk about having my 300th fight in America on a Ricky Hatton undercard. But the geezer who was trying to sort it out found out about my criminal record and couldn't get me a visa to go out there. Then I was told I could have my last fight in my hometown at the Aston Villa Leisure Centre. I accepted without hesitation.

CHAPTER 16

Final fight and post-retirement

There were a few times I thought I was going to pack it in. Sometimes I was getting bored of it and would end up boxing like shit because of my boredom. There was a guy called Michael Grant from London, another ABA champion who had good ability. I boxed him on a dinner show down in London and he beat me easily that night. It was my 257th fight and it was getting harder to box, with these fresh, ambitious lads starting out in their boxing careers. When it came to my 300th contest, I knew it would be the last time I would fight.

I boxed Lee Selby the week before my last fight, which I lost on points. Soon after, it was my final fight.

The build-up to it was mad. My opponent for my final fight, Matin Mohammed, I had fought a few weeks before but they give it a draw. Yet truth be told, I had boxed like shit in that fight. When they said they were going to put him up against me for my last fight, I agreed to it. I had to be 9st 10lbs. It wasn't a problem. Training that week, I was using Stevie B's gym in Acocks Green, just keeping my weight down, doing pads and bags. Just ticking over really. On the day of the weigh-in, I was really nervous. It was like having my first fight all over again. I don't know why as I wasn't bothered about the kid. In my head, I knew it was the last fight I was having. The last chapter of my boxing career. It was like being made redundant from a job. I knew it was my last day going in to work. I had people down at the gym the morning of the fight. I'm sure I did a workout in the morning. Don't know why.

On the day of my last fight I went in the pub and got a pint of beer, downed it, and just sat there for half an hour thinking about what I was going to do after the fight. Then I went home, got my kit and went to my mom's, as that's where Sky TV were picking me up from. They wanted to film my family before the fight and then come to the Villa ground. They filmed me right up to the minute I got in the ring. To tell the truth, they did my head in. I wasn't used to the spotlight like that. Every journalist wanted an interview and they asked the same questions all the time. 'Is this your last fight? What if you win? Will you carry on? How will you feel if you lose?' I had reporters from the local TV news stations wanting to interview me. Reporters were calling me from Germany and even as far away as Japan. I was overwhelmed. It was a lot of pressure and a bit surreal as I wasn't used to getting that much attention. It became a major thing. I think that's why I was nervous as fuck for my last fight. The press attention was just too much for me.

I didn't really think it was a big deal but then everyone was telling me that 300 fights was, in fact, a big deal. It felt a bit mad.

I was never really nervous about my fights. It all depended on who I was fighting. Like when I fought Jon Kays, I wasn't nervous. I was a bit too relaxed, a bit cocky actually. He was a new kid and I knew nothing about him. But he hit me with a right hand in the first round and I thought, 'Fucking hell!' He then hit me with another shot and I again thought 'Fucking hell!' But as I say, generally I wasn't nervous. I hadn't heard of Jon Kays. I knew he beat Sid Razak on points. But I thought that he would be no problem.

On the night, when I went to fight Mohammed, in the changing room I was still really nervous. I really had butterflies and thought that I couldn't lose to this kid in front of my mates and family. I wanted to go out with a win. My mate done a tune for the ring walk for me as he was a DJ. It was a remix of the Fugees track 'Ready or Not'. Usually, music for the ring walks didn't bother me. You see kids flapping about it. They're more worried about what tune they're going in to than the fucking fight. Didn't bother me as I came to fight, not to dance!

The crowd were chanting my name during the fight. There were reporters from abroad who were ringside. As it was in my hometown, I got a good reception from the crowd.

From the start, I felt a little bit tense because of my nerves. I wasn't as relaxed as I normally was. The fight was only scheduled for four-threes. But it took me a round just to loosen up as there was no way I wanted to lose. I then started catching him with some shots as the fight went on. If it had been a six-rounder instead of a four, I think I probably would have gotten him out of there in four rounds. He wasn't strong but he was awkward.

Apart from that, he was a piece of piss to fight. I thought that I'd won every round against him. He wasn't that good, to be honest. When the MC announced me as the winner, it was a great feeling. But I was also sad as I knew that my name would never be announced in a boxing ring again. Happiness came in knowing that my family and friends were there to witness me win my last fight.

After the fight, I was in the changing room and some fans came in and asked me for an autograph. Then, a group of us went to a bar outside the venue for a drink. Some of us even went to a bar the next night.

People still thought that I wasn't going to pack it in then. I was like, 'Nah, that's it.' I was really tired. Nineteen years a pro. It was a long time and I knew that was it. I'd had enough. Towards the end of my career, I was getting hit with shots that I wasn't getting caught with before. I also had a few injuries and was getting pissed off with going training all the time.

* * *

The board weren't going to take my licence away. They just wanted to know how many fights I was going to have as 300 is a ridiculous amount. I'd knocked it on the head at 292, then came back to have eight more fights. All they asked me was what I was going to do after my 300th and I told them that was it. I then remember Robert Smith saying to me the night after my last fight, 'Is that it now, Pete? You ain't coming back next week?'

'Nah,' I said. 'That's it.'

'Promise?' he asked.

'Yeah yeah,' I replied.

I could have carried on fighting. There was no reason to stop me. I got on well with the board. I had a good relationship with them.

The next morning, I woke up thinking, 'What am I going to do now?' It felt like losing your job. For a few weeks, I was a bit lost. I was still getting up and going for a run. But I didn't see the point of why I was doing it. It was just habit as I'd been doing it for that many years. I'd just get up and go for a run and people would see me running.

'Buckley, you having another fight?' some people would shout when they saw me jogging.

Then, about a month after my final fight, I got a phone call asking me if I wanted to fight in Dubai against an Arab fighter. He was connected with something to do with Manchester City. The kid was nothing special but they were offering me silly money to go to Dubai and box him. I was hesitating a little bit.

'Nah, that's it now,' my missus said. 'You're done. What you gonna do? Have 302 fights?'

My mate Karl Taylor had boxed him before. They paid Karl Taylor to lose to this kid. They gave him an extra grand to have a move about with him. Karl could have beat him easy. In the end, I just turned around and said, 'Nah, I'm not doing it.'

I can't remember who phoned me. Some rich kid, I imagine. The guy said it was good money and that I would be flying to Dubai first class. But I rejected their offer and just knocked it on the head. I could have done it and was getting itchy feet, thinking, 'Should I do it?' It would have been quite a bit of money to have a move about with a crap kid. But my missus was adamant.

'You're not doing it,' she said firmly. I needed someone to tell me that I wasn't doing it. I just fucked it off.

I thought, 'If I take this fight now, I will have 301. I'm going to have to have 310 fights then to round it up.' I couldn't do it to my missus and daughter, so I decided to knock it on the head there and then.

After turning that fight down, I still had no idea what I was going to do. I thought I was still going to stay involved in the sport. I used to take fighters in and train them. I didn't miss the fighting as I felt that I'd really slowed down towards the end. I was losing to some people I shouldn't have lost to and was going through the motions just to earn a bit of money. But it wasn't all about just the money. I would miss going to boxing shows most weeks. As I wouldn't be going to shows, I wouldn't see any of the referees and the officials, some of whom I had known since I turned pro. It was a very nice thing when I would go to a boxing show because I still got a lot of respect from the officials. They would ask how I was doing and if I was coming back. I would tell them that this was it. No comeback at all. A few people did think that I was going to come back and have a few more fights, but I promised my missus that I wouldn't fight again, and I wouldn't go back on my word. But it took me about 18 months before it was out of my system. There were times I was tempted to come back but I drew a line under it, though it was still hard. I would watch boxing on TV and think, 'I could go the distance with him easy.' But I thought better of it. I was still doing bits of sparring. I sparred this kid down at this gym about 18 months after retiring. I was playing with him mostly but then he started hitting me with a few shots and I thought, 'Fucking hell. He shouldn't be hitting me with them.' I knew it was time and I couldn't go on forever. I had all my brain scans and they were all clear. I thought it was a good time to get out while I still had my faculties.

I did little bits of running and training but then I would think, 'Why am I training still? I'm not fighting.' This wasn't just a phase for six months but two to three years before I got the running out of my system. I had been boxing from a young age and not fighting anymore felt like I had been made redundant. I don't miss fighting in the ring but I love watching it.

* * *

When I was boxing, there was a bloke on the board called Les Potts. He was an ex-policeman and he would do a lot of schemes based around helping ex-offenders. He said to me once, 'Pete, will you come over to this gym?' I can't remember where it was. Somewhere over near Wolverhampton, I think. It was me just going over and talking to these young lads, taking them on the pads and so on. These kids had been exactly like me when I was 14. Getting in trouble with the police and generally up to no good. I really liked it. I thought that I'd like to do something like this when I packed up boxing but I didn't really know how to go about it. I'd still like to do more of that. It's hard to get into it but it would be really rewarding. When I had the amateur boxing gym, we used to have quite a few kids who had been in trouble. I could relate to them and vice versa. I wasn't one of these people who would say, 'You got to get GCSEs, you got to do this,' as that would be like the pot calling the kettle black. They knew what I'd been through as a kid as I did speak to them about my life, about what I had done. That's why I got a lot of respect from them. I would say to them, 'Look man, you don't need to go out robbing. You have got things to do. You could come to the gym. Come to the gym every night if you want to. If you haven't got money for the gym, don't worry about it. Just get yourself off the streets.' As I say, it was really rewarding.

I ran the Heartlands Gym for a while and also trained my nephew Billy in that time. He boxed at Solihull, at the ABC there. He was unbeaten in about five or six fights. I entered him in the championships. He got to the quarter-finals, where he boxed a kid from Leeds in his hometown. He lost by a point. But he got a bit disheartened. When the club folded, I tried to get him to another club. But he wanted me to train him. He kept saying he was going to have another go but I kept saying to him that he had to do it off his own bat, like I used to do when I was his age. I used to get the bus from Acocks Green to Ladywood to Fiveways, walk up Ladywood Road and go to the canoe centre. I wish he had gone back into it as he had some potential and, in my view, would have been a good boxer. He is about 25 now. He stopped going when he was 16. When I stopped training amateurs, he knocked it on the head.

* * *

Going back to Heartlands, when I got this club I ran it with this geezer, I won't say his name. My brother knew him and gave him my number as this guy wanted me to help him at his gym. So, I met him at his house. I didn't know him but I did know his older brother. This guy was saying that he had these ideas for the gym and talked a good talk. I came down and had a look at the gym. It seemed alright. It was based in a church hall and had a ring and bags.

The guy I was running the club with used his own money to get the club off the ground. I started going down there Monday through Friday, training kids from scratch. This geezer didn't have a fucking clue what he was doing.

I knew he was talking shit soon after I met him. He made out that as an amateur, he had won 100 or so-plus fights. I said to myself that if he had won that many fights, he would have been an ABA champion. But he wasn't. He also said that Mickey Duff and Terry Lawless came to watch his last fight and he was going to go pro with them.

'You're fucking full of shit,' I thought.

I'd heard all this shit before, so I took it with a pinch of salt. I was doing all the work there as he didn't have a fucking clue. I was training the kids down there and progressing with them, and he was trying to teach them a different way. I'm not saying that my way's the right way. But he didn't know what he was doing. He couldn't hold the pads. Just couldn't do fuck all.

He was letting bigger kids spar younger kids, and in turn the bigger kids were bullying the younger ones. There were two brothers, one was sound, whereas the other was an idiot. Their dad was a real nice bloke. The younger brother was bigger than the older brother and he was a bully. In the gym, he was knocking the bollocks out of kids. I said to him, 'Fuck off. Get out of here. I'm not having this.' I didn't like his attitude.

'Get the fuck out the club,' I repeated to the younger brother.

I told his older brother, 'You're alright, but your brother's a fucking idiot. I ain't having him down here. I'm not having any bullying down here.'

Kids came to learn to defend themselves against bullies, not to get beat up by one. What was happening was that I would go to the gym after work. The gym would be open at 5pm and I would be there by 5.45pm. The younger brother would already be sparring the other kids and battering them. The geezer I was running the gym with wouldn't tell the younger brother to stop doing that. He'd keep his mouth shut. As long as he paid the gym fees, he didn't mind. I didn't give a fuck about gym fees.

'If he carries on, I'm fucking him out this gym.' I angrily said to the guy I was supposed to be running the gym with.

On one night I went to the gym, I saw the same idiot, the same younger brother, beat a smaller boy in sparring.

'Get the fuck out of this ring,' I shouted at him. 'Get your stuff and get the fuck out the gym. Just get the fuck out the gym.'

At the end of the session, his dad came in and tried to convince me to keep him on.

'I've had enough of him,' I said. 'He's a fucking bully and I'm not having it.'

Eventually, I did let him back in but told him that if he did it again, he would be out for good. Yet he hadn't learned his lesson. He was back to square one and he was doing it again. So, I told him to fuck off for good.

Then I knocked the amateur boxing training on the head due to falling out with the geezer there. I just started taking pros in again.

While I was at Heartlands, I decided to put a show on at Tyseley Working Men's Club. I had a few of the boxers I trained come round, like Nicky Powell, a big, tall kid with a good jab. He had two pro fights before packing in the sport.

I needed a sponsor for the kit. Then, me and a mate of mine called Micky Boyce were talking one day.

'You have a club. Do you need a sponsor?' he asked. 'If so, I'll get you a new kit.

'Yeah alright,' I said. 'Just get my name on the back.' So, he gave me a cheque for the kit.

Soon after I was going to Nottingham and the person I ran the club with and another person were in the car. The co-trainer was driving. I fell asleep in the car on the way to the show. When I woke up, I heard them talking about the kit. They must have forgotten I was there. They were talking about how much they got the kit for, but it was for lower the amount that the cheque was for. That's how I knew that he wasn't been straight with me. I didn't say anything at the time.

On the night of the show in Tyseley Working Men's Club, we made a few quid. This was because I managed to get sponsors for the various provisions that we needed, such as for a doctor. So really, we got the show for nothing. I had to leave the show early as I was going out with my missus at the end of the night.

The Monday when I went to the gym, I checked the money from the night and realised that it was very light. I knew it was light because the venue on the night was packed, so takings should have been high.

'Where's this money gone?' I asked the person who I was running the gym with.

'Oh oh oh ...' he hesitated.

'Hold on a minute, mate,' I said. 'I got a sponsor for the doctor. I got a sponsor for the ring.' After amateur shows you always feed the kids, so I also got food for the kids.

'Give me the kit. All the gear,' I said angrily. 'You know what, I'm going to pop down tomorrow night and I want all the kit in a bin bag. I fucking want my kit.'

I came down to the gym the next night and he was there.

'What it is,' he said. 'I spoke to my solicitor…'

'Who the fuck are you speaking to a solicitor? It's an amateur boxing club!'

I went around the counter, got all the kit, put it in the bags and fucked off. I never went back there. All the kids were phoning me and asking me to come back. I will not be ripped off by anybody. I can't work with someone I don't trustand I feel isn't being straight with me. He didn't know how to train the boxer. He just didn't have a clue.

He then put on another show and I purposely went down there to see how things would go. Trainers who promote a club show will have 15 fights that they must put on. When we put our show together, we had 15 fights and 11 winners, so we did quite well, but at this show he put on, there was hardly anyone down there and he only had six fights and no winners. I just looked at him, laughed and walked out. Soon, the club folded. He couldn't run it without me. He did not have a clue. But I enjoyed what I was doing. I loved seeing kids who had never boxed before progress in their talent and know that I helped them win fights. I wish I could have done it on my own. It is also what the guy I ran the club with kept saying to me. He was just talking shit! I was running the club – and I enjoyed it while it lasted.

* * *

When I was still boxing for Nobby, he got me a trainer's licence but I did not have to take the required course. By the time I packed boxing in, you had to go on a course to do it. What happened was the Midlands Boxing Board said to me that they wanted me to carry on in the game. 'We're going to pay, you don't have to pay anything, just go down to Manchester, go to the trainer's course and do the first aid course.' They paid for it when it would normally cost me £150. They did it off their own bat as a goodwill gesture as they wanted to keep me in boxing, which was nice of them. I did it for a few years.

When I packed in boxing, I still had my trainer's licence and I was taking fighters in for other people. Errol Johnson, who has got a gym over in Wednesbury in the Black Country, took me in for my last few fights and I knew him quite well. He phoned me and asked if I'd take some lads in for him. I would just take lads around the country fighting and from there, I started helping him out a bit.

* * *

Sid Razak was another journeyman boxer known on the British boxing scene. I knew him for about 25 years and I always got on with him. When he turned pro, he was first trained by former world title challenger Pat Cowdell. He got a few wins under Pat and then was trained by Jon Pegg and Richie Woodhall's dad, Len. After he boxed Stephen Smith on the undercard of my last fight, he decided that he wanted a change of trainer, and that is when I started to train him.

Sid could bang a bit as well. When he got his weight right, which was nine stone – and I wouldn't let him fight at first until he got down to that weight – he would give good lads a test. He also caused a few upsets.

For example, I took him down to Liverpool and he beat a kid called Joe Tonks, who was unbeaten. He also boxed a guy called Dean Anderson, who was one of Errol Johnson's fighters. The fight was on a show promoted by Errol Johnson and Sid knocked the kid out in two rounds. Another fight he had was in London against a guy who had been a top amateur and won silver at the European Championships. Sid knocked him down and Frankie Gavin, the world amateur champion, was ringside cheering him on. As Sid went in for the kill, he looked at Frankie and his opponent put him on his arse. That was one of the only times that he was put over.

When I trained Sid, he had the same mentality as me. That's why we got on so well. He'd fight anyone at an hour's notice. He didn't give a fuck. He was as tough as they come in the ring. Me and Sid had some good laughs when we were fighting. I trained him for about two years, though he was a nightmare to train as he was always late. For example, he would say he was going to come at a certain time but would show up an hour late. Even though he used to frustrate me, he was that laid back and too much of a nice kid that I couldn't stay angry with him. In the end, I would tell him to show up an hour earlier than when training was supposed to start, without letting him know what I was really doing. I would do the same when we had to go to one of his fights. I've told him that he'll be late for his own funeral!

There was one occasion I will never forget, which highlights how late he could be. He called me from Peterborough and told me that he had a fight in Belfast on Saturday, but that we needed to arrive on Friday and we had to be at Birmingham Airport at eight o'clock in the morning to check in. Of course, come Friday morning, Sid was late again and he was due to pick me up. I kept phoning him and there was no answer. He finally answered the phone.

'I'm on my way, Pete,' he said.

'Sid,' I answered. 'You're going to be fucking late.'

'Nah,' he replied. 'We'll be alright, we'll be OK.'

We got to Birmingham Airport and luckily we had no hassle checking in. As soon as we booked in, the airport was calling our names over the tannoy. We literally had to run for the plane but we got to our seats on time.

Another problem Sid had, especially towards the end of his fighting career, was monitoring his weight. He was someone who could lose or gain weight really quickly. He could get away with it but sometimes I'd have to lift him on the back of the scales to help him make weight. For example, for the fight in Belfast, when our plane landed and we were in the car on the way to the hotel, I asked Sid what his weight was like. 'Yeah, yeah, good. I'll be alright, Pete,' he said. He lifted up his top. I looked at him.

'Sid, man. You look fat,' I said.

'Nah, Pete. I'm alright,' he replied.

The next morning, before the weigh-in, I said to Sid that I was going out for something to eat.

'I'll come with you,' he said. We argued back and forth, and in the end he came with me, although I did not let him eat anything. At the weigh-in, Sid was supposed to be 10st 2lbs but came in at 10st 7lbs. 'Oh fucking hell,' I thought. I turned to him and said, 'You made me feel like a right idiot there. You're overweight and everything.'

'We did alright,' he said. 'We took the fight now.'

There is another side to the story of this fight. Sid was there as the fall guy for his opponent, who was going to beat him and was also unbeaten. When the promoters saw that Sid came in overweight, they considered taking some money away but I quickly reminded them of the real reason Sid was there. Come fight night, Sid floored the guy in the first round. Second round, he knocked the guy out. He wasn't supposed to do that! After the fight, which in hindsight made me laugh, he said to me, 'Pete, see if you can get more money off them!'

'For what?' I said. 'You knocked the kid out and you came in half a stone heavier than him! How am I gonna get more money?'

'Ah just try,' he replied.

'Sid, are you being serious? Why would they give us more money? You weighed in heavy and you knocked the kid out! Fuck off!'

After the fight, Sid took me out for a curry. This eventually became a regular thing that Sid would do. He was a good lad like that. We ended up at a really expensive curry house, which also had a cocktail bar. I had a pint and a curry. Sid, without even a care about the weight issues, ordered starters, a curry, puddings and this and that. When the bill came, the total was around £120!

'Fucking hell, Sid. You still paying?' I said.

'Yeah, of course I'm paying,' he replied, and he paid straight away.

Towards the end of his career, he cared less and less about boxing. He was putting on weight and stopped training as hard. It got so bad that once, when he boxed in Rotherham, he was a stone overweight. I said to him, 'Sid, you look a right fat bastard.'

'Pete, it's alright,' he said, laid back as always. When he got into the ring, I had to pull his shorts really high up as the crowd were shouting, 'You fat bastard!' I felt embarrassed. He lost on points but he didn't give two shits. He was a proper lad. A real tough kid.

There was another boxer I used to train, called Matt Seawright. Matt was a Scottish lad who lived in Tamworth. He had over a hundred fights and was a tough guy. I always got on with him as he was a good lad. There was no hassle from him. He would just get into the training and would box anyone. He didn't moan and I think that's why we got on.

I also used to take in Kevin McCauley, who was Errol Johnson's fighter, now and again. He is still boxing now and has had about 250-odd fights. One of the fights he had was at York Hall in London. He was boxing a lad who Ricky Hatton was training. I knew Ricky as he had boxed a few of my gym mates such as Mark Ramsay, Paul Denton and Brian Coleman. The fight started to get rough. Suddenly, Kev put his head on this lad and the ref disqualified him. When you get disqualified, you don't get paid and you have to go in front of the boxing board. Kev asked me to go down to see if he could get paid some of the money for the fight. I rushed down but they only paid the expenses. About a month later, Kev went in front of the board but he just got a telling-off and received all of his purse.

* * *

When I used to box for Nobby, there was a fighter at the gym called Jason Nesbitt, who I became friends with. He had a hard life growing up as he was in care. We used to spar a lot and sometimes he would try and take the piss. During our spars, I always got the better of him and I don't think he liked that. He could really punch with his right hand and if he hit you clean you would know about it as about seven of his ten wins were by knockout.

After I packed it in, Jason was boxing for Errol Johnson and I would take him to fights now and then. He was a tough kid, though he could be hard work sometimes. He was smoking weed a lot and didn't used to train as much. Every time I would pick him up for a fight, there would be some sort of excuse before we got to the fight, so you knew straight away you were on a loser. As soon as I'd pick him up, the excuses would start. He would say that he'd hurt his hand, his leg, or give some other type of excuse. Jason had a very hard life but he would blame the world. He blamed everyone around him and never took well to home truths. Nobby used to tell him that and he didn't like it.

I once took him down to Rotherham for a fight. He boxed this kid called Adam Hague, who was trained by Matthew Hatton. He wasn't anything special. I had a feeling that Jason didn't fancy the fight as he was moaning about all sorts, such as how much he was getting paid. The fight started and he was taking a bit of stick from the crowd. Next thing, the lad hit him with a shot and, because Jason was getting a bit chinny towards the end of his career, he went down heavy on to the canvas. He got up but was soon dropped again. He survived the round and got back to the corner.

'How you feeling?' I asked him, and he didn't know where he was. 'I'm pulling you out, OK.'

'Yeah OK,' he replied.

I called the ref over and pulled him out.

'Good call there, Pete,' said the ref.

As soon as they announced it was stopped, Jason wasn't happy.

'Why did you pull me out?' he complained.

'What you on about, Jase?' I said.

'Why did you pull me out?' he said again.

'Cos you were fucked, mate. You didn't know where you were,' I replied.

Back in the changing room, he was on the phone to his missus.

'Ah, Peter pulled me out,' he told his missus as he was telling her how the fight went.

I was pissed off that he did that. As soon as he got off the phone, I pulled him aside and told him straight

'Listen, alright,' I told him. 'I pulled you out, Jase, as I didn't want to see you get fucking knocked out. So don't make out like you were doing OK in the fight. If I wouldn't have pulled you out, you would have been *carried* out on a fucking stretcher. Like or dislike you, I wasn't going to see you get hurt by a fucking novice.'

The kid was a novice. When a kid that's had one fight can knock you down to the ground and you struggle to recover, it's time to call it a day.

'You want to think about packing it in,' I said.

But Jason didn't think that he needed to retire. He fought 11 more times over the next year or so before he decided to pack it in. But you've got to know when to call it quits. Boxers are the bravest people. Anyone can be a brave cornerman and keep sending their boxer out for round after round. But the cornermen are not the ones taking the punches and I wasn't going to be that brave cornerman.

* * *

I was going down to Stevie B's and I was training a few kids. Not white-collar kids but people who had done MMA. They used to train on the bags and the pads. They would ask me to do the pads for them and offer me £20. So I'd stay for an hour. But after half an hour, they would be blowing out of their arses.

Boxers started coming in there and I had a few boxers phone me, including Sid. Then I renewed my trainer's licence but my first aid certification had expired. I was supposed to go down to Manchester to take the first aid course again but it happened to take place at the same time I got married, so I missed the course. I kept meaning to book it but decided against doing it as by that point I wasn't training fighters. I needed to start earning money, so I just knocked it on the head and got a job, like normal people. People did say to me when I went to boxing shows, 'Pete, do your first aid course and help us out with a few fighters.' But it's hard work without the amateur gym. I was down at the gym Monday through Friday from three o'clock to nine o'clock every night. It doesn't really pay. Plus, I was working and looking after my mom, so I didn't have the time for it. You do amateur boxing for the love of it but it wasn't making me no money.

CHAPTER 17

The press, Norman, marriage and Hollywood

For all the respect I received from people involved in boxing, there has also been a lot of shit written about me. The worst thing that was ever written about me was in the *Sunday Mercury*.

Someone phoned me one day and said, 'Have you read the story in the *Sunday Mercury*? It's a bit of a piss-take.' I hadn't read the story, so I went to the shop and bought a copy.

After I read the article, I was fucking fuming. They wrote a story, which was basically a load of shit and also mentioned my brother, who had died.

I phoned them up and went ballistic.

'I want to speak to the geezer who wrote this story,' I said. The man came on the line and I was still mad.

'Who the fuck's written this story about me? I didn't give my permission for you to write this story.' They said they didn't need my permission.

'You fucking piece of shit!' I was just shouting down the line to him, just fucking angry.

'You don't even know me, mate. No one has spoken to me about doing a story.'

What he wrote was really degrading, and he was full of shit. It was a big story for their paper. It mentioned my upbringing but it was bollocks what they said about it. It also said some things that never happened. It made out that I had come from a broken home, which I don't. It was a load of bullshit from start to finish. They didn't know anything about boxing. He wasn't even a boxing writer, just a fucking idiot. It pissed me off as you don't get to 300 fights if you're the world's worst boxer. You see some of these videos on the internet titled the 'world's worst boxer'. They can't even put a pair of gloves on, let alone throw a punch. To put me in that category was taking the piss. I haven't got the money to sue them for what they did. It's why I don't really believe what I read in the papers as a lot of the time it's bollocks. They say what they want to say.

* * *

As I mentioned when I fought Naseem Hamed, a good mate of mine, who I knew from Nobby's gym, is Norman Dhalie. He also used to go to school with me. He wasn't a bad boxer but he used to think he was Prince Naseem. We used to call him Stormin' Norman. He was a real tough kid but he was nuts. Sometimes when he boxed, he used to stick his chin out and showboat, though he couldn't take much of a shot. But then one time we were in Manchester and he was boxing someone called John White. For the first round and a bit, Norman was battering him as he was so awkward. He then became arrogant and began sticking out his chin. Boom! White punched Norman, put him over and the fight got stopped. As Norman was getting out the ring, someone shouted, 'Ah, you fucking Pa*i.' Norman went for the geezer while he still had his boxing gloves on. He didn't give a fuck.

'Oi! Get back in here!' Nobby said to Norman as he grabbed him and got him out of there.

Another time, he was boxing the late Bradley Stone at the Lewisham Theatre. For three rounds, he was throwing shots from every angle and hitting Bradley everywhere. I was in Norman's corner for that fight and people were giving him a lot of racist abuse throughout. With Bradley Stone, his fans were West Ham. Later in the fight, Stone hit him with a body shot and Norman went down, didn't beat the count and the fight was stopped. As soon as he got out of the ring, the three of us walked back to the changing room. As we were walking back, the racist abuse from the crowd happened again. Norman, who still had his boxing gloves on, walked towards the crowd. Bang! He punched a geezer in the face. This guy's mates all jumped up. Nobby grabbed Norman and ran into the changing rooms. I shit myself! There were loads of them. After we got paid, we had to leave out the back through the fire exit as they were waiting for us at the front.

Norman was a real funny and emotional geezer. Once he took a fight in Solihull. Once again, he went into the ring sticking his chin out and the kid he boxed knocked him out in a round, although Norman didn't have a mark on him. He hated losing and he used to cry when he lost. He came back into the changing rooms crying because he lost. Then he started headbutting the locker and he split his head open. The locker did more damage to him than what happened to him in the ring.

Norman could have £1,000 in his pocket and he'd still rob a Mars bar. That is the type of person he was. We would get paid after a fight and he would go into a shop and literally nick a Mars bar and put it in his pocket. He would come out and say, 'Ah look, I robbed that.' I would reply, 'You got £800 in your pocket. Why rob that?' But we did used to have a laugh. 'If you had brains, you'd be dangerous,' Nobby would say to him.

When you went out with him for a drink, it would always end up in fisticuffs. He just didn't give a fuck. I still see him about now. He's not had the best of luck since he retired from boxing. I used to let him cut my grass and give him 20 quid, so I used to always look after him. A few years ago, he got sectioned at the Queen Elizabeth Hospital. He phoned me up one day while he was in hospital.

'Pete, can you bring some baccy up?' he asked.

'Yeah, of course I can,' I replied. So I went to the hospital.

They let me and my mates into his room. He was a little paranoid when in the ward, thinking people were shouting racist abuse at him. I thought he was going to be in there for 28 days. A few days later, my mobile rang and his name was on the screen.

'Alright, Norm,' I answered. 'You want anything? You run out of baccy?'

'No no no! I'm out of the hospital,' he said.

'What do you mean you're out? I thought you got sectioned for 28 days,' I replied.

'Nah,' he said. 'They just kept me in for a few days and now I'm out.'

They let him out of the hospital without any medication, just fuck all. He was a bit of a danger. Never to me but if you didn't know him, you'd be very wary of him.

He had a flat in Acocks Green for a while and he called me and said that he thought his neighbours were electrocuting him through the wall.

'Nah mate, they ain't,' I said.

'I can feel these electric shocks going through my body,' he told me. 'What I want you to do is to come down, lie on my bed and while they're electrocuting you, I'm gonna go around and smash their head in with a hammer.'

'Your neighbour's not doing that. He's not doing it,' I replied.

In the end, his neighbour ended up phoning the police on him and he got locked up for a while. When he got out, he lost his flat. I still speak to him now but it's a shame as he's a real good lad.

* * *

About four or five years after I retired, I got a message one day on Facebook.

'Hi Pete. My name's Mike Flavin. I work for Straight Street Pictures in America. Have you heard of George Tillman Jr?'

I thought it was a bit of a wind-up, to tell the truth.

Mike continued, 'We'd be interested in a discussion about making a movie of your life story.'

I'm still thinking this is a wind-up but I texted him back.

'What do you mean, mate?' I asked, adding a smiley face. I then send another text.

'What do you mean? Are you being serious or what?' I said, again with a smiley face at the end.

Mike Flavin, 'We're deadly serious. George read your story in the *Washington Post*.'

My last fight was published in that paper as well as in *Ring Magazine*.

Mike Flavin, 'George read your story and he'd be interested in making a movie about you.'

I was still thinking it was a bit of a wind-up, but I replied, 'Oh yeah?'

Mike Flavin, 'Is there any chance he could speak to you? Do you have a contact number?'

I replied, 'Yeah, I'll speak to him.'

I checked George Tillman Jr out and saw that he had made some big movies, such as the *Barbershop* films.

'Is this real or what?' I wondered, but arranged a time for him to ring me. When he rang me, he just started chatting.

'Alright Pete. I read your story and was really inspired by it. I'd like to try and get a movie made about it.'

'Are you being serious?' I said.

'Yeah. I've read a bit about you and googled you. I find it really fascinating that you had that many fights and that you would fight at the drop of a hat this champion and that champion.'

We continued chatting for a few minutes.

'I want to get some writers involved,' he said.

We continued to chat about this and that, sending messages back and forth and him ringing me just asking how I was doing. He mentioned that he was going to send me the names of two writers, along with some of their work, so that I could have a read through it. One of the writers was called Noah and the other was called Bob. I thought Noah was the better writer of the two because I spoke to him and he seemed on my level, and I liked the work I'd read by him. But they went with Bob. He was alright, just not the better of the two.

I started speaking to Bob and he was calling me a couple of times a week for a couple of hours at a time. I just told him about my life story. After a few months of this, the producers called me one day and said they were going to send me a script to read. When I read the script, I really didn't like it because it was not 100 per cent a true story. For example, some of it was about how I met Tania. It made out that I met her at a church dance.

I thought, 'What the fuck?!' So I called them back and complained that the story was not factual.

'We can't make it 100 per cent factual,' they said. 'Every story on television or film is never all true.' The script felt Americanised.

Then they said, 'We can change certain bits that you're not happy with. Put a line under what you don't like, then send it to us and we'll see what we can do.'

When they started talking money, I couldn't believe the amount that was being discussed. My eyes were getting big and I was counting the pound notes before they fell. They said that they were going to get $20 million to make the film but they were talking about it like it was 20 pence. They also mentioned that they were going to try and get some investors. I thought everything sounded good.

I sent the script back and then I spoke to George on the phone, who said that the story wouldn't be 100 per cent true.

'Have you watched *The Fighter*?' he asked.

'Yeah,' I replied.

'Well, a lot of that was changed,' he said.

I asked how long this would all take.

'Well, *The Fighter* took seven years to get off the ground,' he replied.

He explained what they were doing. They also mentioned the actors they were sending the script to. Michael Fassbender's name was one that cropped up. 'They are mentioning some real Hollywood stars here,' I thought. He phoned me again and said that he was going to take it to the Sundance Film Festival to try and get some investors there. Then I didn't hear from them again for six months. They then contacted me and said that they hadn't forgotten about me, they were just trying to get this and that. At that point, they asked me to sign a contract.

'What do you mean a contract?' I said.

They replied, 'It's nothing concrete. All it is, while we're working on this, we don't want you to go to somebody else. We don't want to waste our time and effort and then you turn around and say that you've signed with someone else. If somebody is interested in the story at your end, you can let us know. Then we'll probably negotiate with them.'

This was going on for two to three years. I wasn't exactly getting pissed off but I did ask, 'Is anything happening with this?' He did explain to me that this wouldn't happen overnight and that it could take years. 'Yeah, whatever,' I thought. 'I ain't doing nothing else.'

The last time I spoke to himwhich was around June 2011, he said that they were going to send me another contract, as the previous contract they sent was close to expiring. 'We're just going to send you an 18-month one. If we don't do anything in those 18 months and someone comes to you after 18 months, then do what you like.'

After nine months, I had some contact with George telling me what was happening. I just kept saying, 'Yeah, OK thanks,' as there was nothing I could do. The last time I heard from them was by email, saying that they had tried to get investors, that they had got some of the money but that they needed about $20 million.

'So where would you film this?' I asked.

'We would do part of it in America and part of it in Britain,' George said. 'Not necessarily Birmingham but we'd find somewhere suitable.'

This went on for a while and then one day I just contacted them and asked, 'Is anything going on with this?' as the 18 months were up on the second contract. That was two years ago.

* * *

Tania and I have known each other since we were teenagers and have been together for more than 28 years. One day, I said to her that it was time we got married. She laughed and thought I was joking. Later, she asked if I was serious about getting married.

'Yes, I am,' I said.

A few days later, she phoned me and said that she had booked the registry office and I was like, 'Sound.' The wedding was really nice. We got married in Solihull in the afternoon. She looked beautiful on that day and I am a lucky man. Some family came over from Ireland and from London. My mates were there as well, including Nobby, which I was happy about. My missus organised everything herself. She picked the suit, she picked the car, the music, the DJ and the food. I just handed over money. For the reception, we used the back room of the Westley Arms pub in Acocks Green, which was local to us. We had a band with a singer to provide some live music. After they finished we had a DJ for the rest of the night. The DJ was Tania's cousin and he was brilliant. It was a really good night. We went to Tenerife for our honeymoon. We had gone there 15 years ago.

Epilogue
How I'd like to be remembered

I'd like to be remembered as someone who earned people's respect. I never boxed just to be paid, and I never went into the ring just to fall over. I always gave a good account of myself. Even if I'd been on the piss the night before or took a fight on really short notice, I know I got the boxing community's respect, just by the way people spoke to me. I won two Midlands titles. I fought for a Masters title on a day's notice against Carl Greaves and he always says that I gave him his hardest fight. I was better than what my record shows – 100 per cent better.

Someone said to me, 'Pete, I've watched you box at least 50 times and always thought you should have gotten the decision when you did not. How do you feel about that?' How did I feel? I didn't really feel anything because I was earning and was back in the ring the following week. I know whenever I really won or lost. If I lost, then I got beaten by the better kid. There are two fights, one against Carl Allen and the other against Matt Harris. I was confident I won both. If you listen to the decision, I lost each one by half a point. There is nothing

I can ever do about it. If I'd won half the fights I lost by half a point, my record would have been a lot better than it is. I would have gotten many more wins. That would have been more than most boxers have achieved.

I've had 300 fights, have been retired 11 1/2 years and I still get people phoning me up and wanting to interview me about my career. I've got a DVD about my last fight. In the build-up to it, Sky Sports came to my house to film me with my mom and my missus. Backstage at the fight itself, they filmed me at the Aston Villa Leisure Centre. They were talking to people backstage like Dean Powell and Robert Smith of the British Boxing Board of Control. They say on this DVD how much respect they have for me and that they knew they could phone me up and I would help them out. They spoke to different people within the sport and every single one of them gives me total respect. It's nice to know that the boxing community respects me.

I won certain awards that I never dreamed I would get. I won the Joe Bromley Award. I'm ingrained on that list forever. To me, when I won that Services to Boxing Award, as well as being inducted into the British Boxing Hall of Fame, that showed to me that I had the total respect of the boxing community. Not from the person on the street who says, 'Oh, you had 300 fights and lost 256 of them.' They don't mean nothing to me as they don't understand the boxing game. I don't want their respect. It doesn't mean nothing.

There is a boxing page on Facebook and there isn't one negative comment about me. World champions to European and domestic champions were praising me. There was one comment that said, 'Peter could have gone a long way if he would have chosen it.' But I didn't choose it. I chose the other way when I was fighting in the ring. I didn't want to fight every three to six months. I wanted a fight every week. If I had gone the other way and won a British title, I would be forgotten about now. There are a lot of British champions who no one ever speaks about.

The major thing in my life now that I am retired is my four grandsons, who I think the world of. If they want to box, I wouldn't put them off it. But I would like them to do something else, other than if they were training in a gym. If they had talent, then I would be behind them 100 per cent.

I'd like to be remembered as someone who not only came to fight but fought smart in not taking a beating. Anyone can get in the ring and prove how tough they are but I was better in that I used my brain. I made hard fights easy. Also, the respect I got from top promoters, as well as being invited to the top hotels in London for dinners and awards, no other journeymen had that privilege. I was top of the tree, the number one journeyman for many years. No one else came close.

There was a lad named Ryan from up north. He was fighting one week at a show in Manchester. He was a mouthy lad but I liked him. He was saying in the changing rooms, 'Pete, I'm going to have more fights than you had. I thought, 'Fair play, kid. Good luck.' Mike Goodhall, who's been doing boxing cards as an MC for years, said, 'Let's see if you're as sharp as Pete when you've finished boxing.' Well, the lad got knocked out that night and I remember Mike saying to him, without being cruel, 'I've never seen Peter Buckley get knocked out like you did tonight.' I don't think he boxed many times after that. At every show I was boxing on, people knew who

I was more than they knew who some champions were. I was always being asked for my picture and would I sign this and that, which made me feel famous. It was a great feeling what boxing did for me. That's why I'll always be grateful for boxing. It gave me respect for myself and from other people. I was King of the Journeymen.

Peter Buckley acknowledgements

Firstly, I want to thank my wife Tania for being there through most of my life. If I didn't meet her when I did, I don't know where I would be today. Before I met her, my life was out of control as I was going to prison all the time and just not giving a fuck about anyone apart from my family. We have been through a lot together, both good and bad. But she has been my rock and my soulmate. When I was about to do something stupid, she would straight away talk me out of acting on it. I could be like a bull in a china shop and not think about my actions. She was always the one who would tell me to stop and think about the outcome of what I was about to do. She's one in a billion.

Nobby, for giving me the chance to do something that no one else did. He showed me my life could be better than sitting in a prison cell and wasting away. He gave me lessons in life and showed me that if I treated people with respect, I would get that respect back. 'You have to earn respect,' he would say. 'You don't just get it.' I always wonder where I would have ended up if I hadn't bumped into Rocky Lawlor in a pub one Sunday night. He took the time to knock on my door the following Monday to go to Nobby's gym with him. I know I wouldn't have returned to boxing off my own bat. My mom was so proud when I went back to boxing as she knew I was wasting my life away. I know it made her sad. But the joy I saw in her eyes when I won the Midlands Area title – she was the proudest woman in the world.

All my brothers and sisters who have always supported me, looked out for me, and were there for me when mom died. We are close and that will never change.

My grandsons, who I think the world of, and my daughter for blessing me with them.

Boxing was my second chance in life. As mad as it sounds, I felt safe between the ropes and felt that I belonged there. I can never get that buzz again. It's gone but never forgotten.

Chris Akers acknowledgements

Thank you to the following people:

To my family and friends for the support they have shown me during the writing of this book.

To Michael Angelo Serra for recommending me to Peter when he wanted someone to write his autobiography. Your support has been immense.

To Peter for giving me this opportunity to write his life story.

To Claudia Peterson for the great job she did in editing the book.

To Duncan and Mandy Hamilton for their support and their friendship over the last couple of years.

To Donald McRae and Paul Zanon, who in different ways helped me when I was in the early stages of writing this book.

And finally to all the writers who have given me constructive criticism and encouragement over the years. All of it has been greatly appreciated.

Peter Buckley's record

(source: www.boxrec.com)

Date	*Opponent*	*Location*	*Result*
4/10/89	Alan Baldwin	Stafford	DRAW
10/10/89	Ronnie Stephenson	Wolverhampton	L PTS
30/10/89	Robert Braddock	Birmingham	W PTS
14/11/89	Neil Leitch	Evesham	W PTS
22/11/89	Peter Judson	Stafford	W PTS
11/12/89	Stevie Woods	Bradford	W PTS
21/12/89	Wayne Taylor	Birmingham	W PTS
10/1/90	John O'Meara	Kensington	W PTS
19/2/90	Ian McGirr	Birmingham	L PTS
27/2/90	Miguel Matthews	Evesham	DRAW
14/3/90	Ronnie Stephenson	Stoke-on-Trent	DRAW
4/4/90	Ronnie Stephenson	Stafford	L PTS
23/4/90	Ronnie Stephenson	Birmingham	W PTS
30/4/90	Chris Clarkson	Mayfair	L PTS
17/5/90	Johnny Bredahl	Aars, Denmark	L PTS
4/6/90	Ronnie Stephenson	Birmingham	W PTS
28/6/90	Robert Braddock	Birmingham	W TKO 5
1/10/90	Miguel Matthews	Cleethorpes	W PTS
9/10/90	Miguel Matthews	Wolverhampton	L PTS

17/10/90	Tony Smith	Stoke-on-Trent	W PTS
29/10/90	Miguel Matthews	Birmingham	W PTS
21/11/90	Drew Docherty	Solihull	L PTS
10/12/90	Neil Leitch	Birmingham	W PTS
10/1/91	Duke McKenzie	Wadsworth	L TKO 5
18/2/91	Jamie McBride	Glasgow	L PTS
4/3/91	Brian Robb	Birmingham	W TKO 7
26/3/91	Neil Leitch	Wolverhampton	DRAW
1/5/91	Mark Geraghty	Solihull	W PTS
5/6/91	Brian Robb	Wolverhampton	W PTS
	(for vacant BBBofC Midlands Area super featherweight title)		
9/9/91	Mike Deveney	Glasgow	L PTS
24/9/91	Mark Bates	Basildon	W RTD 5
29/10/91	Johnny Armour	Kensington	L PTS
14/11/91	Mike Deveney	Edinburgh	L PTS
28/11/91	Craig Dermody	Liverpool	L PTS
19/12/91	Craig Dermody	Oldham	L PTS
18/1/92	Alan McKay	Kensington	DRAW
20/2/92	Brian Robb	Oakengates	W TKO 10
	(BBBofC Midlands Area super featherweight title)		
27/4/92	Drew Docherty	Glasgow	L PTS
15/5/92	Ruben Condori	Augsburg, Germany	L PTS
29/5/92	Donnie Hood	Glasgow	L PTS
7/9/92	Duke McKenzie	Bethnal Green	L RTD 3
12/11/92	Naseem Hamed	Liverpool	L PTS
19/2/93	Harald Geier	Wiener Neustadt, Austria	L PTS
26/4/93	Bradley Stone	Lewisham	L PTS
18/6/93	Eamonn McAuley	Belfast	L PTS
1/7/93	Tony Silkstone	York	L PTS
6/10/93	Jon Jo Irwin	Solihull	L PTS
25/10/93	Drew Docherty	Glasgow	L PTS

6/11/93	Michael Alldis	Bethnal Green	L PTS
30/11/93	Barry Jones	Cardiff	L PTS
19/12/93	Shaun Anderson	Glasgow	L PTS
22/1/94	Barry Jones	Cardiff	L PTS
29/1/94	Naseem Hamed	Cardiff	L TKO 4
10/3/94	Tony Falcone	Bristol	L PTS
29/3/94	Conn McMullen	Bethnal Green	W PTS
5/4/94	Mark Bowers	Bethnal Green	L PTS
13/4/94	James Murray	Glasgow	L PTS
6/5/94	Paul Lloyd	Liverpool	L RTD 4
3/8/94	Greg Upton	Bristol	L PTS
26/9/94	John Sillo	Liverpool	L PTS
5/10/94	Matthew Harris	Wolverhampton	L PTS
7/11/94	Marlon Ward	Piccadilly, London	L PTS
23/11/94	Justin Murphy	Piccadilly, London	L PTS
29/11/94	Neil Swain	Cardiff	L PTS
13/12/94	Michael Brodie	Potters Bar	L PTS
20/12/94	Michael Alldis	Bethnal Green	L PTS
10/2/95	Matthew Harris	Birmingham	W TKO 6
	(for BBBofC Midlands Area super bantamweight title)		
23/2/95	Paul Ingle	Southwark, London	L PTS
20/4/95	John Sillo	Liverpool	L PTS
27/4/95	Paul Ingle	Bethnal Green	L PTS
9/5/95	Ady Lewis	Basildon	L PTS
23/5/95	Spencer Oliver	Potters Bar	L PTS
1/7/95	Dean Pithie	Kensington	L PTS
21/9/95	Patrick Mullings	Battersea	L PTS
29/9/95	Marlon Ward	Bethnal Green	L PTS
25/10/95	Matthew Harris	Telford	L PTS
	(for BBBofC Midlands Area super bantamweight title)		
8/11/95	Vince Feeney	Bethnal Green	L PTS
28/11/95	Barry Jones	Cardiff	L PTS

15/12/95	Patrick Mullings	Bethnal Green	L PTS
5/2/96	Patrick Mullings	Bexleyheath	L PTS
9/3/96	Paul Griffin	Millstreet, Ireland	L PTS
21/3/96	Colin McMillan	Southwark	L TKO 3
14/5/96	Venkatesan Devarajan	Dagenham	L PTS
29/6/96	Matt Brown	Erith	W TKO 1
3/9/96	Vince Feeney	Bethnal Green	L PTS
28/9/96	Fabrice Benichou	Barking	L PTS
9/10/96	Gary Marston	Stoke-on-Trent	DRAW
6/11/96	Neil Swain	Tylorstown	L PTS
29/11/96	Alston Buchanan	Glasgow	L PTS
22/12/96	Brian Carr	Glasgow	L PTS
11/1/97	Scott Harrison	Bethnal Green	L PTS
29/1/97	Carl Allen	Stoke-on-Trent	L PTS
12/2/97	Ronnie McPhee	Glasgow	L PTS
25/2/97	Dean Pithie	Sheffield	L PTS
7/3/97	Jason Booth	Northampton	L PTS
20/3/97	Thomas Bradley	Newark	W PTS
8/4/97	Sergey Devakov	Bethnal Green	L PTS
25/4/97	Matthew Harris	Cleethorpes	L PTS
8/5/97	Gregorio Medina	Mansfield	L RTD 2
13/6/97	Mike Deveney	Paisley	L PTS
19/7/97	Richard Evatt	Wembley Arena	L PTS
30/8/97	Michael Brodie	Cheshunt	L PTS
6/10/97	Brendan Bryce	Piccadilly	W PTS
20/10/97	Kelton McKenzie	Leicester	L PTS
20/11/97	Ervine Blake	Solihull	L PTS
6/12/97	Danny Adams	Wembley Arena	L PTS
13/12/97	Gary Thornhill	Sheffield	L PTS
31/1/98	Scott Harrison	Picketts Lock	L PTS
5/3/98	Steve Conway	Leeds	L PTS
18/3/98	Ervine Blake	Stoke-on-Trent	L PTS

26/3/98	Graham McGrath	Solihull	W RTD 4
11/4/98	Salim Medjkoune	Southwark	L PTS
18/4/98	Tony Mulholland	Manchester	L PTS
27/4/98	Alston Buchanan	Glasgow	L PTS
11/5/98	Jason Squire	Leicester	W RTD 2
21/5/98	Lee Armstrong	Bradford	L PTS
6/6/98	Tony Mulholland	Liverpool	L PTS
14/6/98	Lee Armstrong	Shaw	L PTS
21/7/98	David Burke	Widnes	L PTS
5/9/98	Michael Gomez	Telford	L PTS
17/9/98	Brian Carr	Glasgow	L PTS
3/10/98	Justin Murphy	Crawley	L PTS
5/12/98	Lehlo Ledwaba	Bristol	L PTS
19/12/98	Acelino Freitas	Liverpool	L RTD 3
9/2/99	Chris Jickells	Wolverhampton	L PTS
16/2/99	Franny Hogg	Leeds	L PTS
26/2/99	Richard Evatt	Coventry	L TKO 5
17/4/99	Martin O'Malley	Dublin, Ireland	L TKO 3
29/5/99	Richie Wenton	Halifax	L PTS
14/6/99	Carl Allen	Birmingham	L PTS
26/6/99	Paul Halpin	Millwall, London	L PTS
15/7/99	Salim Medjkoune	Peterborough	L PTS
7/8/99	Steve Murray	Dagenham	L PTS
12/9/99	Kevin Gerowski	Nottingham	L PTS
20/9/99	Matt Zegan	Peterborough	L PTS
2/10/99	Jason Cook	Cardiff	L PTS
9/10/99	Brian Carr	Manchester	L PTS
19/10/99	Gary Steadman	Bethnal Green	L PTS
27/10/99	Miguel Matthews	Birmingham	W PTS
20/11/99	Carl Greaves	Grantham	L PTS
11/12/99	Gary Thornhill	Liverpool	L PTS
29/1/00	Bradley Pryce	Manchester	L PTS

19/2/00	Gavin Rees	Dagenham	L PTS
29/2/00	Tony Mulholland	Widnes	L PTS
20/3/00	Carl Greaves	Mansfield	L PTS
27/3/00	James Rooney	Barnsley	L PTS
8/4/00	Delroy Pryce	Bethnal Green	L PTS
17/4/00	Franny Hogg	Glasgow	L PTS
11/5/00	Craig Spacie	Newark	L PTS
25/5/00	Jimmy Phelan	Hull	DRAW
19/6/00	Delroy Pryce	Burton-on-Trent	L PTS
1/7/00	Richard Evatt	Manchester	L PTS
16/9/00	Lee Meager	Bethnal Green	L PTS
23/9/00	Gavin Rees	Bethnal Green	L PTS
2/10/00	Brian Carr	Glasgow	L PTS
14/10/00	Gareth Jordan	Wembley	L PTS
13/11/00	Kevin Lear	Bethnal Green	L PTS
24/11/00	Leeroy Williamson	Hull	L PTS
9/12/00	Leo O'Reilly	Southwark	L PTS
15/1/01	Eddie Nevins	Manchester	L PTS
23/1/01	David Burke	Crawley	L PTS
31/1/01	Tony Montana	Piccadilly	L PTS
19/2/01	Kevin England	Glasgow	W PTS
12/3/01	Carl Allen	Birmingham	L PTS
19/3/01	Duncan Armstrong	Glasgow	L PTS
27/3/01	Carl Allen	Brierley Hill	L PTS
5/5/01	Danny Hunt	Picketts Lock	L PTS
9/6/01	Gary Thornhill	Bethnal Green	L PTS
21/7/01	Scott Miller	Sheffield	L PTS
28/7/01	Kevin Lear	Wembley	L PTS
25/9/01	Ricky Eccleston	Liverpool	L PTS
7/10/01	Nigel Senior	Wolverhampton	L PTS
31/10/01	Woody Greenway	Birmingham	L PTS
16/11/01	Jimmy Beech	West Bromwich	L PTS

1/12/01	Chill John	Bethnal Green	L PTS
9/12/01	Nigel Senior	Shaw	W PTS
26/1/02	Scott Lawton	Bethnal Green	L PTS
9/2/02	Sam Gorman	Coventry	L PTS
23/2/02	Alex Moon	Nottingham	L PTS
4/3/02	Leo Turner	Bradford	L PTS
11/3/02	Martin Watson	Glasgow	L PTS
26/4/02	Scott Lawton	Coventry	L PTS
10/5/02	Lee Meager	Bethnal Green	L PTS
8/6/02	Bradley Pryce	Glasgow	L TKO 1
20/7/02	Jeff Thomas	Bethnal Green	L PTS
23/8/02	Ben Hudson	Bethnal Gren	DRAW
6/9/02	Dave Stewart	Bethnal Green	L PTS
14/9/02	Peter McDonagh	Bethnal Green	L PTS
20/10/02	James Paisley	Southwark	L PTS
12/11/02	Martin Hardcastle	Leeds	DRAW
29/11/02	Daniel Thorpe	Hull	L PTS
9/12/02	Nicky Leech	Nottingham	L PTS
16/12/02	Joel Viney	Cleethorpes	L PTS
28/1/03	Billy Corcoran	Nottingham	L PTS
8/2/03	Colin Toohey	Liverpool	L PTS
15/2/03	Terry Fletcher	Wembley	L PTS
22/02/03	Dean Lambert	Huddersfield	L PTS
5/3/03	Billy Corcoran	Bethnal Green	L PTS
18/3/03	Nathan Ward	Reading	L PTS
5/4/03	Baz Carey	Manchester	L PTS
15/5/03	Mike Harrington	Bristol	W PTS
27/5/03	Dave Stewart	Dagenham	L PTS
7/6/03	Rimell Taylor	Coventry	DRAW
12/7/03	George Telfer	Glasgow	L PTS
22/7/03	Chas Symonds	Bethnal Green	L PTS
1/8/03	Jaz Malik	Bethnal Green	W PTS

6/9/03	John Murray	Huddersfield	L PTS
13/9/03	Issac Ward	Wakefield	L PTS
25/9/03	Gary Woolcombe	Bethnal Green	L PTS
6/10/03	Scott Haywood	Barnsley	L PTS
20/10/03	Joel Viney	Bradford	W PTS
29/10/03	David Kehoe	Leicester Square, London	L PTS
7/11/03	Femi Fehintola	Sheffield	L PTS
14/11/03	Dave Stewart	Bethnal Green	L PTS
21/11/03	Henry Castle	Canary Wharf	L PTS
28/11/03	Lee Meager	Derby	L PTS
13/12/03	Derry Mathews	Manchester	L PTS
21/12/03	Daniel Thorpe	Bolton	L PTS
16/1/04	Nadeem Siddique	Bradford	L PTS
16/2/04	Scott Haywood	Scunthorpe	L PTS
29/2/04	Gary O'Connor	Shaw	L PTS
3/4/04	Stevie Bell	Manchester	L PTS
16/4/04	Issac Ward	Hartlepool	L PTS
23/4/04	Colin Bain	Glasgow	L PTS
6/5/04	Aamir Ali	Barnsley	L PTS
13/5/04	Lee Beavis	Bethnal Green	L PTS
4/6/04	Tristan Davies	Dudley	L PTS
3/7/04	Barrie Jones	Newport	L PTS
3/9/04	Stefy Bull	Doncaster	L PTS
10/9/04	Tiger Matthews	Liverpool	L PTS
17/9/04	Kell Brook	Sheffield	L PTS
24/9/04	Ceri Hall	Dublin, Ireland	L PTS
11/10/04	Darren Johnstone	Glasgow	L PTS
22/10/04	Jonathan Whiteman	Mansfield	L PTS
29/10/04	Colin Bain	Glasgow	L PTS
9/11/04	Tom Hogan	Leeds	L PTS
21/11/04	Chris McDonagh	Bracknell	L PTS
10/12/04	Craig Johnson	Mansfield	L PTS

17/12/04	Stephen Mullin	Liverpool	L PTS
12/2/05	Jay Morris	Portsmouth	L PTS
21/2/05	Stuart Green	Glasgow	L PTS
5/3/05	Paul Buckley	Southwark	L PTS
23/3/05	Ryan Barrett	Leicester Square, London	L PTS
9/4/05	Nadeem Siddique	Norwich	L PTS
25/4/05	Jimmy Gilhaney	Glasgow	L PTS
14/5/05	James Gorman	Dublin, Ireland	L PTS
27/5/05	Alan Temple	Spennymoor	L PTS
4/6/05	Patrick Hyland	Dublin, Ireland	L PTS
25/6/05	Sean Hughes	Wakefield	DRAW
24/7/05	Scott Lawton	Sheffield	L PTS
3/9/05	Jackson Williams	Norwich	L PTS
19/9/05	Ryan Brawley	Glasgow	L PTS
14/10/05	Jimmy Gilhaney	Motherwell	L PTS
23/11/05	Shane Watson	Mayfair	L PTS
2/12/05	Billy Corcoran	Nottingham	L PTS
14/12/05	Stephen Burke	Blackpool	L PTS
23/1/06	David Appleby	Glasgow	L PTS
2/2/06	Michael Grant	Holborn	L PTS
18/2/06	Jimmy Doherty	Stoke-on-Trent	L PTS
4/3/06	Stevie Bell	Manchester	L PTS
13/3/06	Gary McArthur	Glasgow	L PTS
25/3/06	Brian Murphy	Irvine	L PTS
2/4/06	Barry Downs	Shaw	L PTS
13/4/06	Paul Newby	Leeds	L PTS
28/4/06	Gary O'Connor	Manchester	L PTS
6/5/06	Ian Clyde	Stoke-on-Trent	L PTS
20/5/06	Stephen Haughian	Belfast	L PTS
9/6/06	Wes Miller	Doncaster	L PTS
18/6/06	James Brown	Manchester	L PTS
29/6/06	Rob Hunt	Dudley	L PTS

10/7/06	Carlvin White	Manchester	L PTS
9/9/06	Stuart Green	Inverurie	L PTS
18/9/06	Stuart Green	Glasgow	L PTS
29/9/06	Mitch Prince	Motherwell	L PTS
3/11/06	Mitch Prince	Glasgow	L PTS
12/11/06	Danny Harding	Manchester	L PTS
24/11/06	Adam Kelly	Hull	L PTS
6/12/06	Daniel Thorpe	Thurcroft	L PTS
19/2/07	Mark Hastie	Glasgow	L PTS
3/3/07	Wayne Downing	Burton-on-Trent	L PTS
11/3/07	Shinny Baayar	Shaw	L PTS
26/3/07	Charlie King	Glasgow	L PTS
20/4/07	Kevin Buckley	Dudley	L PTS
28/4/07	Furhan Rafiq	Clydebank	L PTS
3/6/07	Andy Ward	Barnsley	L PTS
24/6/07	Jon Kays	Wigan	L PTS
23/9/07	Shane Watson	Heathrow	L PTS
7/10/07	Darren Askew	Shaw	L PTS
17/11/07	Chris Goodwin	Stoke-on-Trent	L PTS
28/11/07	Kim Poulson	Piccadilly	L PTS
10/12/07	Leonard Lothian	Leicester	L PTS
11/7/08	Ali Shah	Wigan	L PTS
24/7/08	Scott Evans	Wolverhampton	L PTS
12/9/08	Chris Lewis	Wolverhampton	L PTS
19/9/08	Joe Elfidh	Doncaster	L PTS
26/9/08	Dean Arnold	Wolverhampton	L PTS
5/10/08	Matin Mohammed	Nottingham	DRAW
12/10/08	Pete Leworthy	Bristol	L PTS
24/10/08	Lee Selby	Newport	L PTS
31/10/08	Matin Mohammed	Birmingham	W PTS